INTRODUCTION to ARITHMETIC for DIGITAL SYSTEMS DESIGNERS

INTRODUCTION to ARITHMETIC for DIGITAL SYSTEMS DESIGNERS

SHLOMO WASER

Monolithic Memories Incorporated

and

MICHAEL J. FLYNN

Stanford University

HOLT, RINEHART AND WINSTON

New York   Chicago   San Francisco   Philadelphia
Montreal   Toronto   London   Sydney   Tokyo
Mexico City   Rio de Janeiro   Madrid

Library of Congress Cataloging in Publication Data

Waser, Shlomo.
   Introduction to arithmetic for digital systems
designers.

   Bibliography: p.
   Includes index.
   1. Computer arithmetic and logic uints.   I. Flynn,
M. J. (Michael J.), 1934–   II. Title.
TK7895.A65W37   1982   621.3819'582   82-12163

ISBN 0-03-060571-7

Printed in the United States of America

Published simultaneously in Canada

2 3 4 5   039   9 8 7 6 5 4 3 2 1

CBS COLLEGE PUBLISHING
Holt, Rinehart and Winston
The Dryden Press
Saunders College Publishing

PREFACE

The advent of large scale integrated silicon circuitry has made complex technology increasingly available to digital systems designers. Special numeric applications such as signal processing, statistical data analysis, etc., can be expedited by an order of magnitude by a specially designed processor. Such an approach may represent the only feasible solution in certain real-time environments. However, it is certainly not the purpose of this book to address such direct applications. Rather, it is to provide a basic understanding of number representations and basic arithmetic operations using these representations. Thus, we hope to give designers an introduction to the possibilities of using modern techniques and technology in their applications.

Arithmetic is sometimes a tricky business—things are not as simple as they seem and the details assume an out of proportion significance. Many excellent texts on computer organization provide considerable introductory material on arithmetic. Yet since their focus is on broader issues the treatment lacks the detail needed to be immediately useful to a designer.

Our purpose is to provide sufficient detail of both theory and practice to adequately prepare a digital logic designer with a familiarity of the issues and an awareness of the state of the art in algorithms for basic arithmetic operation design. The algorithms presented were selected within the framework and limitations of MSI and LSI technology. We have not tried to be comprehensive in the review of computer arithmetic literature, as there are other texts designed to serve this purpose (see, for example, the work by Hwang, [HWA 78]). A special feature of this book is an extensive appendix containing the specifications on currently available MSI and LSI integrated circuits related to arithmetic design. This is intended for use in practical design situations as are the design exercises at the end of each chapter. These design problems involve practical implementation issues and are intended for students already well versed in logic design (at least one course).

When preparing this material, we had the following four uses in mind.

1. It could be used as a supplementary text in a course on computer organization. Such a course could be either at an intermediate level (perhaps covering only Chapter 1 of our text) or at a more advanced level (stressing the latter chapters).

2. The nucleus text could be employed in a course on arithmetic. Depending on the amount of time available, this text material could be supplemented with recent papers in the field.

3. It can be utilized as a text on the design of arithmetic functional units. By emphasizing the design exercises the text provides basis for learning both theory and practice of arithmetic design.

4. Also practicing designers can use it as a reference.

We have tried to stress information of practical implementation value without ignoring theoretic foundations. However, we have purposely omitted long proofs of theorems (especially Winograd's bounds) in an effort at conciseness.

This text is an evolution of material originally presented as part of a course on Advanced Computer Organization at Stanford University (EE482) in the form of notes and reprints of papers. Further impetus came from a special seminar on Computer Arithmetic which Professor Harvey Garner (visiting Stanford at the time) helped us organize. The collection and drafting of the material in its preliminary form was part of a thesis at Stanford for the Engineer's Degree. During this evolution, however, the focus remained constant: that this work should present what every digital engineer should know about arithmetic and perhaps didn't know who to ask for it.

ACKNOWLEDGMENTS

Writing this book required a considerable amount of time, certainly more than either author expected. We gratefully acknowledge a number of sources of support, including Stanford University (especially the Computer Systems Laboratory and the Electrical Engineering Department), Monolithic Memories Incorporated (MMI), and Trinity College, Dublin. Academic research support has been provided by grants from the Army Research Office (Durham) and the National Board for Science and Technology, Ireland. Don Knuth and his colleagues also deserve an acknowledgment for permitting us the use of his TEX formatting system and the computer equipment involved in producing this manuscript.

The book, in its present form, is also the result of the work and encouragement of many individuals.

Some of the artwork and all of the technical specifications in the Appendix were provided by Monolithic Memories Inc., (MMI). Murray Siegel of MMI was particularly supportive of these efforts. All other artwork (that was not typeset) was completed by Willem Terluin and Stephanie Williams, both illustrators at Stanford Word Graphics. The figures they produced were always carefully drawn in an efficient period of time.

Len Trubisky of Honeywell was quite helpful in forming the discussion on byte division. The design of a combinatorial floating point processor was influenced by many discussions with Daniel Gajski and Tor Undheim (who implemented the design in the Norsk Data Computer). Many other useful discussions help shape the book, and we are grateful to the following people: Dennis Allison, David Birkner, Chuck Hastings, Ravi Iyer, Graham Jullien, Gerald Shapiro, George Taylor and John Wakerly. Also Harvey Garner, Herschel Loomis and T. R. N. Rao provided many constructive insights and suggestions for the manuscript.

We are also deeply indebted to the staff and students at Stanford University who encouraged the book's production. Frances Ferguson and Moira Lieberman generously offered their time and administrative support. Scott Wakefield and Robert Wedig patiently assisted with technical problems and questions concerning the automatic editors. The students in two successive offerings of the EE382 Course (Advanced Computer Architecture) at Stanford University contributed to the editorial process with their constructive suggestions, criticisms, and questions.

The editors must also be commended. Barbara Laddaga managed the initial text entry and early design. Kathleen Flynn was responsible for additional text entry, all changes, the typeset figures and tables, final book design and production arrangements.

Finally we would like to thank our families for their patience and support during the long period it took to write this book.

TABLE OF CONTENTS

ABBREVIATIONS AND SYMBOLS

$x \bmod y$	least positive remainder of $\frac{x}{y}$
$x = y$	x is equal to y or x is congruent to y
$\{x_i\}$	the set of elements, x_i for specified index values, i
MSB	Most Significant Bit
MSD	Most Significant Digit
LSB	Least Significant Bit
LSD	Least Significant Digit
RC	Radix Complement
DRC	Diminished Radix Complement
TC	Two's Complement
OC	One's Complement
$\lfloor x \rfloor$	Greatest integer contained by x
$\lceil x \rceil$	Least integer containing x
C_{in}	Carry-in
C_{out}	Carry-out
$\oplus$	Exclusive OR
OVR	Overflow detection
β	Radix

max	Largest representable number
min	Smallest representable (absolute) number (excluding zero)
NAN	Not A Number
RND(x)	Rounded value of x
∇a	Downward directed rounding
Δa	Upward directed rounding
T	Truncation; round to zero
RZ	Round to zero
A	Augmentation; round away from zero
RN	Round to closest machine number
o	overflow indicator
u	underflow indicator
i	infinity indicator
MRRE	Maximum Relative Representable Error
ARRE	Average Relative Representable Error
ROM	Read Only Memory
$X = [x_1, \ldots x_n]$	Residue Representation of X
X^c	Complement of X
fan-in	maximum number of inputs to a logic element
fan-out	maximum number of outputs from a logic element
ALU	Arithmetic Logic Unit
CLA	Carry-look-ahead Adder
CPA	Carry-propagate Adder
CSA	Carry-save Adder
Q	Quotient (full value)
q_i	bit i of signed digit quotient representation
k_i	bit i of binary representation of quotient

PLA   Programmed Logic Array

PROM   Programmable Read Only Memory

PAL*   Programmable Array Logic

        * PAL is a registered trademark of MMI Corporation

SSI   Small-scale integrated logic

MSI   Medium-scale integrated logic

LSI   Large-scale integrated logic

Chapter 1

NUMERIC DATA REPRESENTATION

The main problem in computer arithmetic is the mapping from the human infinite number system to the finite representational capability of the machine. Finitude is the principal characteristic of a computer number system. Almost all other considerations are a direct consequence of this finitude. For example, overflow is simply an unsuccessful attempt to map from the infinite to the finite number system.

The common solution to this problem is the use of modular arithmetic. In this scheme, every integer from the infinite number set has one unique representation in a finite system. However, now a problem of interpretation is introduced, that is, in a modulo 8 system the number 9 is mapped into the number 1. As a result of mapping the number 1 corresponds in the infinite number system to 1, 9, 17, 25, etc.

1.1 NUMBER SYSTEMS

1.1.1 Natural Numbers

The historical need for and the use of numbers were for counting; even nowadays, the child's numerical development starts with counting. The counting function is accomplished by the infinite set of numbers 1, 2, 3, 4, ..., which are described as natural numbers. These numbers have been used for thousands of years, and yet only in the last century were they described precisely by Peano (1858–1932). The following description of Peano's postulates is adapted from Parker [PAR 66].

POSTULATE 1: For every natural number x there is a unique natural number which we call the successor of x and which is denoted by x'.

POSTULATE 2: There is a unique natural number which we call 1.

POSTULATE 3: The natural number 1 is not the successor of any natural number.

POSTULATE 4: If two natural numbers x and y are such that $x' = y'$, then $x = y$.

POSTULATE 5: (Principle of Mathematical Induction): Let M be a subset of the natural numbers with the following properties: (a) 1 is a member of M; (b) for any x which belongs to M, x' also belongs to M. Then M is the set of natural numbers.

Later on, there will be a description of other number systems (negative, real, rational), and it will be shown that all other number systems can be described in terms of natural numbers. At this point, our attention is on the problem of mapping from the infinite set to a finite set of numbers.

1.1.2 Finitude

Garner [GAR 65] has shown that the most important characteristic of machine number systems is finitude. Overflows, underflows, scaling, and complement coding are consequences of this finitude.

1.1.3 Modular Arithmetic—Informal Description

Informally, the infinite set of natural numbers needs to be represented by a finite set of numbers. Arithmetic that takes place within a closed set of numbers is known as "Modular Arithmetic." Brennan [BRE 68] provides the following examples of modular arithmetic in everyday life: The clock tells time in terms of the closed set (modules) of 12 hours, and the days of the week all fall within modulo 7. If the sum of any two numbers within such a modulus exceeds the modulus, only the remainder number is considered; e.g., eight hours after seven o'clock the time is three o'clock, since

$$(8 + 7) \text{ modulo } 12 = \text{remainder of } \frac{15}{12} = 3.$$

Seventeen days after Tuesday, the third day of the week, the day is Friday, the sixth day of the week, since

$$(17 + 3) \text{ modulo } 7 = \text{remainder of } \frac{20}{7} = 6.$$

1.1.4 Modular Arithmetic—Formal Description

In modular arithmetic the property of congruence (having the same remainder) is of particular importance. By definition [STE 71]:

> If m is a positive integer, then any two integers N and M are congruent; modulo m, if and only if there exists an integer K such that $N - M = Km$ or

$$N \bmod m \equiv M \bmod m,$$

where m (a positive integer) is called the modulus.

Informally, the modulus is the quantity of numbers within which a computation takes place. $(0, 1, 2, 3, \ldots, m - 1.)$

Example:
If $m = 256$ and $M = 258$, $N = 514$, then

$$514 \bmod 256 \equiv 2$$

and

$$258 \bmod 256 \equiv 2;$$

i.e., they are congruent mod 256 and

$$514 - 258 = 1 \cdot 256,$$

i.e., $K = 1$.

1.1.5 Properties

Congruence has the same properties with respect to the operations of addition, subtraction, and multiplication, or any combination.

If $N = N' \bmod m$ and $M = M' \bmod m$, then

$$(N + M) \bmod m \equiv (N' + M') \bmod m,$$
$$(N - M) \bmod m \equiv (N' - M') \bmod m,$$
$$(N * M) \bmod m \equiv (N' * M') \bmod m.$$

Example:
$m = 4$, $N' = 11$, $N = 3$, $M' = 5$, $M = 1$; then

$$3 + 1 \bmod 4 \equiv (11 + 5) \bmod 4 \equiv 0,$$
$$3 - 1 \bmod 4 \equiv (11 - 5) \bmod 4 \equiv 2,$$
$$3 \times 1 \bmod 4 \equiv (11 \times 5) \bmod 4 \equiv 3.$$

What if N is negative in the operation $N \bmod m$? We could choose from several conventions; for example,

$$-7 \bmod 3 \equiv -1 \quad \text{or} \quad +2,$$

since

$$-7/3 = -2 \quad \text{quotient}, \ -1 \quad \text{remainder}$$

or

$$-7/3 = -3 \quad \text{quotient}, \ +2 \quad \text{remainder}.$$

For modulus operations the usual convention is to choose *the least, positive residue (including zero)*. We will assume this convention unless otherwise specified throughout this book, even if the modulus is negative; for example, $-7 \bmod -3 = +2$. That is,

$$\frac{-7}{-3} = +3 \quad \text{quotient}, \ +2 \quad \text{remainder}.$$

In terms of conventional division this is surprising since one might expect

$$\frac{-7}{-3} = +2 \quad \text{quotient}, \ -1 \quad \text{remainder}.$$

We will distinguish between the two division conventions by referring to the former as *modulus division* and the latter as *signed division*. This distinction follows the work of Warren and his colleagues, [WAR 79].

The division operation is defined as

$$\frac{a}{b} = q + \frac{r}{b},$$

where q is the quotient and r is the remainder. But even the modulus division operation does not extend as simply as the other three operations; for example,

$$\frac{3}{1} \neq \frac{11}{5} \bmod 4.$$

Nevertheless, division is a central operation in modular arithmetic. It can be shown that for any modulus division M/m there is a unique quotient-remainder pair and the remainder has one of the m possible values $0, 1, 2, \ldots, m-1$. This leads to the concept of *residue class*.

A residue class is the set of all integers having the same remainder upon division by the modulus m. For example, if $m = 4$, then the numbers 1, 5, 9, 13... are of the same residue class. Obviously, there are exactly m residue classes, and each integer belongs to one and only one residue class. Thus, the modulus m partitions the set of all integers into m distinct and disjoint subsets called residue classes.

Example:
If $m = 4$, then there are four residue classes which partition the integers:

$$\{\ldots, -8, -4, 0, 4, 8, 12, \ldots\}$$

$$\{\ldots, -7, -3, 1, 5, 9, 13, \ldots\}$$

$$\{\ldots, -6, -2, 2, 6, 10, 14, \ldots\}$$

$$\{\ldots, -5, -1, 3, 7, 11, 15, \ldots\}$$

In conclusion, by not dealing with individual integers but only with the residue class of which an integer is a member, the problem of working with an infinite set is reduced to one of working with a finite set.

1.1.6 Extending Peano's Numbers

Peano's numbers are the natural integers 1, 2, 3, ..., but in real life we deal with more numbers. The historic motivation for the extension can be understood by studying some arithmetic operations. The operations of addition and multiplication (on Peano's numbers) result in numbers that are still described by the original Peano's postulates. However, subtraction of two numbers may result in negative numbers or zero. Thus, the extended set of all integers is

$$-\infty, \ldots, -2, -1, 0, 1, 2, \ldots + \infty,$$

and natural integers are a subset of these integers. The operation of division on integers may result in noninteger numbers; by definition such a number is a rational number, which can be represented exactly as a ratio of two integers. However, if the rational number is to be approximated as a single number, an infinite sequence of digits may be required for such a number, for example, $1/3 = 0.33333\ldots$. Between any two rational numbers, however small but finite their difference, lies an infinite number of other rational numbers and infinitely more numbers which cannot be expressed as rationals. We call these latter numbers *real* numbers and they include such constants as π and e. Real numbers can be viewed as all points along the number axis from $-\infty$ to $+\infty$.

Real numbers need to be represented in a machine with the limitation of finitude. This is accomplished by approximating real and rational numbers, by terminating sequences of digits. Thus, all numbers (real, rational, and integers) can be operated on as if they were integers (provided scaling and rounding are done properly).

1.2 INTEGER REPRESENTATION

The data representation to be described here is a weighted positional representation. The development for a weighted system was a particular breakthrough in ancient man's way of counting. To count 17 stones he may have counted the first ten and marked something in the sand (to indicate 10) and then counted the remaining 7 stones. If his mark on the sand happened to look like 1, he could have easily generated the familiar weighted positional number system. Our base

10 system (sometimes called the Arabic system), comes to us from India via North Africa, and was quite an improvement over earlier schemes such as Roman numbers.

In a weighted positional system, the number N is the sequence of $m + 1$ digits $d_m, d_{m-1} \ldots, d_2, d_1, d_0$, which in base b can be computed to give $N = d_m \cdot b^m + d_{m-1} \ldots b^{m-1} + \ldots d_1 \cdot b + d_0$. The digit values for d_i may be any integer between 0 and $b - 1$. For example, in the familiar decimal system, the base is $b = 10$, and the 4-digit number 1736 is:

$$N = 1736 = 1 \times 10^3 + 7 \times 10^2 + 3 \times 10^1 + 6.$$

In the binary system $b = 2$, and the 5-digit number 10010 is:

$$N = 1 \times 2^4 + 0 \times 2^3 + 0 \times 2^2 + 1 \times 2 + 0 = 18 \quad \text{(base 10)}.$$

Other common number bases are octal (base $= 8$) and hexadecimal (base $= 16$).

The leading digit, d_m, is the most significant digit (MSD) or the most significant bit (MSB) for binary base—similarly d_0 is designated as the least significant digit or bit—(LSD) or (LSB).

The above positional number system does not include a representation of negative numbers. Two methods are commonly used to represent signed numbers [GAR 65].

a. *Magnitude plus sign*: digits are represented according to the simple positional number system; an additional high-order symbol represents the sign. This code is natural for humans but unnatural for a modular computer system.

b. *Complement codes*: two types are commonly used, namely, *radix complement* code (RC) and *diminished radix* complement code (DRC). Complement coding is natural for computers, since no special sign symbology or computation is required. In binary arithmetic (base $= 2$) the RC code is called *two's complement* and the DRC is called *one's complement*.

1.2.1 Radix Complement Code—Subtraction Using Addition

Suppose N is a positive integer of the form

$$N = d_m \cdot b^m + d_{m-1} \cdot b^{m-1} + \cdots + d_0.$$

The maximum value N may assume is $b^{m+1} - 1$; i.e., where all the digit values, d_i, are equal to $b - 1$, their maximum value. Thus, $b^{m+1} > N \geq 0$.

Now suppose we wish to represent $-N$, a negative $m + 1$ digit number. We define the radix complement of N as

$$RC(N) = b^{m+1} - N.$$

Clearly the RC(N) is a nonnegative integer.

For ease of representation let $n = m + 1$; then $RC(N) = b^n - N$. Assume b is even and suppose M and N are n-digit numbers. We wish to compute $M - N$ using the addition operation. M and N may be either positive or negative numbers so long as

$$\frac{b^n}{2} - 1 \geq M, N \geq \frac{-b^n}{2}.$$

Then

$$M - N$$

is more accurately

$$(M - N) \bmod b^n,$$

and

$$(M - N) \bmod b^n = (M \bmod b^n - N \bmod b^n) \bmod b^n.$$

But if we replace $-N$ with $b^n - N$, the equality is unchanged; that is by taking

$$(M \bmod b^n + (b^n - N) \bmod b^n) \bmod b^n,$$

we get

$$M \bmod b^n - N \bmod b^n.$$

The computation of $b^n - N$ is relatively straightforward. For N less than b^n, let N be represented as $X_m \ldots X_0$, and the operation $b^n - N$ is actually

$$n \text{ digits}$$

$$\overbrace{\hspace{4cm}}$$

$$
\begin{array}{cccccccc}
1 & 0 & 0 & 0 & 0 & \ldots & 0 \\
- & X_m & X & X & X_i & \ldots & X_0 \\
\end{array}
$$

$$\text{recall } m = n - 1.$$

Now the radix complement of any digit X_i is designated $RC(X_i)$. For all lower order digits which satisfy

$$X_0 = X_1 = \cdots = X_i = 0,$$

the $RC(X_i)$ is

$$RC(X_0) = RC(X_1) = \cdots = RC(X_i) = 0.$$

That is,

$$
\begin{array}{r}
0\ 0 \\
-\ 0\ 0 \\
\hline
0\ 0.
\end{array}
$$

For $X_{i+1} \neq 0$, the first (lower order) nonzero element in N,

$$RC(X_{i+1}) = b - X_{i+1};$$

and for all elements X_j thereafter, $m \geq j \geq i + 2$,

$$RC(X_j) = b - 1 - X_j.$$

For example, in a three-position decimal number system, the radix complement of the positive number 245 is $1000 - 245 = 755$. This illustrates that by properly scaling the represented positive and negative numbers about zero, no special treatment of the sign is required. Thus, in radix complement code, the most significant digit indicates the sign of the number. In the base 10 system, the digits 5, 6, 7, 8, 9 (in the most significant position) indicate negative numbers; i.e., the three digits represent numbers from $+499$ to -500, and in the binary system, the digit 1 is an indication of negative numbers.

Example:

$M = +250$, $N = +245$; compute $M - N$.

$$
\begin{array}{rcr}
250 & \Rightarrow & 250 \\
-245 & & +755 \\
\hline
& & 1005 \quad \text{mod } 1000 \equiv 5.
\end{array}
$$

For the familiar case of even radix, a disadvantage of the radix complement code is the asymmetry around zero, that is, the number of negative numbers is greater by one than the number of positive numbers. But this shortcoming is not a serious one, especially if the number zero is viewed as a positive number; then there are as many positive numbers as there are negative numbers.

The greatest disadvantage of the two's complement number system is the difficulty in converting from positive to negative numbers and vice versa. This difficulty is the motivation [STO 75] for developing the diminished radix complement code.

1.2.2 Diminished Radix Complement Code

By definition, the diminished radix complement of the previously defined number N, DRC(N) is $b^n - 1 - N$. In a decimal number system, this code is called nine's complement, and in binary system, it is called one's complement.

The computation of the diminished radix complement (DRC) is simpler than that of the radix complement. Since, if $N \bmod b^n = X_{n-1} X_{n-2} \ldots X_0$, then for all

X_i $(n - 1 \geq i \geq 0)$

$$DRC(X_i) = b - 1 - X_i.$$

Since $b - 1$ is the highest valued symbol in a radix b system, no borrows can occur and the DRC digits can be computed independently.

This simplicity of complement computation comes at some expense in arithmetic operation since the arithmetic logic itself is always mod b^p, (where $p > n$). Consider the computation P mod $(b^n - 1)$. If P were initially represented as a mod b^p number or the result of addition or subtraction of two numbers mod b^n, then the conversion to a mod $b^n - 1$ number, P', would be

$$\text{If } P < b^n - 1 \quad \text{then} \quad P = P'.$$

That is,

$$P \bmod b^n \equiv P \bmod (b^n - 1) = P'.$$

If $P > b^n - 1$, then P' must be increased by 1 (called the end around carry) for each multiple of $b^n - 1$ contained in P. Thus,

$$P' = P + \left\lfloor \frac{P}{b^n - 1} \right\rfloor.$$

That is, P' is P plus the largest integer contained by $\frac{P}{b^n - 1}$.

(Throughout this book we use two symbols, $\lceil x \rceil$ and $\lfloor x \rfloor$, respectively the ceiling and the floor of the real number x. The ceiling function is defined as the smallest integer which properly contains x, eg., if $x = 1.33$, then $\lceil x \rceil = \lceil 1.33 \rceil = 2$. The floor function is defined as the largest contained by x; eg., $\lfloor x \rfloor = \lfloor 1.33 \rfloor = 1$.)

Finally, if

$$P = k(b^n - 1),$$

k equal to any integer, then

$$P' = 0.$$

Example:

Suppose we have two mod 99 numbers A' and B', having the following operations performed mod 1000, and then corrected to mod 100 and then to a mod 99 result:

(i) A' $= 47$, B' $= 24$; find $(A' + B') \bmod 99$.

$$\begin{array}{r} 47 \\ +24 \\ \hline 071 \end{array}$$

71 mod 100 $\equiv$ 71 mod 99 = result.

(ii) A′ = 47, B′ = 57; find (A′ + B′) mod 99.

$$\begin{array}{r} 47 \\ +57 \\ \hline 104 \\ +1 \\ \hline 05 \end{array}$$ 4 mod 100 ≡ 5 mod 99 = result.

(iii) A′ = 47, B′ = 52; find (A′ + B′) mod 99.

$$\begin{array}{r} 47 \\ +52 \\ \hline 099 \end{array}$$ 99 mod 100 ≡ 0 mod 99 = result.

Since $b^n - 1$ is a represented element in n-digit arithmetic (mod b^n arithmetic), we have two representations for zero: $b^n - 1$ and 0.

While the problem of $b^n - 1$ and b^n modular compatibility will be of interest to us in Chapter 2, the use of DRC in subtraction provides a more restricted version of this problem. In order to represent negative numbers using the DRC we will partition the range of b^n representation as follows:

$$b^n - 1, \ldots\ldots\ldots, \frac{b^n}{2} \qquad \frac{b^n}{2} - 1, \ldots\ldots\ldots, 1, 0$$
$$\ \ \ 0 \qquad\qquad\qquad \text{max.} \qquad\ \text{max.} \qquad\qquad\qquad 0$$
$$\qquad\qquad\qquad\quad \text{neg.} \qquad\ \text{pos.}$$
$$\qquad\text{negative} \qquad\qquad\qquad\qquad \text{positive}$$

Thus any m-digit $(m = n - 1)$ number M must be in the following range:

$$\frac{b^n}{2} - 1 \geq \text{M} \geq \frac{-b^n}{2} + 1.$$

Note that $\frac{b^n}{2}$ is congruent to (lies in the same residue class as) $\frac{-b^n}{2} + 1$ modulo $b^n - 1$; since

$$\frac{-b^n}{2} + 1 \bmod b^n - 1 \equiv (b^n - 1) - \frac{b^n}{2} + 1 \bmod b^n - 1 \equiv \frac{b^n}{2} \bmod b^n - 1.$$

So long as b has 2 as a factor there will be a unique set of leading digit identifiers for negative numbers. For example, if $b = 10$, a negative (nonpositive) number will have 5, 6, 7, 8, 9 as a leading digit.

Consider the computation M − N using the diminished radix complement (DRC) with mod b^n arithmetic logic to be corrected to mod $b^n - 1$. M and N lie within the previously defined range.

$$(\text{M} - \text{N}) \bmod (b^n - 1) \equiv (\text{M} \bmod (b^n - 1) - \text{N} \bmod (b^n - 1)) \bmod (b^n - 1).$$

Then

$$M \bmod (b^n - 1) \equiv M,$$

and

$$-N \bmod (b^n - 1) = b^n - 1 - N,$$

$$M - N = M + b^n - 1 - N;$$

that is,

$$M + \mathrm{DRC}(N).$$

Since the basic addition logic is performed mod b^n, we correct the mod b^n difference, D, as follows to find D', the mod $b^n - 1$ difference,

$$D = M + b^n - 1 - N.$$

If $D > b^n - 1$, then

$$D' = D + 1; \qquad \text{i.e., } M - N > 0.$$

If $D < b^n - 1$, then

$$D' = D; \qquad \text{i.e., } M - N < 0.$$

If $D = b^n - 1$, then

$$D' = 0; \qquad \text{i.e., } M = N,$$

and *the result is zero* (i.e., one of the two representations).

In summary, in the decimal system $-43 \Rightarrow 99 - 43 = 56$, and in the binary system $-3 \Rightarrow 111 - 011 = 100$. These examples illustrate the advantage of the diminished radix complement code—the ease of initial conversion from positive to negative numbers; the conversion is done by taking the complement of each digit. Of course, in the binary system, the complement is the simple Boolean NOT operation.

A disadvantage of the system is illustrated by taking the complement of zero; for example, in a 3-digit decimal system, complement of zero $= 999 - 000 = 999$. Thus, the number zero has two representations 000 and 999. (Note: the complement of the new zero is $999 - 999 = 000$.)

Another disadvantage is that the arithmetic logic requires correction of results (end-around carry).

1.3 IMPLEMENTATION OF INTEGER OPERATIONS

For each integer data representation, five operations will be analyzed: addition, subtraction, shifting, multiplication, and division. Most of the discussion will assume binary arithmetic (radix 2).

Addition and subtraction will be treated together, since the subtraction is the same as addition of two numbers of opposite signs. Thus, subtraction is performed by adding the negative of the subtrahend to the minuend. Therefore, the first thing to be addressed is the negation operation in each data representation.

1.3.1 Negation

In a one's complement system, negation is a simple Boolean NOT operation. Negation in a two's complement (TC) system can be viewed as

$$TC(N) = 2^n - N = (2^n - 1 - N) + (1),$$

where n is the number of digits in the representation. It may look awkward in the equation, but in practice this form is easier to implement, since the first term is the simple one's complement (i.e., NOT operation) and the second term calls for adding one to the least significant bit (LSB). The discussion of one's and two's complement operations follows Stone [STO 75].

1.3.2 Two's Complement Addition

Two's complement addition is performed as if the two numbers were unsigned numbers; that is, no correction is required. However, it is necessary to determine when an overflow occurs. For the two summands B and C, there are four cases to consider:

Case	B	C	Comments
1	Positive	Positive	
2	Negative	Negative	
3	Negative	Positive	$|B| > |C|$
4	Negative	Positive	$|B| < |C|$

For positive numbers, the sign bit (the MSB) is zero, and for negative numbers, the sign bit is one. The sign bit is added just like all the other bits. Thus, the sign bit of the final result is made up of the sum of the summands' sign bits plus the carry into the sign bit. In the first case, the sum of the sign bits is zero $(0+0=0)$, and if a carry is generated by the remaining bits, the resultant sign bit will become one. That is, the result overflows (since adding the two positive numbers generated a negative number). The rest of the cases are analyzed in a similar fashion and summarized in the following table:

Case	B	C	Sum of Signs	Carry-in to Sign Bit C_{in}	Carry-out of Sign Bit C_{out}	Overflow	Notes
1a	Pos	Pos	0	0	0	no	
1b	Pos	Pos	0	1	0	yes	
2a	Neg	Neg	0	1	1	no	
2b	Neg	Neg	0	0	1	yes	
3	Neg	Pos	1	0	0	no	$|B| > |C|$
4	Neg	Pos	1	1	1	no	$|B| < |C|$

Two observations can be made from the above table: first, it is impossible to overflow the result when the two summands have different signs (this is quite clear intuitively); second, the overflow condition can be stated in terms of the carries in and out of the sign bit—that is, overflow occurs when these carries are different. The Boolean expression for this condition is ($\oplus$ is the exclusive OR operation):

$$\text{OVERFLOW} = C_{in} \oplus C_{out}.$$

1.3.3 One's Complement Addition

It was mentioned earlier that addition in one's complement representation requires correction. An insight into the reason for correction can be obtained by analyzing the four cases as was done for the two's complement addition (for simplicity the overflow cases are ignored).

Case 1: Same as two's complement addition and no correction is required.

Case 2: Adding two negative numbers B, C;

$$\text{DRC}(|B|) + \text{DRC}(|C|) = \text{DRC}(|B| + |C|)$$
$$\text{where } \text{DRC}(|x|) = 2^n - 1 - |x|.$$

$$
\begin{array}{r}
2^n - 1 - |B| \\
+2^n - 1 - |C| \\
\hline
2^{n+1} - 2 - (|B| + |C|)
\end{array}
$$

In modulo 2^n, the number 2^{n+1} is represented by its congruent 2^n. Thus, the sum is $2^n-2-(|B|+|C|)$, but it should have the one's complement format $2^n-1-(|B|+|C|)$. Therefore 1 must be added to the LSB to have the correct result.

Case 3: B negative, C positive, $|B| > |C|$.

$$
\begin{array}{r}
2^n - 1 - |B| \\
+ \qquad |C| \\
\hline
2^n - 1 - (|B| - |C|)
\end{array}
$$

This form requires no correction.

Case 4: B negative, C positive, $|B| < |C|$.

$$DRC(|B|) + |C| = |C| - |B|.$$

$$
\begin{array}{r}
2^n - 1 - |B| \\
+ \qquad |C| \\
\hline
2^n - 1 + (|C| - |B|)
\end{array}
$$

But this result has to be positive and correction is required. After the correction, the result is $2^n + (|C| - |B|)$, which is congruent to $|C| - |B|$.

The implementation of the correction term is relatively easy. Whenever correction is necessary there is a carry-out of the sign bit. Thus, in hardware the carry-out of the sign bit is added to the LSB (if no correction is required, zero is added to the LSB). The correction term is the end-around carry, and it causes one's complement addition to be slower than two's complement addition.

Overflow detection in one's complement addition is the same as in two's complement addition, that is, $OVR = C_{in} \oplus C_{out}$.

1.3.4 Computing Through the Overflows

This subject is covered in detail by Garner [GAR 78]. Here we just state the main property. In complement-coded arithmetic it is possible to perform a chain of additions, subtractions, multiplications, or any combination that will generate a final correct (representable) result even though some of the intermediate results have overflowed.

For example, in 4-bit two's complement representation, where the range of representable numbers is -8 to $+7$, consider the following operation:

$$+5 + 4 - 6 = +3.$$

$$
\begin{array}{ll}
\underline{0101} & +5 \\
\underline{0100} & +4 \\
1001 & \text{Overflow} \\
\underline{1010} & -6 \\
0011 & +3 \,(\text{correct})
\end{array}
$$

1.3.5 Arithmetic Shifts

The arithmetic shifts are discussed as an introduction to the multiplication and division operations. An arithmetic left shift is equivalent to multiplying by the radix (assuming the shifted result does not overflow), and an arithmetic right shift is equivalent to dividing by the radix. In binary, shifting p places is equivalent to multiplying or dividing by 2^p. In left shifts (multiplying), zeros are shifted into the least significant bits, and in right shifts, the sign bit is shifted into the most significant bit (since the quotient will have the same sign as the dividend).

The difference between a logical and an arithmetic shift is important to note. In a logical shift *all bits* of a word are shifted right or left by the indicated amount with zeros filling unreplaced end bits. In an arithmetic shift the sign bit is fixed and the sign convention must be observed when filling unreplaced end bits. Thus, a right shift (divide) of a number will fix the sign bit and fill the higher order unreplaced bits with either ones or zeros in accordance with the sign bit. With arithmetic left shift the lower order bits are filled with zeros regardless of the sign bit. So long as a p place left shift does not cause an overflow—that is, $2^p *$ original value $\leq$ maximum representable number in the word—arithmetic left shift is the same as logical left shift.

In two's complement right shift there is an asymmetry between the shifted results of positive and negative numbers:

$$-13/2 \Rightarrow 10011 \text{ right shift } 11001 \quad -7;$$

$$+13/2 \Rightarrow 01101 \text{ right shift } 00110 \quad +6.$$

This, of course, relates to the asymmetry of the two's complement data representation, where the quantity of negative numbers is larger by one than the quantity of positive numbers.

By contrast, the one's complement right shift is symmetrical:

$$-13/2 \Rightarrow 10010 \text{ right shift } 11001 \quad -6;$$

$$+13/2 \Rightarrow 01101 \text{ right shift } 00110 \quad +6.$$

Notice that the asymmetric resultant quotients correspond to modular division; i.e., creating a quotient so that the remainder is always positive. Similarly, symmetric quotients correspond to signed division—the remainder assumes the sign of the dividend.

1.3.6 Multiplication

In unsigned data representation, multiplying two operands, one with n bits and the other with m bits, requires that the result will be $n + m$ bits. If each of the two operands is n bits, then the product has to be $2n$ bits. This, of course, corresponds to the common notion that the multiplication product is a double length operand. This should be clear from analyzing the multiplication of the two largest representable unsigned operands:

$$P = (2^n - 1) * (2^n - 1) = 2^{2n} - 2^{n+1} + 1 = 2^{2n-1} + 2^{2n-1} - 2^{n+1} + 1.$$

Positive number

Thus, the largest product P is $2^{2n} > P > 2^{2n-1}$, so $2n$ bits are necessary and sufficient to represent it.

In signed numbers, where the MSB of each of the operands is a sign bit, the product should require only $2n - 1$ bits since the product has only one sign bit. However, in the two's complement code there is one exceptional case: multiplying -2^n by -2^n results in $+2^{2n}$. But this positive number is not representable in $2n - 1$ bits. This latter case is treated many times as an overflow, especially in fractional representation where both operand and results are restricted to the range: $-1 \leq R < +1$. Thus, multiplying -1 times -1 gives the unrepresentable $+1$.

1.3.7 Division

Division is the most difficult operation of the four basic arithmetic operations. Two properties of the division are the source for this difficulty:

1. Overflow—Even when the dividend is n bits long and the divisor is n bits long, an overflow may occur. A special case is a zero divisor.

2. Inaccurate results—In most cases, dividing two numbers gives a quotient that is an approximation to the actual rational number.

In general, one would like to think of division as the converse operation to multiplication but, by definition:

$$\frac{A}{B} = Q + \frac{R}{B}$$

or

$$A = B * Q + R,$$

where A is the dividend, B is the divisor, Q is the quotient, and R is the remainder. When $R = 0$, there is a subset of cases for which division is the exact converse of multiplication.

In terms of the natural integers (Peano's numbers), all multiplication results are still integers, but only a small subset of the division results are such numbers. The rest of the results are rational numbers, and to represent them accurately a pair of integers is required.

In terms of machine division, the result has to be expressed by one finite number. Going back to the definition of division,

$$\frac{A}{B} = Q + \frac{R}{B},$$

it is observed that the same equation holds true for any desired finite precision.

Example:

In decimal arithmetic, if $A = 1$, $B = 7$, then $1/7$ is computed as follows:

$A/B = Q + R/B$	or $A = B * Q + R$	
$1/7 = 0.1 + 0.3/7$	or $1 = 0.7 + 0.3$	$Q = 0.1$
$1/7 = 0.14 + 0.02/7$	or $1 = 0.98 + 0.02$	$Q = 0.14$
$1/7 = 0.142 + 0.006/7$	or $1 = 0.994 + 0.006$	$Q = 0.142$
$1/7 = 0.1428 + 0.0004/7$	or $1 = 0.9996 + 0.0004$	$Q = 0.1428$

In implementing a simple subtractive division algorithm, a difficulty of the division becomes evident. Multiplication can be thought of as successive additions, and division is similarly successive subtractions. But while in multiplication it is known how many times to add, in division the quotient digits are not known in advance. It is not absolutely certain how many times it will be necessary to subtract the divisor from a given order of the dividend. Therefore, in these algorithms, which are trial and error processes, it is not known that the divisor has been subtracted a sufficient number of times until it has been subtracted once too often.

One more difficulty in division is the multiplicity of valid results depending upon the sign conventions, e.g., signed vs. modular division. Thus, if one wishes a signed division using the two's complement code, a negative quotient requires a correction by adding one to the least significant bit.

The difficulties encountered in performing division as a trial and error shift and subtract process are eliminated when a different approach to implementation is taken. The division of A/B can be treated as multiplication of A times the reciprocal of B, $(1/B)$. Thus, the problem is reduced to the computation of a reciprocal which will be discussed in the chapter on division algorithms.

1.4 FLOATING POINT NUMBER REPRESENTATION

1.4.1 Motivation and Terminology

So far, we have discussed fixed point numbers where the number is written as an integer string of digits and the radix point is a function of the interpretation. The problem with fixed point arithmetic is the lack of dynamic range, which can be illustrated by the following example in the decimal number system.

> Assume that there are four decimal digits, then the dynamic range, 9999 to 0, is $\simeq 10,000$. This range is independent of the decimal point position, that is, the dynamic range of 0.9999 to 0.0000 is also $\simeq 10,000$. Since this is a 4-digit number we may want to represent during the same operation both 9999 and 0.0001; but this is impossible to do in fixed point arithmetic without scaling.

The above example illustrates the motivation for floating point representation: dynamic range. Floating point representation is similar to scientific notation, that is,

$$\text{fraction} \times (\text{radix})^{\text{exponent}}.$$

For example, the number 9999 is expressed as 0.9999×10^4. In a computer with floating point instructions the radix is implicit, so only the fraction and the exponent need to be represented explicitly.

The floating point format for the above 4 decimal digits could be like this:

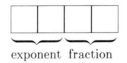

exponent fraction

Now let's examine the dynamic range in this representation (assume positive numbers and positive exponents only).

> Smallest (nonzero) number $= 0.01 \times 10^0 = 0.01$.
> Largest number $= 0.99 \times 10^{99}$ approximately 10^{99}.
> Therefore, the dynamic range is $10^{99}/0.01$, approximately 10^{101}.

Thus, in floating point representation the dynamic range is several orders of magnitude larger then that of fixed point representation.

In practice, floating point numbers may have a negative fraction and negative exponent. There are many formats to represent these numbers, but most of them have the following properties in common:

a. The fraction is an unsigned number called the *mantissa*;

b. The exponent is represented by a *characteristic* which is an excess code to accommodate both polarities of the exponents;

c. The sign of the entire number is represented by the most significant bit of the number.

For example, the following format is an extension of the previous example:

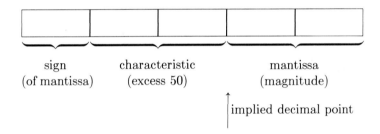

The excess code is a method of representing both negative and positive exponents by adding bias to the exponent:

$$\text{bias} = \frac{1}{2}\beta^s,$$

where

$$\beta = \text{radix},$$
$$s = \text{number of exponent digits}.$$

For the above format:

$$\text{bias} = \frac{1}{2}(10)^2 = \frac{1}{2}(100) = 50;$$

and the biased exponent is called the characteristic and is defined as follows:

$$\text{characteristic} = \text{exponent} + \text{bias}.$$

Example:

Exponent $= 2$, will result in

$$\text{characteristic} = 2 + 50 = 52.$$

The mantissa is the magnitude of the fraction, and its sign is the MSD of the format. Numbers are defined as normalized if the MSD of the mantissa is nonzero. The number zero is represented by a zero mantissa and any characteristic; thus, there is no unique representation for zero. However, by definition, a normalized zero has zero exponent characteristic, and a zero in the sign position. Following are some examples:

$$
\begin{array}{lll}
0\ 51\ 78 \rightarrow +.78 \times 10^1 & = +7.8 & \\
0\ 52\ 07 \rightarrow +.07 \times 10^2 & = +7.0 & \text{unnormalized} \\
0\ 47\ 12 \rightarrow +.12 \times 10^{-3} & = .00012 & \text{negative exponent} \\
1\ 51\ 78 \rightarrow -.78 \times 10^1 & = -7.8 & \text{negative number} \\
0\ 52\ 00 \rightarrow +.00 \times 10^2 & = +0.0 & \text{unnormalized zero} \\
0\ 00\ 00 \rightarrow +0.0 \times 10^0 & = +0.0 & \text{normalized zero}
\end{array}
$$

The same approach can be used in binary floating point numbers. Consider a 32-bit word, where 24 bits are the unsigned mantissa, 7 bits are the characteristic, and the MSB is the sign of the number as follows:

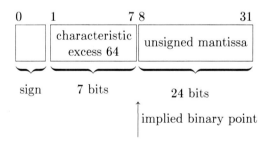

The range of the representable numbers as determined by the exponent in this format is:

The largest exponent is $127 - 64 = 63$ and $2^{+63} \simeq 10^{+19}$.

The smallest exponent is $0 - 64 = -64$ and $2^{-64} \simeq 10^{-21}$.

1.5 PROPERTIES OF FLOATING POINT REPRESENTATION

1.5.1 Lack of Unique Representation

Generally a floating point number is evaluated by this equation:

$$M \times \beta^e,$$

where

$$M = \text{Mantissa},$$
$$\beta = \text{Radix},$$
$$e = \text{exponent}.$$

In a 5-digit decimal floating point representation, the number 9 can be written as 0.9×10^1 or as 0.09×10^2. The lack of unique representation makes comparison of numbers difficult. Consequently floating point numbers are usually represented in normalized form, where the mantissa is always represented by a nonzero most significant digit. Obviously, this rule could not apply to the case of zero. Therefore, by definition, normalized zero is represented by all zero digits (which simplify zero detection circuitry). It is interesting to note that a normalized zero in floating point representation is designed to be identical to the fixed point representation of zero.

1.5.2 Range and Precision

Range is a pair of numbers (smallest, largest) which bounds all representable numbers in a given system. Precision is the gap between any two such representable numbers.

The largest number representable in any normalized floating point system is approximately equal to the radix raised to the power of the maximum positive exponent, and the absolute value of the smallest nonzero number is approximately equal to the radix raised to the power of the maximum negative exponent.

Let us translate the above paragraph into equations.

$$\boxed{max = \beta^{e_{\max}} * M_{\max}}$$

where

$$max = \text{largest representable number},$$
$$\beta = \text{Radix},$$
$$e_{\max} = \text{largest exponent},$$
$$M_{\max} = \text{largest Mantissa}.$$

$$\boxed{min = \beta^{e\text{min}} * \mathrm{M_{min}}}$$

where

$min=$ smallest number (absolute value),
$e_{\text{min}}=$ smallest exponent,
$\mathrm{M_{min}}=$ smallest Mantissa (normalized).

Example:

The following IBM System 370 (short) format is similar to the binary format at the end of the last section, except that the IBM radix is 16.

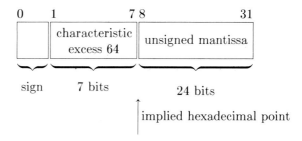

Since

$$\beta = 16,$$

then

$$e_{\text{max}} = 63; \qquad \mathrm{M_{max}} = 1 - 16^{-6}.$$

Therefore the largest representable number is

$$max = 16^{63} * (1 - 16^{-6}) \simeq 7.23 \times 10^{75}.$$

And the smallest positive normalized number is

$$min = 16^{-64}(16^{-1}) \simeq 5.4 \times 10^{-79},$$

since

$$e_{\text{min}} = -64; \qquad \mathrm{M_{min}} = 16^{-1}.$$

For a given radix, the range is mainly a function of the exponent. By contrast, the precision is a function of the mantissa. *Precision* is the resolution of the system, and it is defined as the minimum difference between two mantissa representations, which is equal to the value of the least significant bit of the mantissa. In the IBM short format, there are 24 bits in the mantissa, therefore, the precision is 16^{-6}(or 2^{-24}) $\simeq 0.6 \times 10^{-7}$, or approximately seven significant decimal digits.

Example:

More precision is obtained by extending the number of bits in the mantissa, for example, in the IBM System 370, one more word is added to the mantissa in its long format, that is, 32 more bits. The mantissa is 56 bits long and the precision is 16^{-14}(or 2^{-56}) $\simeq 10^{-17}$. The format with an extended mantissa is commonly called double precision, but in reality the precision is more than doubled. In the IBM case this is 17 vs. 7 decimal digits.

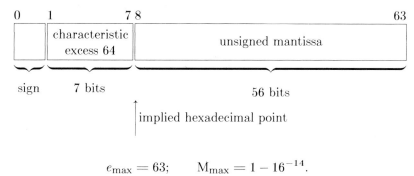

$$e_{\max} = 63; \qquad M_{\max} = 1 - 16^{-14}.$$

The largest representable number is

$$max = 16^{63}*(1 - 16^{-14}).$$

and the smallest positive normalized number is, as before,

$$min = 16^{-64}(16^{-1}).$$

1.5.3 Mapping Errors: Overflows, Underflows, and Gap

Just as in fixed point system, the finitude of the machine number system is a problem in floating point representation. In practice, the problem of overflow in a floating point system is much less severe than in a fixed point system, and most business-type applications are never aware of it. For example, the budget of the U.S. Government, while in hundreds of billion dollars, requires only 11 decimal digits to represent, well within the capability of the IBM/370 floating point format. By contrast, in many scientific applications [STE 74], the computation results in overflows; for example, $e^{200} > 10^{76}$, therefore, e^{200} cannot be represented in the IBM floating point system. Similarly $(0.1)^{200}$ cannot be represented either, since $(0.1)^{200} = 10^{-200}$ and the smallest representable number is approximately 10^{-76}. The latter situation is called *underflow*. Thus, mapping from the human infinite number system to a floating point system with finite range may result in an unrepresentable exponent (exponent spill). The exponent spill is called overflow if the absolute value of the result is larger than *max*, and it is called underflow if the absolute value of the result is smaller than *min*. In order to allow the computation to proceed in a reasonable manner after an exponent spill, the following approximations can be used: underflow is replaced by a normalized zero, and overflow is replaced by the largest signed representable number. However, the CDC 6600 produces a bit pattern representing ∞, and from that point on this overflow is treated as a genuine ∞, for example, $X \div \infty = 0$. These approximations should not be confused with the computations through overflows in fixed point representation. The latter always produce a correct result whereas the floating point approximation of overflow and underflow always produces an incorrect result, but this incorrect result may have an acceptable error associated with it. For example, in computing a function using polynomial approximation some of the last terms may underflow, but by setting them to zero, no significance is lost. The case in point [STE 74] is $\sin X \simeq X$, which for $|X| < .25 \times 16^{-32}$ is good to over 65 hexadecimal digits. So far, we have discussed the consequences of mapping out of range numbers, and have shown that the resulting overflow or underflow is a function of the range, that is, the exponent portion of the floating point number. Now consider the consequences of the fact that the floating point number system can represent only a finite subset of R, the set of real numbers. For simplicity assume that the set R is within the range of floating point numbers, thus, the error in mapping is a function of the mantissa resolution. Garner [GAR 76] has shown that for a base β floating point number system, with a $p -$ bit mantissa, the value of the gap between normalized floating point numbers is $2^{-p}\beta^e$ where e is the value of the unbiased exponent. The magnitude of the mapping error is some fraction of the gap value. For example, in the range of 0.5 to 0.999... the IBM short format has a maximum mapping error (gap) of $2^{-24} \times 16^0 = 2^{-24} \simeq 10^{-7}$ while the long IBM format reduces the mapping error to $2^{-56} \simeq 10^{-17}$.

1.6 FLOATING POINT OPERATIONS

In this section the four basic arithmetic operations are discussed in just enough detail so that the resulting consequences can be analyzed. All operations assume normalized operands:

$$\text{radix}^{-1} \leq \text{mantissa} < 1.$$

Example:

In the binary system radix $= 2$ and $0.5 \leq \text{mantissa} < 1$.

1.6.1 Addition and Subtraction

Addition and subtraction require that the exponents of the two operands be equal. This alignment is accomplished by shifting the mantissa of the smaller operand to the right, while proportionally increasing its exponent until it is equal to the exponent of the larger number. (In general scientific notation the alignment could be accomplished by the converse operation, that is, shift the mantissa of the larger number left, while decreasing its exponent. However, this is impossible in a normalized floating point system, since a left-shifted normalized mantissa has to be larger than 1, but $1 - 2^{-p}$ is the largest representable $p - $ bit mantissa.) After the alignment the two mantissas are added (or subtracted) and the resultant number, with the common exponent, is normalized. The latter operation is called postnormalization. In the addition operation, the postnormalization is a maximum of one right-shifted digit. Since the range of one mantissa is $0.5 \leq |m_1| < 1$ and the other unnormalized mantissa has the range of $0 \leq |m_2| < 1$, the range of the sum $0.5 \leq |m_1 + m_2| < 2$, may require no shift for $0.5 \leq |m_1 + m_2| < 1$ or may require one position right shift for $1 \leq |m_1 + m_2| < 2$. In the latter case the exponent is increased by 1. If this results in exponent spill, the postnormalization sets the number to its largest possible value. In subtraction, the maximum shift required on postnormalization is equal to the number of mantissa bits. Subtraction may produce this special case of zero result, whereby the postnormalization, instead of shifting, generates a normalized zero.

1.6.2 Multiplication

Multiplication in floating point is conceptually easier than addition. No alignment is necessary. The mantissas are multiplied as if they were fixed point integers and the exponents are simply added. Postnormalization is made up of one of the following cases.

Case 1. Resultant mantissa is in the range of $0.5 \leq |m_1 * m_2| < 1$, in which case no shifting is required.

Case 2. $0.25 \leq |m_1 * m_2| < .5$ requires one place left shift and reducing the resultant exponent by one. (Cases 1 and 2 are justified since $0.5 \leq |m_1| < 1$, $0.5 \leq |m_2| < 1$, then $0.25 \leq |m_1 * m_2| < 1$.)

Case 3. If either operand is zero, then the postnormalization produces a normalized zero.

Case 4. If either Case 1 or Case 2 (after exponent reduction) generates an exponent spill, then the postnormalization forces the largest absolute value with the sign bit set to the proper sign (the EXCLUSIVE-OR of the two operand signs).

1.6.3 Division

To perform floating point division F_1/F_2, the mantissas are divided (m_1/m_2) and the exponent of the divisor is subtracted from the exponent of the dividend. Since $0.5 \leq |m_1| < 1$ and $0.5 \leq |m_2| < 1$, then $0.5 \leq |m_1/m_2| < 2$.

Case 1. If $m_1 < m_2$, then $0.5 < |m_1/m_2| < 1$ and no postnormalization is required.

Case 2. If $m_1 \geq m_2$, then $1 \leq |m_1/m_2| < 2$ postnormalization is done by shifting the mantissa one place to the right, and increasing the exponent by one.

Case 3. If the dividend is zero, postnormalization produces normalized zero.

Case 4. If the divisor is zero, the result overflows and the postnormalization forces the largest representable value.

Case 5. If both dividend and divisor are zero, then the result is undefined. (Later on we will call such a result NAN = Not A Number.)

Case 6. If the postnormalized exponent is out of bound, the result is overflow or underflow.

1.7 PROBLEMS IN FLOATING POINT COMPUTATIONS

1.7.1 Loss of Significance

The following example [HAS 77] illustrates the loss of significance problem. Assume that two numbers are different by less than 2^{-24}. (The representation is the IBM System 370 short format.)

$$A = 0.100000 \times 16^1$$
$$B = 0.\text{FFFFFF} \times 16^0.$$

When one is subtracted from the other, the smaller must be shifted right to align the radix points. (Note that the least significant digit of B is now lost.)

$$A = 0.100000 \times 16^1$$
$$B = 0.0\text{FFFFF} \times 16^1$$
$$\overline{A - B = 0.000001 \times 16^1} = .1 \times 16^{-4}.$$

Now, let's calculate the error generated due to loss of digits in the smaller number. The result is (assuming infinite precision):

$$A = 0.1000000 \times 16^1$$
$$B = 0.0\text{FFFFFF} \times 16^1$$
$$\overline{A - B = 0.0000001 \times 16^1} = .1 \times 16^{-5}.$$

$$\text{ERROR} \quad = 0.1 \times 16^{-4} - 0.1 \times 16^{-5} = 0.\text{F} \times 16^{-5}.$$

Thus, the loss of significance (error) is $.F \times 16^{-5}$. An obvious solution to this problem is a guard digit, that is, additional bits are used to the right of the mantissa to hold intermediate results. In the IBM format an additional 4 bits (one hexadecimal digit) are appended to the 24 bits of the mantissa. Thus, with a guard digit the above example will produce no error. On first thought one might think that in order to obtain maximum accuracy it is necessary to equate the number of guard bits to the number of bits in the mantissa. However, Yohe [YOH 73] has proven that two guard digits are always sufficient to preserve maximal accuracy. This is also supported by the previous analysis showing that, in addition, the postnormalization has a maximum of one left shift. Thus, no more than one guard digit will enter the final significant result. However, to insure an unbiased rounding a third digit, (sticky digit) has to be added beyond the two guard digits. Rounding and sticky digits will be described in detail in the next section.

The following example illustrates another loss of significance inherent in the floating point number system.

$$
\left.
\begin{array}{l}
A = 0.100000 \times 16^1 \\
B = \underline{0.100000 \times 16^{-10}}
\end{array}
\right\}
\begin{array}{l}
\text{Original} \\
\text{Operands}
\end{array}
$$

$$
\left.
\begin{array}{l}
A = 0.100000000000 \times 16^1 \\
B = \underline{0.000000000001 \times 16^1}
\end{array}
\right\}
\text{Alignment}
$$

$$
\begin{array}{ll}
A + B = 0.100000000001 \times 16^1 & \text{Addition} \\
A + B = 0.100000 \times 16^1 & \text{Postnormalization}
\end{array}
$$

Thus, $A + B = A$ while $B \neq 0$. This violation of a basic law of algebra is characteristic of the approximation used in the floating point system.

1.7.2 Rounding: Mapping the Reals into the Floating Point Numbers

Rounding in floating point arithmetic and associated error analysis, are probably the most discussed subjects in floating point literature. References include [YOH 73, MAR 73]; for a more complete list see Garner [GAR 76].

The following formal definition of rounding is taken from Yohe [YOH 73]:

Let R be the real number system and let M be the set of machine representable numbers. A mapping RND: R → M is said to be rounding if, for all $a \in R$, $b \in R$, $RND(a) \in M, RND(b) \in M$ we have:

$$\text{RND } (a) \leq \text{RND } (b) \text{ whenever } a \leq b \, .$$

Further: A rounding is called optimal if for all $a \in R$ and for $RND(a) \in R \cap M$, $RND(a) = a$.

This implies that if $a \in R$ and m_1, m_2 are consecutive members of M with $m_1 < a < m_2$ then $RND(a) = m_1$ or $RND(a) = m_2$. Rounding is symmetric if $RND(a) = -RND(-a)$. For example, RND $(39.2) = -RND(-39.2) = 39$.

Yohe defines a total of five rounding modes for all $a \in R$, including three optional symmetric roundings T, A, and RN.

1.   Downward directed rounding: $\nabla a \leq a$.

2.   Upward directed rounding: $\Delta a \geq a$.

3.   Truncation, T, rounding toward zero.

4.   Augmentation, A, rounding away from zero.

5.   RN, rounding which selects the closest machine number, and in the case of a tie selects the number whose magnitude is larger. This rounding is the most frequently used since it produces maximum accuracy.

The directed rounding, while not provided in any production computer, is very important in interval arithmetic. Interval arithmetic is a procedure for computing an upper and lower bound on the true value of a computation. These bounds define an interval which contains the true result. Yohe claims that hardware designed to produce these roundings would enable interval operations to be executed in one tenth to one fifth of the time normally required to execute them with simulated floating point arithmetic.

The above five rounding methods are illustrated in the following example for decimal arithmetic.

	∇	Δ	T	A	RN
+39.7	+39	+40	+39	+40	+40
+39.5	+39	+40	+39	+40	+40
+39.2	+39	+40	+39	+40	+39
+39.0	+39	+39	+39	+39	+39
−39.0	−39	−39	−39	−39	−39
−39.2	−40	−39	−39	−40	−39
−39.5	−40	−39	−39	−40	−40
−39.7	−40	−39	−39	−40	−40

In order to handle overflow and underflow, Yohe describes hardware architecture that includes an indicator digit representing one of four conditions:

1. o = overflow indicator.

2. u = underflow indicator.

3. i = infinity indicator.

4.   representable number (none of the above).

The largest positive floating point number is denoted by *max*, and the smallest normalized positive floating point number by *min*.

The effects of the five rounding methods are summarized in Table 1, while Figure 1–1 partitions graphically the infinite space of the reals into several ranges. All together, 17 cases are tabulated. Case 1 gives the same result for all five rounding methods since it is an exact normalized machine number. In this table, m_1 and m_2 represent consecutive positive normalized floating point numbers with $m_1 < m_2$. Cases 5, 6, 13, and 14 show the rounding effect for $m_1 \leq R \leq m_2$. All the remaining cases overflow or involve underflow. For example, in the overflow cases, the rounding algorithm will set the exponent overflow indicator. If the rounding option implies rounding toward zero, the result will be $\pm$ *max*. If the rounding option implies rounding away from zero, the infinity indicator is set and the result is replaced by the particular bit configuration used to represent infinity.

TABLE 1
Effects of Rounding according to Yohe [YOH 73]

Case	R — Range of Values	Δ Value	Δ Ind*	∇ Value	∇ Ind	T Value	T Ind	A Value	A Ind	O Value	O Ind	Case
1	$R = m$	m		m		m		m		m		1
2	$max + \beta^{e_{max}-p} \leq R$	∞	o, i	max	o	max	o	∞	o, i	∞	o, i	2
3	$max + \frac{1}{2}\beta^{e_{max}-(p+1)} \leq R < max + \beta^{e_{max}-p}$	∞	o, i	max	o	max	o	∞	o, i	∞	o, i	3
4	$max \leq R < max + \frac{1}{2}\beta^{e_{max}-(p+1)}$	∞	o, i	max	o	max	o	∞	o, i	max		4
5	$\frac{1}{2}(m_1 + m_2) \leq R < m_2$	m_2		m_1		m_1		m_2		m_2		5
6	$m_1 \leq R < \frac{1}{2}(m_1 + m_2)$	m_2		m_1		m_1		m_2		m_1		6
7	$min - \frac{1}{2}\beta^{e_{min}-(p+1)} \leq R < min$	min	u	0	u	0	u	min	u	min	u	7
8	$\frac{1}{2} min \leq R < min - \frac{1}{2}\beta^{e_{min}-(p+1)}$	min	u	0	u	0	u	min	u	min	u	8
9	$0 \leq R < \frac{1}{2} min$	min	u	0	u	0	u	min	u	0	u	9
10	$-\frac{1}{2} min < R \leq 0$	0	u	$-min$	u	0	u	$-min$	u	0	u	10
11	$-min + \frac{1}{2}\beta^{e_{min}-(p+1)} < R \leq -\frac{1}{2} min$	0	u	$-min$	u	0	u	$-min$	u	$-min$	u	11
12	$-min < R \leq -min + \frac{1}{2}\beta^{e_{min}-(p+1)}$	0	u	$-min$	u	0	u	$-min$	u	$-min$	u	12
13	$-\frac{1}{2}(m_1 + m_2) < R \leq -m_1$	$-m_1$		$-m_2$		$-m_1$		$-m_2$		$-m_1$		13
14	$-m_2 < R \leq -\frac{1}{2}(m_1 + m_2)$	$-m_1$		$-m_2$		$-m_1$		$-m_2$		$-m_2$		14
15	$-max - \frac{1}{2}\beta^{e_{max}-(p+1)} < R \leq -max$	$-max$	o	$-\infty$	o, i	$-max$	o	$-\infty$	o, i	$-max$		15
16	$-max - \beta^{e_{max}-p} < R \leq -max - \frac{1}{2}\beta^{e_{max}-(p+1)}$	$-max$	o	$-\infty$	o, i	$-max$	o	$-\infty$	o, i	$-\infty$	o, i	16
17	$R \leq -max - \beta^{e_{max}-p}$	$-max$	o	$-\infty$	o, i	$-max$	o	$-\infty$	o, i	$-\infty$	o, i	17

(The Δ, ∇, T, A, and O groups are subheadings under "Rounding Option.")

Note: The left column which describes the range of the real numbers, is illustrated graphically in Figure 1–1.

*i represents the infinity indicator; o represents the overflow indicator; and u represents the underflow indicator.

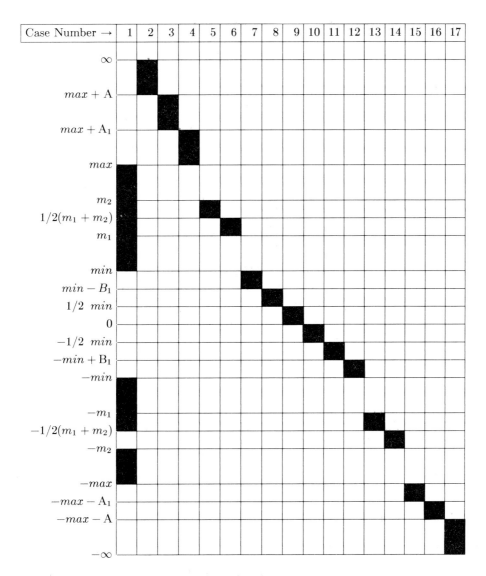

Figure 1–1.   Graphical illustration of the 17 different cases of the positive range of the reals.

The following shorthand notation is used in Figure 1–1.

$$A = \beta^{e_{\max} - p},$$
$$A_1 = \frac{1}{2}\beta^{e_{\max} - (p+1)},$$
$$B_1 = \frac{1}{2}\beta^{e_{\min} - (p+1)},$$

where:

$$\beta = \text{radix},$$
$$e_{\max} = \text{maximum possible exponent},$$
$$e_{\min} = \text{minimum possible exponent},$$
$$p = \text{number of } \beta\text{-base mantissa digits}.$$

Note that A corresponds to $\beta^{e_{max}} \cdot \beta^{-p}$, a number with maximum exponent and least possible (unnormalized) mantissa. A_1 and B_1 represent quantities with mantissas out of range of the indicated exponent.

1.7.3 Radix Trade-offs and Error Analysis

So far, the range and significance were discussed independently, but for a given number of bits there is a trade-off between them. Recall the previously mentioned 32-bit format with 24 bits of unsigned mantissa, 7 bits of exponent, and one sign bit. The trade-offs between range and significance are illustrated by comparing a system with a radix of 16 (hexadecimal) against a system with a radix of 2 (binary system).

	Largest Number	Smallest Number	Precision
Hexadecimal system	7.2×10^{75}	5.4×10^{-79}	24 Bits
Binary system	9.2×10^{18}	2.7×10^{-20}	24 Bits

While the hexadecimal system has the same precision as binary, hex-normalization may result in three leading zeros whereas nonzero binary normalization never has leading zeros. The above table indicates that for a given word length there is a trade-off between range and accuracy; more accuracy (base 2) is associated with less range and vice versa (base 16). But there is quite a bit of sacrifice in range for a little accuracy. Cody [COD 73] tabulates the error as a function of the radix for three 32-bit floating point formats having essentially identical range.

Base	Exponent Bits	Range	Mantissa Bits	Maximum Relative Error	Average Relative Error
2	9	$2^{255} \simeq 6 \times 10^{76}$	22	0.5×2^{-21}	0.18×2^{-21}
4	8	$4^{127} \simeq 3 \times 10^{76}$	23	0.5×2^{-21}	0.14×2^{-21}
16	7	$16^{63} \simeq 0.7 \times 10^{76}$	24	2^{-21}	0.17×2^{-21}

The relative error of $X \in R$ in the right columns is defined as the magnitude of the representable error divided by X (with exponents x). The maximum relative representation error (MRRE) over all normalized fractions is computed below (obviously the maximum representable error is $\frac{1}{2}$ of the gap):

$$\text{MRRE} = \frac{\text{maximum representable error}}{\text{smallest normalized fraction}} = \frac{\frac{1}{2} * 2^{-p} * \beta^x}{\frac{1}{\beta} * \beta^x} = \frac{1}{2} 2^{-p} \beta.$$

For example, in the hexadecimal system

$$\text{MRRE} = \frac{1}{2} \times 2^{-24} \times 16 = 2^{-25} \times 2^4 = 2^{-21}.$$

The average relative representation error (ARRE) assumes a logarithmic distribution for floating point number and a uniformly distributed minimum representation error.

From the above table the binary system seems better in range and accuracy than the hexadecimal system. So, why use hexadecimal radix at all? The answer is in the higher computational speed associated with larger base value as illustrated by the following example.

Example:

Assume a 24-bit mantissa with all bits zero except the least significant bit. Now compare the maximum number of shifts required for each case of postnormalization.

Case 1: Binary system: radix $= 2$. In this case, 23 shifts are required.

Case 2: Hexadecimal system: radix $= 16$. In this case we shift 4 bits at a time (since each hexadecimal digit is made of 4 bits). Therefore, the maximum number of shifts is five.

Thus the hexadecimal shifting is several times faster than the binary.

Garner [GAR 76] summarizes the trade-offs:

> "... the designer of a floating number system must make decisions affecting both computational speed and accuracy. Better accuracy is obtained with small base values and sophisticated round-off algorithms while computational speed is associated with larger base values and crude round-off procedures such as truncation."

1.8 TOWARD A STANDARD FLOATING POINT REPRESENTATION

1.8.1 Background

Presently there are more then 20 different floating point formats in use by various computer manufacturers. We illustrate below the formats of three computers which are popular for scientific computing, using the following general terminology. Exponent will represent all forms of biased and unbiased exponents while significand represents the mantissa independent of the location of the radix point.

S	E	F

S = Sign bit (indicates the sign of the significand).

E = Biased Exponent.

F = Significand.

Figure 1–2 shows further details of the three formats; from it we can see that there is hardly any similarity between the various formats. This situation, which prohibits data portability produced by numerical software, was the main motivation for setting up in 1978 an IEEE (Computer Society) committee to standardize floating point arithmetic. The main goal of the standardization efforts is to establish a standard which will allow communication between systems at the data level without the need for conversion.

	IBM/370	DEC PDP-11	CDC Cyber 70
	S = Short L = Long	S = Short L =Long	
Word length	S: 32 bits L: 64 bits	S: 32 bits L: 64 bits	60 bits
Exponent	7 bits	8 bits	11 bits
Significand	S: 6 digits L: 14 digits	S: (1)+23 bits L: (1)+55 bits	48 bits
Bias of exponent	64	128	1024
Radix	16	2	2
Hidden '1'	No	Yes	No
Radix point	Left of Fraction	Left of hidden '1'	Right of MSB of Fraction
Range of Fraction (F)	$(1/16) \leq F < 1$	$0.5 \leq F < 1$	$1 \leq F < 2$
F representation	Signed magnitude	Signed magnitude	One's complement
Approximate max. positive number	$16^{63} \simeq 10^{76}$	$2^{127} \simeq 10^{38}$	$2^{1023} \simeq 10^{307}$
Precision	S: $16^{-6} \simeq 10^{-7}$ L: $16^{-14} \simeq 10^{-17}$	S: $2^{-24} \simeq 10^{-7}$ L: $2^{-56} \simeq 10^{-17}$	$2^{-48} \simeq 10^{-14}$

Figure 1–2. Comparison of floating point specification of three popular computers.

In addition to the respectable goal of "the same format for all computers," the committee wanted to ensure that it would be the best possible standard for a given number of bits. Specifically, the concern was to ensure correct results, that is, the same as those given by the corresponding infinite precision with an error of 1/2 of the LSB. Furthermore, to ensure portability of all numerical data, the committee specified exceptional conditions and what to do in each case (overflow, underflow, etc.). Finally, it was desirable to make possible future extensions of the standard such as interval arithmetic.

The motivation of this section is quite independent of the potential adoption of this standard. Rather, one can view the standard as an "ideal" numeric representation largely derived without implementation or compatibility constraints. It then serves (at the least) as the basis for comparison with actual floating point formats.

Before we describe the details of the proposed standard, let's analyze the good and bad points of each of the above three popular formats.

Representation Error: According to Ginsberg [GIN 77] the combination of base 16, short mantissa size, and truncated arithmetic should definitely be avoided. This criticism is of the IBM short format where, due to the hexadecimal base, the MRRE is 2^{-21}. By contrast, the 23 bits combined with the hidden '1' as on PDP-11 seems to be a more sensible trade-off between range and precision in a 32-bit word, with MRRE of 2^{-24}.

Range: While the PDP-11 scores well on its precision on the single format, it loses on its double format. In a 64-bit word the trade-off between range and precision is inadequate and more exponent range should be given at the expense of precision. The exponent range of the CYBER 70 seems to be more appropriate for the majority of scientific applications.

Rounding: None of the three formats uses an *unbiased* rounding to the nearest machine number in case of ties, [GIN 77].

1.8.2 The Proposal

The IEEE Computer Society received several proposals for standard representations for consideration, however, the most complete has been the one prepared by Kahan, Coonen, Stone, and Palmer [COO 79]. Several references have called this the "KCS proposal" after Kahan, Coonen, and Stone, but we shall refer to it simply as the "Kahan proposal."

We first describe the Kahan proposal and then we point out some controversial issues, with the pros and cons for each such issue.

Data Formats: The floating point data format is made up of three parts (from left to right): sign bit, biased exponent (characteristics), and significand (mantissa):

S	E	F

where

$S = $ Sign bit (indicates the sign of the significand),

$E = $ Biased exponent,

$F = $ Significand;

then

$e = $ true exponent $ = E - $ bias,

$f = $ true significand $ = 1.F$.

A normalized nonzero number, X, has the following interpretation.

$$X = (-1)^S * 2^{E-bias} * (1.F).$$

This format has three levels of precision as outlined in Figure 1–3: SINGLE, DOUBLE and QUAD.

	Single	Double	Quad
Word length	32 bits	64 bits	128 bits
Sign	1-bit	1-bit	1-bit
Biased exponent	8 bits	11 bits	15 bits
Significand	(1) + 23 bits	(1) + 52 bits	112 bits
Bias of Exponent	127	1023	16383
Ranges:			
(a) Approximate* max. positive number	$2^{128} \simeq 1.7 * 10^{38}$	$2^{1024} \simeq 9 * 10^{307}$	$2^{16384} \simeq 1.2 * 10^{4932}$
(b) Minimum positive normalized number	$2^{-126} \simeq 1.2 * 10^{-38}$	$2^{-1022} \simeq 2.2 * 10^{-308}$	$2^{-16383} \simeq 1.6 * 10^{-4932}$
Precision	$2^{-23} \simeq 10^{-7}$	$2^{-52} \simeq 10^{-15}$	$2^{-112} \simeq 10^{-33}$

*Actual maximum positive number is slightly smaller. For example, in the single precision it is: $2^{127}(2 - 2^{-23})$.

Figure 1–3.   The three levels of precision of the floating point data format.

Note: The first version of the proposal was drafted in April 1978 by Harold Stone and the final version was published in March of 1981 in *Computer*. The original draft included a QUAD format while the final one omitted it. We include the description of the QUAD format as it is instructive of the suggested range and precision for 128 bits.

To simplify the discussion only the SINGLE precision is described. Of the 32 bits, 1 is used for the sign, 8 for the biased exponent and 23 for the significand. The significand (F) is represented by a sign-magnitude notation, with an implied leading one (hidden '1') and an implied binary point to the right of the hidden '1'. By now it should be clear that the format (at least on SINGLE precision) is very similar to that of the PDP-11 and the VAX from Digital Equipment Corporation (DEC), but it is not identical. For example, the Kahan true significand is in the range $1 \leq f < 2$, whereas the DEC significand is $0.5 \leq f < 1$. Other differences will be pointed out later on. The biased exponent is an 8-bit number of the range $0 < E < 255$ (the values of 0 and 255 are for reserved operands), and it is biased by the value 127. Thus, the true exponent has the range $-127 < e < 128$, as shown in the following table.

Biased Exponent	True Exponent	
	Kahan	DEC PDP-11
E	Bias = 127	Bias = 128
0	Reserved Operand	Reserved Operand
1	−126	−127
2	−125	−126
⋮	⋮	⋮
127	0	−1
128	1	0
129	2	1
⋮	⋮	⋮
254	127	126
255	Reserved Operand	Reserved Operand

The different decoding of the reserved operands are compared in Figure 1–4.

S	Biased Exp	Significand	Interpretation	
0	0	0	+Zero	
1	0	0	−Zero	
0/1	0	Not 0	±Denormalized Numbers	KAHAN
0	255	0	+Infinity	
1	255	0	−Infinity	
X	255	Not 0	NAN (Not a Number)	
S	Biased Exp	Significand	Interpretation	
0	0	Don't care	Unsigned zero	DEC
1	0	Don't care	General purpose reserved operands	

Figure 1–4. Kahan and DEC decoding of the reserved operands (Illustrated with the SINGLE format, i.e., $E_{max} = 255$)

1.8.3 Extended Formats

The Kahan proposal does not require but recommends the use of extended formats for temporary results. This mechanism reduces the chance of an intermediate overflow of a computation whose result would have been representable in a basic format. It also reduces the round-off error introduced during a long chain of operations.

Each of the two basic formats has associated with it an extended format; thus we have single-extended and double-extended formats as follows (note that the hidden bit is not used here since it has sufficient significand bits).

	Single-extended	Double-extended
Word length $\geq$	44 bits	80 bits
S = Sign	1-bit	1-bit
E = Exponent	11 bits	15 bits
F = Significand $\geq$	31 bits	63 bits

Arithmetic Operations. The Kahan proposal specifies the following operations:

1. Numerical operations
   - Add
   - Subtract
   - Multiply
   - Divide
   - Square Root
   - Remainder

2. Conversion operations
   - Floating point $\leftrightarrow$ Integer
   - Binary (integer) $\leftrightarrow$ Decimal (integer)
   - Binary (floating) $\leftrightarrow$ Decimal (floating)

3. Miscellaneous operations
   - Move from one format width to another
   - Compare and set condition code
   - Find integer part

Rounding. There are four rounding modes

1. RN = Unbiased rounding to nearest (in case of a tie round to even).

2. RZ = Round toward zero (chop, truncate).

3. RM = Round toward minus infinity.

4. RP = Round toward plus infinity.

Of the four only the first is mandatory and the rest are optional. Unbiased rounding is very similar to the conventional round to nearest which is implemented by adding 1/2 of the digit to be discarded and then truncate to the desired precision.

Example:

$$
\begin{array}{ll}
39.2 & 39.7 \\
\underline{0.5\quad\ } & \underline{0.5\quad\ } \\
39.7 \to 39 & 40.2 \to 40.
\end{array}
$$

But, suppose the number to be rounded is exactly half way between two numbers, which one is the nearest? To answer the question let us add the same 0.5 to the two following numbers:

$$
\begin{array}{ll}
38.5 & 39.5 \\
\underline{0.5\quad\ } & \underline{0.5\quad\ } \\
39.0 \to 39 & 40.0 \to 40.
\end{array}
$$

Notice that in both cases we rounded up even though each number was exactly half way between smaller and larger numbers. Therefore, by simply adding 0.5 and truncating a biased rounding is generated. In order to have unbiased rounding we round to even whenever there is a tie between two numbers. Now, using the previous numbers we get:

$$38.5 \to 38$$
$$39.5 \to 40.$$

In the first case the number is rounded down and in the second case the number is rounded up. Therefore, we have statistically unbiased rounding. Of course, the same unbiased rounding could be obtained by rounding to odd (instead of even) in the tie case. This time the rounding looks like this:

$$38.5 \to 39$$
$$39.5 \to 39.$$

However, rounding to even is preferred because it may result in "nice" integer numbers as in the following examples:

$$1.95 \to 2$$
$$2.05 \to 2.$$

Whereas rounding to odd results in the more frequent occurrence of noninteger numbers:

$$1.95 \to 1.9$$
$$2.05 \to 2.1.$$

Now, we illustrate the implementation of the unbiased rounding to even, and introduce the so called "sticky bit".

The conventional system for rounding is to add 1/2 of the LSD position of the desired precision, to the MSD of the portion to be discarded. But this scheme has a problem as is illustrated below (the XXXX are additional bits). Thus:

$$
\begin{array}{ll}
38.5 \text{ XXXXXX} & \leftarrow \text{Raw number} \\
\underline{0.5} & \leftarrow \text{Add } 0.5 \\
39.0 & \leftarrow \text{Result} \\
39 & \leftarrow \text{Truncate}
\end{array}
$$

Two cases have to be distinguished.

Case 1: XXXXXX $\neq 0$ (at least one X $= 1$) and the rounding is correct since 39 is nearest $38.5 + \Delta$, where $0 < \Delta < 0.5$.

Case 2: XXXXXX $= 0$ (all bits are X $= 0$). Now the rounding is incorrect because we have a tie case which requires the result to be rounded to even (38).

It is obvious that regardless of the number of X bits, all possible permutations can be mapped into one of the two above cases. Therefore, one bit can be used to distinguish between Case 1 and Case 2. This bit is called the "sticky bit", and it has the value one for Case 1 and the value zero for Case 2. The logic implementation of the sticky bit is simply ORing of the bits to the right of the second guard bit, as illustrated below for the addition/subtraction operation.

1.		G	R	S

|← —— desired precision —— →|

where

$$
\begin{array}{l}
G = \text{first guard bit,} \\
R = \text{second guard bit,} \\
S = \text{sticky bit.}
\end{array}
$$

In the case of a left shift (normalization after subtraction), S does not participate in the left shift, but instead zeros are shifted into R. But, in the case of a right shift due to a significand overflow (during magnitude addition), the R guard bit is ORed into S during the shift.

The above format (with two guard bits) is necessary only during the addition/subtraction process; the final result just before rounding has only one guard bit and the sticky bit.

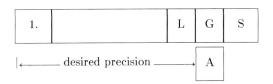

where

$$L = \text{LSB of the significand before rounding,}$$
$$G = \text{guard bit,}$$
$$S = \text{sticky bit,}$$
$$A = \text{bit to be added to G for proper rounding.}$$

The proper action to obtain unbiased rounding-to-even is determined from the following table.

L	G	S	Action	A
X	0	0	Exact result. Obviously no rounding is necessary	X
X	0	1	Inexact result, but significand is rounded properly	X
0	1	0	The tie case with even significand. No rounding needed	0
1	1	0	The tie case with odd significand. Round to nearest even	1
X	1	1	Round to nearest by adding 1 to the L-bit	1

So far we have addressed only the unbiased rounding, but there are three more optional modes. The round to zero (RZ) is simply a truncation which is used in certain integer related operations (actually most present day computers provide truncation as the only rounding option). The remaining two rounding modes are rounding toward $+\infty$ and rounding toward $-\infty$. These two directed roundings are used in interval arithmetic where one computes the upper and lower bounds of an interval by executing the same sequence of instructions twice, rounding up during one pass and down the next. The sticky bit, introduced previously, is also essential for the correct direct rounding as illustrated below for rounding upward.

Example:

Directed Upward Rounding;

> **Case 1:** No sticky bit is used:
> $38.00001 \rightarrow 38$
> $38.00000 \rightarrow 38$.
> **Case 2:** Sticky bit is used:
> $38.00001 \rightarrow 39$ (sticky bit $= 1$)
> $38.00000 \rightarrow 38$ (sticky bit $= 0$, exact number).

1.8.4 Exceptions and What to Do in Each Case

The Kahan proposal specifies five exceptional conditions that may arise during an arithmetic operation (the sixth is applicable only to QUAD precision):

1. INVALID OPERATION and NANs,

2. OVERFLOW,

3. DIVISION BY ZERO,

4. UNDERFLOW,

5. INEXACT RESULT,

6. UNNORMALIZED RESULT (applicable only to QUAD).

Exceptions are handled in one of two ways (except unnormalized)

1. TRAP and supply the necessary information to correct the fault. For example:

   What instruction caused the TRAP?
   What were the values of the input operands?
   Etc.

2. DISABLE TRAP, but deliver a specified result. For example on UNDERFLOW: "Set result to zero and continue".

In either case there is a corresponding exception—the flag is set and it remains set until cleared by the user.

EXCEPTION 1: **INVALID OPERATION and NANs**.

The INVALID OPERATION exception occurs during a variety of arithmetic operations which do not produce valid numerical results.

Example:

$$\sqrt{-5}$$
$$(+\infty) + (-\infty)$$
$$0 * \infty$$

Operations like the above generate an entity called NAN (Not a Number), which is one class of the reserved operands (Figure 1–4a). This class is characterized by a biased exponent of $111\ldots111$, and a nonzero significand. Therefore, there are (in the SINGLE precision format) $2^{23} \simeq 8$ million members in the NAN class. These NANs can be used (if the trap is enabled) to communicate information to the user program. For example, the result of any of the above operations may be a pointer to the offending line of code. The Kahan proposal suggests, but does not specify the exact information to be contained in the NANs, since this type of information is highly system dependent.

Since the NAN is a valid result of an arithmetic operation, it is necessary to specify exactly what to do if a NAN appears as an input operand. Generally, the NAN will simply propagate through the arithmetic operation.

Example:

$$5 + \text{NAN} \rightarrow \text{NAN}$$
$$3 * \text{NAN} \rightarrow \text{NAN}$$
$$\sqrt{\text{NAN}} \rightarrow \text{NAN}$$

In case both of the input operands are NANs, the result is the NAN with the smaller significand. However, the INVALID OPERATION FLAG is set any time any input operand is a NAN.

EXCEPTION 2: **OVERFLOW and infinities.**

The OVERFLOW FLAG is set whenever the exponent of the result exceeds the allowed range for the corresponding precision. For example, in SINGLE precision OVERFLOW occurs if E $>$ 254. If the OVERFLOW trap is enabled, the exponent is wrapped around into the desired range since it can be out of range, at most, by a factor of two (because every arithmetic operation's result goes to a destination no narrower then its input operands). The exponent is wrapped around by a bias adjust. For example, in the SINGLE precision the bias is 192, rather then 127. In this way the overflowed result (after scaling) is placed away from the OVERFLOW threshold, as illustrated below for multiplying two large numbers:

$$2^{127} * 2^{127} = 2^{254} \leftarrow \text{overflow.}$$

If the bias were the usual 127 than the scaled result is:

$$2^{254-127} = 2^{127},$$

which is very close to the overflow threshold. By contrast using 192 as a bias gives:

$$2^{254-192} = 2^{62},$$

which is not as close to the threshold.

If the OVERFLOW trap is disabled, then infinity with the sign of the overflowed result, is delivered as the final result. The $\pm$ infinity is also a reserved operand with the exponent of $111\ldots111$ (just like NANs) but with a zero significand (see Figure 1–4a). There are two ways to deal with the infinities.

1.   Affine closure (signed infinities);

$$-\infty < \text{ Real numbers } < +\infty.$$

2.   Projective closure (unsigned infinities);

$$+\infty = -\infty = \infty.$$

Comparison between a real number and infinity (other then EQUALITY) results in INVALID OPERATION. Of the two modes the Affine mode is the default since it is appropriate for many engineering computations.

We saw previously that NANs are valid input operands. Similarly the infinities are valid operands, and while they activate the INVALID OPERATION FLAG they generate the specified result. The most obvious example is dividing by $\pm$ infinity, which generates a $\pm$ zero.

EXCEPTION 3: **DIVISION BY ZERO.**

The division by zero is a special case of the OVERFLOW. It happens in a division operation when the divisor is zero and the dividend is a nonzero number (including infinity). If the trap is disabled the delivered result is a signed infinity.

EXCEPTION 4: **UNDERFLOW and DENORMALIZED numbers.**

The UNDERFLOW exception occurs whenever the biased exponent becomes zero or negative, that is, $E < 1$. If the UNDERFLOW trap is enabled, then the exponent is wrapped around into the desired range with a bias adjust similar to the technique used in the OVERFLOW case.

If the UNDERFLOW trap is disabled then the number is denormalized by right shifting the significand and correspondingly incrementing the exponent until it reaches the minimum allowed exponent ($E = 0$). The following example, [COO 79], illustrates the denormalizing process.

Example:

Assume (for simplicity) that we have a SINGLE precision exponent and a significand of 6 bits.

$$Z = 2^{-130} * 1.01101. \,|\, .. \qquad -130 < -126 \text{ so we denormalize}$$
$$Z = 2^{-126} * 0.000101 \,|\, 101... \qquad \text{we round (to nearest, say)}$$
$$X = 2^{-126} * 0.000110| \qquad = \text{the result to be delivered.}$$

The denormalization as a result of UNDERFLOW has been called GRADUAL UNDERFLOW or GRACEFUL UNDERFLOW. Of course, this approach merely postpones the fatal underflow which occurs when all the nonzero bits have been right shifted out of the significand. Note that since denormalized numbers and $\pm$ zero have the same exponent ($E = 0$), such a fatal underflow would automatically produce the properly signed zero. Use of a signed zero indicator is an interesting example of taking a potential disadvantage—two representations for the same value—and turning it (carefully!) into an advantage.

When denormalized numbers are input operands, they are treated the same as normalized numbers if the operation is ADD/SUBTRACT. However, the situation is different in MULTIPLY/DIVIDE, where multiplying a SINGLE precision denormalized number by a large power of 2, and attempting to store the result in SINGLE activates the INVALID OPERATION exception. The reason for the exception is to prevent normalizing a denormalized number that lost part of its precision during prior UNDERFLOW merely by multiplication.

EXCEPTION 5: **INEXACT RESULT**.

Exact result is obtained whenever both the guard bit and the sticky bit are each equal to zero. Any other combinations of the guard and sticky bit implies that a round-off error has taken place, in which case the INEXACT RESULT FLAG is set. The purpose of this flag is to allow integer calculations with a floating point execution unit.

EXCEPTION 6: **UNNORMALIZED RESULT**.

Unnormalized results are valid numbers only when the MSB of the significand is explicit (as in the QUAD precision). But, first let us distinguish between unnormalized and denormalized numbers. Denormalized numbers are only those numbers with the smallest possible exponent ($E = 0$). For example, in SINGLE precision the following are some denormalized numbers:

$$2^{-126} * 0.00110,$$
$$2^{-126} * 0.00011.$$

By contrast, unnormalized numbers may have any allowed exponent and unlike the denormalized numbers, they don't have a unique representation. For example, the following unnormalized numbers are the same:

$$2^{-5} * 0.001,$$
$$2^{-4} * 0.0001,$$
$$2^{-3} * 0.00001.$$

The unnormalized numbers can be generated only by the operations: MULTIPLY, DIVIDE and MOVE. If the destination is QUAD (explicit significand MSB) then the UNNORMALIZED RESULT FLAG is set, and the corresponding trap, if enabled, is activated. If the destination is SINGLE or DOUBLE, where unnormalized numbers don't exist, then an INVALID OPERATION is generated.

1.8.5 Analysis of the Kahan Proposal

There seems to be a general agreement that the following features of the proposed standard are the best for the given number of bits.

- The format of

- The three levels of precision (SINGLE, DOUBLE and QUAD)

- The various rounding modes

- The specification of arithmetic operations

- Condition causing exceptions

However, on a more detailed level there seem to be many controversial issues which we will outline next.

Gradual underflow. This is the area where the most controversy exists. The obvious advantage of the GRADUAL UNDERFLOW is the extension of the range for small numbers and similarly the compression of the gap between the smallest representable number and zero. For example, in SINGLE precision the gap is $2^{-126} \simeq 1.2 * 10^{-38}$ for normalized numbers, whereas the use of denormalized numbers narrows the gap to $2^{-149} \simeq 1.4 * 10^{-45}$. However, Kahan states that GRADUAL UNDERFLOW is needed not so much to extend the exponent range, but rather to allow further computation with some sacrifice of precision in order to defer as long as possible the need to decide whether the UNDERFLOW will have significant consequences.

By contrast with Kahan there are several objections to this GRADUAL UNDERFLOW.

1. Payne [PAY 78] maintains that the range is extended only from 10^{-38} to 10^{-45} (coupled with complete loss of precision at 10^{-45}) and it makes sense only if SINGLE precision frequently generates intermediate results in the range 10^{-38} to 10^{-45}. However, for such cases she believes that the use of SINGLE precision (for intermediate results) is generally inappropriate.

2. Fraley [FRA 78] objects to the use of GRADUAL UNDERFLOW for three reasons:

    a. There are nonuniformities in the treatment of GRADUAL UNDERFLOW;

    b.   There is no sufficient documented need for it;

    c.   There is no mechanism for the confinement of these values.

We will demonstrate only his first objection, that is, the nonuniformities.

Example:

Consider the sum: AB + CD.

    Assume: SINGLE precision;

    Assume: A $\simeq 1.2 * 10^{-38}$ (very close to the underflow threshold but still normalized);

    Assume: B = 17.

There are two cases:

    Case 1: AB $\ll$ CD, AB is so much smaller than CD that it could be eliminated without having any effect on the sum.

    Case 2: AB $\simeq$ CD, therefore, AB contributes significantly to the sum.

Now, let's reduce A so that it underflows; at the same time we increase B by the same factor. If A is represented by a denormalized number then AB is a NAN (since multiplication by a number greater than 4 yields NAN, which is propagated through the sum). The result is annoying if Case 1 holds since the term was irrelevant; but it is desirable if Case 2 holds.

Now, let's reduce A even further, so it can no longer be represented using denormalized numbers; A becomes zero, and so does the product AB. This is fine in Case 1, but it produces the wrong answer in Case 2.

3.   Reinsch [REI 79] also objects to the nonuniform treatment of denormalized numbers. He questions a system which allows a user to double a number by addition ($y = x + x$) but not by multiplication ($y = 2x$). Of course, that is the case with the Kahan proposal where denormalized numbers may be multiplied by factors smaller than 2 only.

4.   The last objection to the GRADUAL UNDERFLOW is the increased implementation cost in floating point hardware. It is much more economical and faster to simply generate a zero output on underflow, and not have to recognize a denormalized number as a valid input.

An alternative approach to denormalized numbers is the use of pointer to a heap on occurrence of underflow [PAY 78]. In this scheme, a temporary extension of range can be implemented on occurrence of either underflow or overflow without sacrifice of precision. Furthermore, multiplication (and division) work as well as addition and subtraction. While this scheme seems adequate, or even better than GRADUAL UNDERFLOW, it also has the same cost disadvantage outlined in number 4 above.

Significand range and exponent bias. The Kahan proposal has a significand $1 \leq F < 2$, and the exponent is biased by 127 (in the SINGLE precision). These yield a number system with a magnitude between 2^{-126} and $\approx 2^{128}$, thus the system is asymmetric in such a way that overflow is less likely to happen then underflow. However, if GRADUAL UNDERFLOW is not used then the above rationale disappears and one can go back to a PDP-11 format with significand of $0.5 \leq F < 1$ and an exponent biased by 128. The PDP-11 SINGLE precision numbers have a magnitude between 2^{-128} and $\approx 2^{128}$ such that overflows and underflows are equally likely to occur.

Zeros and infinities. The Kahan proposal has two zero values $+0$ and -0 and two infinities $+\infty$ and $-\infty$, and it has been called two zero system. An alternate approach, the three zero system, was suggested by Fraley [FRA 78]. His system has values $+0$, -0, 0, $+\infty$, $-\infty$, and ∞.

The basic properties of the two systems are shown below:

2 Zero	3 Zero	Difference
$+0 = -0$	$-0 < 0 < +0$	
$-\infty < +\infty$	$-\infty < +\infty$	
or	or	
$-\infty = +\infty$	∞ not comparable	3 zero system
$x - x = +0$	$x - x = 0$	introduces an
$1/+0 = +\infty$	$1/+0 = +\infty$	unsigned zero
$1/-0 = -\infty$	$1/-0 = -\infty$	
	$1/0 = \infty$	

The main advantage of the three zeros system is the availability of a true zero and a true infinity in the algebraic sense. This is illustrated by the following two examples.

1.   Suppose $f(x) = e^{1/x}$. In the two zeros system we have:

$$f(-0) = 0,$$
$$f(+0) = +\infty;$$

thus $f(-0) \neq f(+0)$, even though $-0 = +0$.

This, of course, is a contradiction of the basic theorem:

$$\text{if } x = y \text{ then } f(x) = f(y).$$

By contrast, in the three zeros system this theorem holds since:

$$-0 \neq +0.$$

2. The two zeros system fails to distinguish zeros that result from underflow from those which are mathematically zero. The result of $x-x$ is $+0$ in the two zeros system. In the three zeros system $x - x = 0$, whereas $+0$ is the result of an underflow of a positive number; that is,

$$0 < +0 < \text{smallest representable number.}$$

1.9 ADDITIONAL READINGS

Sterbenz [STE 74] is an excellent introduction to the problem of floating point computation—a comprehensive treatment of the earlier approaches to floating point representation and their difficulties.

The January 1980, and March 1981 issues of the IEEE *Computer* have several valuable articles on the proposed standard; [STE 81] is a precise description of the proposed IEEE 754 standard, with good introductory remarks by David Stevens.

Cody [COD 81] provides a detailed analysis of the three major proposals and shows the similarity between all of them.

Coonen [COO 81] gives an excellent tutorial on underflows and denormalized numbers. He attempts to clear the misconceptions about gradual underflows and shows how it fits naturally into the proposed standard.

Hough [HOU 81] describes applications of the standard for computing elementary functions such as trigonometric and exponential functions. This interesting article also explains the need for some of the unique features of the standard: extended formats, unbiased rounding, and infinite operands.

Coonen [COO 80] also published a guide for the implementation of the standard. His guide provides practical algorithms for floating point arithmetic operations and suggests the hardware/software mix for handling exceptions. His guide also includes a narrative description of the standard including the QUAD format. For actual hardware implementation of the proposed IEEE Standard, see the list in Section 5.4.5.

1.10 SUMMARY

In arithmetic, the representation of integers is a key problem. Machines by their nature have a finite set of symbols or codes upon which they can operate as contrasted with the infinity that they are supposed to represent. This finitude defines a modular form of arithmetic widely used in computing systems. The familiar modular system, a single binary base, lends itself readily towards compliment coding schemes which serve to scale negative numbers into the positive integer domain.

Pairs of *signed* integers can be used to represent approximations to real numbers called floating point numbers. Floating point representations broadly involve tradeoffs between precision, range and implementation problems. With the relatively decreasing importance of implementation costs, the possibility of defining more suitable floating point representations has led to recent efforts toward a standard floating point representation.

1.11 EXERCISES

1. Consider the operation of integer division: $\pm11 \div \pm5$; that is, find the quotient and remainder for each of the four sign combinations.

   a.   For signed integers.

   b.   For modulus division.

2. If we denote $\div_m$ as modulus division and $\div_s$ denotes signed division find the relationships between these two operations where n and d are numerator and denominator respectively.

3. Another type of division is possible; this is called "floor division." In this the quotient is the greatest integer that is contained by the numerator divided by the denominator, (note that minus 3 is greater than minus 4). Compare this to the results in problem 2.

4. Find an algorithm for computing X mod M, for known M, using only the addition, subtraction, multiplication, and comparison operations. You should not make any assumptions as to the relative size of X and M in considering this problem.

5. Find an algorithm for multiplication with negative numbers using an unsigned multiplication operation. Show that either nothing need be done or describe in detail what must be done to the product of the two numbers one or both of which may be in complement form.

     a.   For radix complement.

     b.   For diminished radix complement.

6. For a variety of reasons, a special purpose machine is built that uses 32-bit representation for floating point numbers. A minimum of 24 bits of precision is required. Compare a 370-like (truncation) system with a simple binary system.

7. Repeat the previous problem changing the binary system to a modified version of the IEEE standard. Compare the IBM/370 format to the IEEE standard format as to the (a) associative, (b) commutative, (c) distributive properties of basic arithmetic operations. In which cases do the properties fail?

8. Find the value of *max* and *min* (largest and smallest representable numbers) for single and double precision.

     a.   IEEE standard.

     b.   System/370.

     c.   PDP-11.

1.12 DESIGN EXERCISES

Note: use data in Design Appendix.

1. Design a circuit to convert a 32-bit two's complement integer into a normalized floating point number in the System/370 short format. Both the initial integer and the floating point result are in 32-bit registers. Use programmed arrays logic. Compute delay in the worst case path.

Chapter 2

RESIDUE NUMBERS AND
THE LIMITS OF FAST ARITHMETIC

In this chapter we are concerned about the speed of arithmetic. In most arithmetic systems the speed is limited by the nature of the building block which makes logic decisions and the extent to which decisions of low order numeric significance can affect results of higher significance. This latter problem is best illustrated by the addition operation in which a low order carry can have a rippling effect on a sum.

We begin by examining ways of representing numbers, especially in so far as they can reduce the sequential effect of carries on digits of higher significance. Carry-independent arithmetic (called residue arithmetic) is possible within some limits. This residue arithmetic representation is a way of approaching a famous bound on the speed at which addition and multiplication can be performed.

This bound (called Winograd's bound) determines a minimum time for arithmetic operations and is an important basis for determining the comparative value of various implementation algorithms to be discussed in subsequent chapters.

For certain operations, storage, especially a Read Only Memory (ROM), can be used to "look-up" a result or partial result. Since very dense ROM technology is now available, the last section of this chapter develops a performance model of ROM access. Unlike Winograd's work, this is not a strict bound but rather an approximation to the retrieval time.

2.1 THE RESIDUE NUMBER SYSTEM

2.1.1 Representation

The number systems considered in the last chapter are linear, positional and weighted, in which all positions derive their weight from the same radix (base). In the binary number systems, the weights of the positions are 2^0, 2^1, 2^2, etc. In the decimal number system, the weights are $10^0 = 1$, $10^1 = 10$, $10^2 = 100$, $10^3 = 1000$, etc.

The residue number system [GAR 59], [GSC 67] usually uses positional bases that are relatively prime to each other, for example, 2, 3, 5. For instance, if the number 8 is divided by the base 5, residue is 3. The table below lists the numbers 0 to 29 and their residues to bases 2, 3, and 5. (The number of unique representations is $2 \times 3 \times 5 = 30$.)

N	Residue to base			N	Residue to base			N	Residue to base		
	5	3	2		5	3	2		5	3	2
0	0	0	0	10	0	1	0	20	0	2	0
1	1	1	1	11	1	2	1	21	1	0	1
2	2	2	0	12	2	0	0	22	2	1	0
3	3	0	1	13	3	1	1	23	3	2	1
4	4	1	0	14	4	2	0	24	4	0	0
5	0	2	1	15	0	0	1	25	0	1	1
6	1	0	0	16	1	1	0	26	1	2	0
7	2	1	1	17	2	2	1	27	2	0	1
8	3	2	0	18	3	0	0	28	3	1	0
9	4	0	1	19	4	1	1	29	4	2	1

The residues in the above table uniquely identify a number. The configuration $[2, 1, 1]$ represents the decimal number 7 just as uniquely as binary 111.

To convert a conventionally weighted number, X, to the residue system, we simply take the residue of X with respect to each of the positional moduli.

Example:
To convert the decimal number 29 to a residue number we do the following:

$$R_5 = 29 \bmod 5 = 4,$$
$$R_3 = 29 \bmod 3 = 2,$$
$$R_2 = 29 \bmod 2 = 1;$$

and the decimal number 29 is represented by $[4, 2, 1]$ in the above residue number system.

The main advantage of the residue number system is the absence of carries between columns in addition and in multiplication. Arithmetic is closed (done completely) within each residue position. Therefore, it is possible to perform addition and multiplication on long numbers at the same speed as on short numbers since the speed will be determined by the largest modulus position. Recall that in the conventional linear weighted number system, an operation on long words is slower due to the carry propagation.

2.1.2 Operations in the Residue Number System

Examples of additions in $5, 3, 2$ residue arithmetic are:

$$
\begin{array}{rclcrcl}
9 & \rightarrow & [4, 0, 1] & & 8 & \rightarrow & [3, 2, 0] \\
\underline{+16} & \rightarrow & \underline{[1, 1, 0]} & & \underline{+19} & \rightarrow & \underline{[4, 1, 1]} \\
25 & \rightarrow & [0, 1, 1] & & 27 & \rightarrow & [2, 0, 1] \\
\text{decimal} & & \text{residue} & & \text{decimal} & & \text{residue} \\
& & 5, 3, 2 & & & & 5, 3, 2
\end{array}
$$

Note that each column was added modulo its base, disregarding any interposition carries. An example of multiplication is:

$$
\begin{array}{rclcl}
7 & \rightarrow & & [2, 1, 1] \\
\underline{\times 4} & \rightarrow & \times & \underline{[4, 1, 0]} \\
28 & & & [3, 1, 0]
\end{array}
$$

Again, each column is multiplied modulo its base, disregarding any interposition carries, for example, $2 \times 4 \,(\mathrm{mod}\ 5) = 8 \,(\mathrm{mod}\ 5) = 3$.

The uniqueness property is the result of the famous Chinese Remainder Theorem.

Theorem: Given a set of relatively prime moduli $m_1, m_2, \ldots, m_i, \ldots, m_n$, then for any $X < M$ the set of residues $\{X \bmod m_i \mid 1 \le i \le n\}$ is unique; where

$$
M = \prod_{i=1}^{n} m_i.
$$

The proof is straightforward. Suppose there were two numbers Y and Z that have identical residue representations, i.e for each i, where $y_i = z_i$.

$$
y_i = Y \bmod m_i.
$$

$$
z_i = Z \bmod m_i.
$$

Then $Y - Z$ is a multiple of m_i, and $Y - Z$ is a multiple of the least common multiple of m_i. But since the m_i are relatively prime, their least common multiple is M. Thus, $Y - Z$ is a multiple of M, and Y and Z cannot both be less than M, [STO 73].

Subtraction: Since $a \bmod m - b \bmod m = (a - b) \bmod m$, the subtraction operation poses no problem in residue arithmetic, but the representation of negative numbers requires use of complement coding.

Following our earlier discussion on complementation, we create a signed residue system by designating numbers $X < M/2$ as positive and $X \ge M/2$ as negative (for all $X < M$). That is, a number $X \ge M/2$ is treated as $X - M$, which is equivalent mod M;

$$
(X - M) \bmod M = X \bmod M,
$$

and the complement of $X \bmod M$ is

$$(M - X) \bmod M.$$

In residue representation $X = [x_i]$; where $x_i = X \bmod m_i$ and the complement of X is the complement of $[x_i]$. Call the complement of X, X^c and of x_i is x_i^c. Then

$$x_i^c = (m_i - x_i) \bmod m_i,$$

and

$$[x_i]^c = [x_i^c] = X^c,$$

since $-x_i$ and $m_i - x_i$ are congruent mod m_i.

Example:
In the 5,3,2 residue system $M = 30$ and integer representations 0 thru 14 are positive and 15 thru 29 are negative i.e., represents numbers -15 thru -1. Now

$$8 = [3, 2, 0],$$

and

$$9 = [4, 0, 1].$$

$$(8)^c = [2, 1, 0]; \quad \text{i.e., } 5 - 3, 3 - 2, \text{ and } (2 - 0) \bmod 2.$$

$$(9)^c = [1, 0, 1].$$

$$
\begin{array}{rcl}
8 = & 8 & = & [3, 2, 0] \\
\underline{-9} = & (9)^c & = & \underline{+[1, 0, 1]} \\
-1 & & & [4, 2, 1] = 29 \text{ or } -1.
\end{array}
$$

2.1.3 Selection of the Moduli

Certain moduli are more attractive than others for two reasons.

1. They are efficient in their binary representation; that is, n binary bits can represent approximately 2^n distinct residues.

2. They provide straightforward computational operations using binary adder logic.

Moduli of the form 2^{k_1}, $2^{k_1} - 1$, $2^{k_2} - 1$, $\ldots 2^{k_n} - 1$ ($k_1, k_2, \ldots, k_n$ are integers) were suggested by Merrill [MER 64] as meeting the above criteria.

Note that not all numbers of the form $2^k - 1$ are relatively prime. In fact, if k is even.

$$2^k - 1 = (2^{k/2} - 1)(2^{k/2} + 1).$$

If k is an odd composite, $2^k - 1$ is also factorable, and for $k = p$, with p a prime, the resulting numbers may or may not be prime. These are famous numbers called Mersenne's numbers [NEW 56];

$$M_p = 2^p - 1 \quad (p \text{ a prime}).$$

Mersenne asserted (1644) that the only p's for which M_p is prime are:

$$p = 2, 3, 5, 7, 13, 17, 19, 31, 67, 127, 257.$$

The conjecture stood for almost 300 years. F. N. Cole in 1903 showed in a historic paper, that M_{67} was not a prime.

Listed below is a table of factors for numbers of the form $2^k - 1$. Note that any 2^n will be relatively prime to any $2^k - 1$. The table is from Merrill [MER 64].

A Partial List of Moduli of the Form 2^k and $2^k - 1$
and Their Prime Factors

Moduli	Prime Factors
3	–
7	–
15	3,5
31	–
63	3,7
127	–
255	3,5
511	7,73
1023	3,11,31
2047	23,89
4095	3,5,7,13
8191	–
$2^k (k = 1, 2, 3, 4 \ldots)$	2

Since the addition time is limited in the residue system to the time for addition in the largest module, we should select moduli as close as possible to limit the size of the largest modulus. Merrill suggests the largest be of the form 2^k and the second largest of the form $2^k - 1$. The remaining moduli should avoid common factors. He cites some examples of interest.

Bits to represent	Moduli set
17	32, 31, 15, 7
25	128, 127, 63, 31
28	256, 255, 127, 31

If the moduli are relatively prime, we can "almost" represent as many objects as the pure binary representation. For example, in the 17-bit case, instead of 2^{17}

code points, we have

$$2^5(2^5 - 1)(2^4 - 1)(2^3 - 1) = 2^{17} - \mathcal{O}(2^{14}),$$

where $\mathcal{O}(2^{14})$ indicates a term of the order of 2^{14}. Thus, we have lost less than 1 bit of representational capability (a 1-bit loss would correspond to an $\mathcal{O}(2^{16})$ loss).

2.1.4 Operations with General Moduli

With the increasing availability of ROM (Read Only Memory) technology, the restriction to moduli forms 2^k or $2^k - 1$ is less important. Thus addition, subtraction, and multiplication can be done by table look-up. In the most straightforward implementation, separate tables are kept for each modulus, and the arguments x_i and y_i (both mod m_i) are concatenated to form an address in the table that contains either the proper sum or product.

Example:
A table of 1024 or 2^{10} entries can be used for moduli up to 32, or 2^5; i.e., if x_i and y_i are 5-bit arguments, then their concatenated 10-bit value forms an address into a table of results.

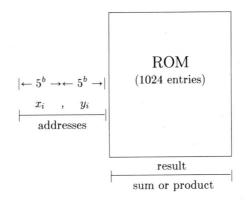

In this case, addition/subtraction and multiplication are accomplished in one access time to the table. Note that since access time is a function of table size and since the table size grows at 2^{2n} (number of bits to represent a number), residue arithmetic has a considerable advantage over conventional representation in its use of table look-up techniques.

2.1.5 Conversion To and From Residue Representation

Conversion from an ordinary weighted number representation into a residue representation is conceptually simple—but implementations tend to be somewhat less obvious.

Conceptually, we could just divide the number to be converted by each of the respective moduli and the remainders would form the residues. This process is usually too slow, however, and the integer to be converted is decomposed (as in the $2^k - 1$ case) and its components are converted and summed modulo the respective base. Thus an integer, A, can be represented in familiar weighted positional notation;

$$A = \sum_{i=0}^{n} A_i R^{n-i},$$

where

$$R = \text{radix},$$
$$A_i = \text{the value of the } i^{\text{th}} \text{position.}$$

It is decomposed with respect to radix position, or pairs of positions, simply by the ordered configuration of the digits.

In the usual case, the radix and the modular base are relatively prime, and for single-position conversion we would have:

$$x_{ji} = A_i R^{n-i} \bmod m_j,$$

where x_{ji} is the ith component of the m_j residue of A; then, x_j the residue of A mod m_j is

$$x_j = \left(\sum_i x_{ji} \right) \bmod m_j.$$

The process can be quickly implemented. Since

$$x_{ji} = (A_i \bmod m_j \cdot R^{n-i} \bmod m_j) \bmod m_j,$$

the $R^{n-i} \bmod m_j$ term is precomputed and included in a table that maps A_i into x_{ji}. Thus, x_{ji} is derived from A_i in a single table look-up.

Example:
Compute the residue mod 7 of the radix 10 integer 826.

$$826 = 8 \times 100 + 2 \times 10 + 6,$$
$$= A_0 \times 10^2 + A_1 \times 10 + A_2.$$

Now:

$$100 \bmod 7 = 2,$$
$$10 \bmod 7 = 3;$$

thus, we have the following tables.

A_0	X_{j0}	A_1	X_{j1}	A_2	X_{j2}
0	0	0	0	0	0
1	2	1	3	1	1
2	4	2	6	2	2
3	6	3	2	3	3
4	1	4	5	4	4
5	3	5	1	5	5
6	5	6	4	6	6
7	0	7	0	7	0
8	2	8	3	8	1
9	4	9	6	9	2

From this, $826 \bmod 7 = (2 + 6 + 6) \bmod 7 = 0$. Larger tables reduce the number of additions required and thus may improve the speed of conversion.

There is an important special case of conversion into a residue system: converting a mod 2^n number into a residue representation mod 2^k or mod $2^k - 1$. This case is important because of the previously mentioned coding efficiency with these moduli and because mod 2^n numbers arise from arithmetic operations using conventional binary type logic.

The conversion process from a binary representation (actually a residue mod 2^n) to a residue of either 2^k or $2^k - 1$ $(n > k)$ is as follows: partition the n bits into m digits of size k bits; that is, $m = \lceil \frac{n}{k} \rceil$. Then a binary number X (mod 2)^n is

$$X_{\text{base } 2} = X_{n-1} 2^{n-1} + X_{n-2} 2^{n-2} + \cdots + X_0;$$

and it can be rewritten as

$$X_{\text{base } 2^k} = X_{m-1} \left(2^k\right)^{m-1} + X_{m-2} \left(2^k\right)^{m-2} + \cdots + X_0.$$

This is a simple regrouping of digits. For example, consider a binary 24-bit number arranged in eight 3-bit groups.

$$X_{\text{base } 2} = 101\ 011\ 111\ 010\ 110\ 011\ 110\ 000.$$

This may be rewritten in octal $(k = 3)$ as $\lceil \frac{n}{k} \rceil = \lceil \frac{24}{3} \rceil$ digits:

$$X_{\text{base } 8} = 5\ 3\ 7\ 2\ 6\ 3\ 6\ 0.$$

The residue $X \bmod 2^k = X_0$ (the least significant octal digit) since all other digits in the representation are $0 \bmod 2^k, (k = 3)$.

Now the residue of $X_{\text{base } 2^k} \bmod (2^k - 1)$ can be computed directly from the mod 2^k representation. If X is a base 2^k number with n digits $(X_{n-1} \ldots X_0)$ and X_i is its ith digit:

$$X \bmod (2^k - 1) = \left(\sum_{i=0}^{n-1} X_i (2^k)^i \bmod (2^k - 1) \right) \bmod (2^k - 1).$$

For $X_0 \bmod (2^k - 1)$, the residue is the value X_0 for all digit values except $X_0 = 2^k - 1$, where the residue is 0. For $X_1 2^k \bmod 2^k - 1$, similarly, the residue is X_1 (1 for each 2^k multiple) unless X_1 itself is $2^k - 1$, in which case the residue is 0. And for $X_i (2^k)^i \bmod 2^k - 1$ the residue $= X_i$ where $X_i \neq 2^k - 1$ and the residue $= 0$ if $X_i = 2^k - 1$. This is the familiar process of "casting-out" $(b-1)$. In the previous example (X in octal)

$$X = 5\,3\,7\,2\,6\,3\,6\,0,$$

$$x = X \bmod 7 = (5 + 3 + 0 + 2 + 6 + 3 + 6 + 0) \bmod 7.$$

Now, pair-sum $\bmod 7$ can be directly computed from a $\bmod 8$ adder by recognizing three cases:

1. $a + b < 2^k - 1$ that is, $a + b < 7$, then $(a + b) \bmod 7 = a + b \bmod 8 = a + b$.

2. $(a + b) = 2^k - 1$, $a + b = 7$; then, $(a + b) \bmod 7 = 0$ that is, cast out 7's.

3. $a + b > 2^k - 1$, that is, $a + b > 7$; then $(a+b) \bmod 7 = a+b+1$. A carry-out occurs in a $\bmod 8$ adder. This end-around carry must be added to the $\bmod 8$ sum. If $a+b > 7$ then $a+b+1 = (a + b) \bmod 7$, i.e., we use end-around carry.

In our example,

$$x = X \bmod 7 = (5 + 3 + 0 + 2 + 6 + 3 + 6 + 0) \bmod 7.$$

	$5 + 3$	$0 + 2$	$6 + 3$	$6 + 0$
octal	10	2	11	6
mod 7	$1 + 0 = 1$	2	$1 + 1 = 2$	6
octal		$1 + 2 = 3$		$2 + 6 = 10$
mod 7		3		$1 + 0 = 1$
octal			$3 + 1 = 4$	
mod 7			4	

and $x = 4$

Conversion from residue representation is conceptually more difficult; however, the implementation is also straightforward [STO 73].

First the integer that corresponds to the residue representation that has a "1" in the jth residue position and zero for all other residues is designated the *weight* of the jth residue, w_j. The ordering of the residues (the "j"s) is unimportant, since however they are ordered, only one integer (mod the product of relatively prime moduli) will have a residue representation of 0, 0, 1, 0 ... 0. That is, it would have a zero residue for all positions $\neq j$ and a residue $= 1$ at j. Now the problem is to scale the weighted sum of the residues up to the integer representation modulo M, the product of the relatively prime moduli. By construction of the weights, w_j, the product

$$\sum_k (x_j \cdot w_j) \bmod m_k = x_j,$$

since w_j is a multiple of all m_k ($k \neq j$) and $(x_j \cdot w_j) \bmod m_j = X \bmod m_j$ for all j. Thus, to recover the integer X from its residue representation, all we do is to sum the weighted residue modulo M:

$$X \bmod M = \sum_j (w_j x_j) \bmod M.$$

Example:

Suppose we wish to encode integers with the relatively prime moduli 4 and 5. The product M, is 20. Thus, we encode integers 0 through 19 in residue representation as follows.

	Residues	
X	$x \bmod 4$	$x \bmod 5$
0	0	0
1	1	1
2	2	2
3	3	3
4	0	4
5	1	0
6	2	1
7	3	2
8	0	3
9	1	4
10	2	0
11	3	1
12	0	2
13	1	3
14	2	4
15	3	0
16	0	1
17	1	2
18	2	3
19	3	4

where

$$w_1 = \text{Value of X for which residue representation is } [1,0] = 5,$$
$$w_2 = [0,1] = 16.$$

Suppose we encode two integers 5 and 13 in this representation:

$$5 = [1,0],$$
$$13 = [1,3].$$

If we now wished their sum, we would get:

$$
\begin{array}{r}
[1,\ 0] \\
+\ [1,\ 3] \\
\hline
[2,\ 3].
\end{array}
$$

And to convert this to integer representation:

$$(x_1 w_1 + x_2 w_2) \bmod 20 = X,$$
$$(2 \cdot 5 + 3 \cdot 16) \bmod 20 = 18.$$

2.1.6 Using the Residue Number System

In the past, the importance of the residue system lay in its theoretic significance rather than in its fast arithmetic capability. While multiplication is straightforward, division is not and comparisons are quite complex. This coupled with conversion problems has limited the applicability of residue arithmetic. With the availability of powerful arithmetic technology this may change for suitable algorithms and applications. In any event, it remains an important theoretic system, as we shall see when determining the computational time bounds for arithmetic operations.

Another important application of residue arithmetic is error checking. If in an n-bit binary system

$$
\begin{array}{r}
a \bmod 2^n \\
+b \bmod 2^n \\
\hline
c \bmod 2^n,
\end{array}
$$

then it also follows that

$$
\begin{array}{r}
a \bmod (2^k - 1) \\
+b \bmod (2^k - 1) \\
\hline
c \bmod (2^k - 1).
\end{array}
$$

Since 2^n and $2^k - 1$ are relatively prime a small k-bit adder ($n \gg k$) can be used to check the operation of the n-bit adder. In practice, $k = 2, 3, 4$ is most commonly used. The larger k's are more expensive, but since they provide more unique representations, they afford a more comprehensive check of the arithmetic. For more information on using residue arithmetic in error checking see the paper by Watson and Hastings [WAT 66].

2.2 THE LIMITS OF FAST ARITHMETIC

2.2.1 Background

The purpose of this section is to present the theoretic bounds on the speed of arithmetic operations, so they can be compared against the state of art in arithmetic algorithms. These bounds serve as a yardstick to measure practical results, and provide a clear understanding of how much more speed improvement can be obtained.

2.2.2 Speed in terms of Gate Delays

The execution speed of an arithmetic operation is a function of two factors. One is the circuit technology and the other is the algorithm used. It can be rather confusing to discuss both factors simultaneously; e.g., a ripple-carry adder implemented in ECL technology may be faster than a carry-look-ahead adder implemented in CMOS. In this section, we are interested only in the algorithm and not in the technology, therefore, the speed of the algorithms will be expressed in terms of gate delays. Using this approach, the carry-look-ahead adder will be faster than the ripple-carry adder. Simplistically translating gate delays for a given technology to actual speed is done by multiplying the gate delays by the gate speed, e.g., 2 ns per ECL gate, 100 ns per CMOS gate, etc.

2.2.3 The model—(r, d) Circuit

Much of the original work to determine a minimum bound on arithmetic speed was done by Winograd [WIN 65], [WIN 67]. In his model the speed (in gate delays) of any logic and arithmetic operation is a function of three items:

Number of digits in each operand $= n$;

Fan-in of the gate (circuit) $= r =$ maximum number of logic inputs or arguments for a logic element;

The radix of the arithmetic $= d =$ number of truth values in the logic system.

Definition: (r,d) circuit is a d-valued logical circuit in which each element has fan-in at most r and can compute any r-argument d-valued logical function in unit time.

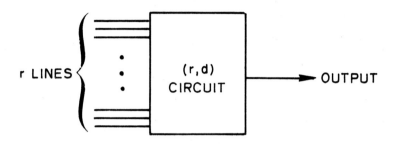

Figure 2–1.   The (r, d) circuit.

In any practical technology, logic path delay depends upon many factors: the number of gates (circuits) that must be serially encountered before a decision can be made, the logic capability of each circuit, cumulative distance among all such serial members of a logic path, the electrical signal propagation time of the medium per unit distance, etc. In many high speed logic implementations, especially those using ECL, the majority of total logic path delay is frequently attributable to delay external to logic gates. Thus, a comprehensive model of performance would have to include technology, distance, geography and layout, as well as the electrical and logical capabilities of a gate. Clearly, the inclusion of all these variables makes a general model of arithmetic performance infeasible. Winograd's (r,d) model of a logic gate is idealized in many ways.

1.   There is zero propagation delay between logic blocks.

2.   The output of any logic block may go to any number of other logic blocks without affecting the delay; I.e., the model is *fan-out* independent. The fan-out of a gate refers to its ability to drive from output to input a number of other similar gates. Practically speaking any gate has a maximum limit on the number of circuits it may communicate based on electrical considerations. Also as additional loads are added to a circuit, its delay is adversely affected.

3.   The (r,d) circuit can perform any logical decision in a unit delay—more comments on this below.

4.   Finally, delay in, and indeed feasibility of, implementations are frequently affected by mechanical considerations such as the ability to connect a particular circuit module to another or the number of connectors through which such an electrical path might be established. These, of course, are ignored in the (r,d) model.

Despite these limitations, the (r,d) model serves as a useful first approximation in the analysis of delay/performance of arithmetic algorithms in most technologies. The effects of propagation delay, fan-out, etc. are merely averaged out over all blocks to give an initial estimate as to the delay in a particular logic path. Thus in a particular technology such as ECL, the basic delay within a block may be one nanosecond. But the effect of delay, including average path lengths, line loading effects, fan-out, etc., might be closer to 3 and 3.5 nanoseconds. Still the number of blocks encountered between functional input and final result is an important and primary determinant (again for most technologies), in determining speed.

The (r,d) model is a fan-in limited model, the number of inputs to a logical gate is limited at r inputs, each gate has one output and all gates take a unit delay time, given valid inputs, to establish an output. The model allows for multivalued logic, where d is the number of values in the logic system. The model further assumes that any logic decision capable of being performed within an r input d-valued truth system is available in this unit time. This is an important premise. For example in a 2 input binary logic system ($r = 2$, $d = 2$) there are 16 distinct logic functions (AND, OR, NOT, NOR, NAND, EQUALITY, IMPLICATION, etc.). In fact, in general there are d^{d^r} distinct logic functions in a general (r, d) logic system. In any practical logic system, only a small subset of these are available. These are chosen in such a way as to be *functionally complete*; i.e., able to generate any of the other logic expressions in the system. However, the functionally complete set will not in general perform a required arbitrary logic function in unit delay, e.g. NOR's implementing EXCLUSIVE OR requires two unit delays. Thus, the (r,d) circuit is a lower bound on a practical realization. What we will discover in later chapters is that familiar logic subsets (e.g. NOR) can by themselves come quite close to the performance predicted by the (r,d) model.

2.2.4 First Approximation to the Lower Bound

Spira [SPI 73] has shown that if a d-valued output, f, is a function of all n arguments (d-valued inputs), then t, the computation time, is

$$t \geq \lceil \log_r n \rceil,$$

in units of (r,d) circuit delay.

Example:

$$n = 10,$$
$$r = 4,$$
$$d = 2;$$

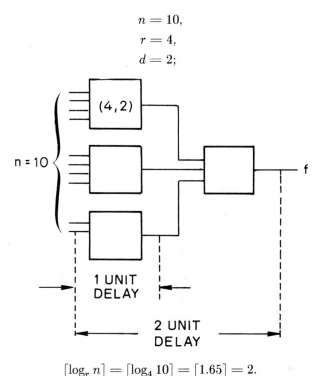

$$\lceil \log_r n \rceil = \lceil \log_4 10 \rceil = \lceil 1.65 \rceil = 2.$$

Proof: Spira's bound can be proved by induction and follows from the definition of the (r,d) circuit. The (r,d) circuit has a single output and r inputs, thus a single level $(t = 1)$ has r inputs. Let f_t designate a circuit with n inputs and t units of delay.

Consider the case of unit delay; i.e., $t = 1$. Since the fan-in in a unit block is r, then, if the number of inputs n is less than or equal to r,

$$1 \geq \lceil \log_r n \rceil,$$

because we have to have at least one gate to define the function f. Now suppose Spira's bound is correct for delays in a $t-1$ circuit (f_{t-1}). Let us find the resulting delay in the network (see Figure 2–2) for f_t. We are given that f_{t-1} is a function of n/r inputs. Now we have:

$$t - 1 \geq \lceil \log_r(n/r) \rceil = \lceil \log_r(n) - log_r(r) \rceil = \lceil \log_r(n) \rceil - 1;$$

and

$$t \geq \lceil \log_r(n) \rceil.$$

This proves the bound.

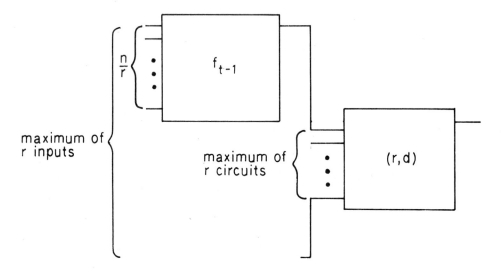

Figure 2–2.   The (r, d) network.

Now we can derive the lower bound for addition in the residue number system.

2.2.5 Spira's Bound Applied to Residue Arithmetic (Winograd's Bound)

The time for addition using (r,d) circuits and the residue system is at least

$$t \geq \lceil \log_r 2 \lceil \log_d \alpha(\mathrm{N}) \rceil \rceil,$$

where $\alpha(\mathrm{N})$ is the number of elements representable by the largest of the relatively prime moduli.

Clearly, since arithmetic is carry-independent between the various moduli we only need concern ourselves with the carry and propagation delay for the largest of the moduli. If this is N, then $\alpha(\mathrm{N})$ is the number of distinct numbers that this modulus can represent. Now $\log_d \alpha(\mathrm{N})$ is the number of d-valued lines required to represent a number for this modulus. Thus an addition network for this modulus will have $2\lceil \log_d \alpha(\mathrm{N}) \rceil$ input lines. In the addition operation a low order 1 can, for certain configurations of input line configurations, affect the most significant output line. The most significant output line then depends upon all input lines. Thus by Spira's bound we have:

$$t \geq \lceil \log_r 2 \underbrace{\lceil \log_d \alpha(\mathrm{N}) \rceil}_{\text{number of digits}} \rceil$$

$$\underbrace{\phantom{t \geq \lceil \log_r 2 \lceil \log_d \alpha(\mathrm{N}) \rceil \rceil}}_{\text{input lines}}$$

Winograd's theorem is actually more general than the above, since it shows that the bound is valid not only for the residue arithmetic but for any arithmetic representation obeying group theoretic properties. In the general case of modular addition the $\alpha(N)$ function needs more clarification. In modular arithmetic we are operating with single arguments mod A^n. If A is prime then $\alpha(N)$ is simply A^n, but if A is composite (i.e., not a prime) then $A = A_1 A_2 \ldots A_m$ and arithmetic can be decomposed into simultaneous operations mod A_1^n, mod $A_2^n, \ldots$ mod A_n^n. In this case $\alpha(N)$ is A_i^n where A_i is the largest prime element composing A.

For example, in decimal arithmetic $A = 10^n = 2^n \cdot 5^n$ and independent-pair arithmetic can be defined for A_2^n and A_5^n, limiting the carry compution to the largest modules; in this case $\alpha(10^n) = 5^n$.

Example:

    1. modular representation:

$$\text{prime base} \quad \alpha(2^{12}) = 2^{12},$$
$$\text{composite base} \quad \alpha(10^{12}) = 5^{12};$$

    2. residue representation:

$$\alpha(> 2^{16}); \text{ using set } \{2^5, 2^5 - 1, 2^4 - 1, 2^3 - 1\} = 2^5;$$

where $\alpha(> X)$ is defined as the composite number greater than X, which has the minimum greatest prime factor.

Note $minimum\ \alpha(> 2^k) = p_n$ where p_n is the nth prime in the product function defined as the smallest product of consecutive primes p_i, or *powers of primes*, that equal or exceed 2^{16};

$$\prod_{i=1}^{n} p_i \geq 2^{16}.$$

The selection of moduli to minimize the α function, is best illustrated by an example.

Example:
Suppose we wish to design a residue system that has $M \geq 2^{47}$, i.e., about 2^{47} unique representations. We wish to minimize the largest factor of M, $\alpha(M)$, in order to assure fast arithmetic. If we simply selected the product of the primes we would have:

$$2 \times 3 \times 5 \times 7 \times 11 \times 13 \times 17 \times 19 \times 23 \times 29 \times 31 \times 37 \times 41 > 2^{47}.$$

That is, the $\alpha(> 2^{47})$ for this selection would be 41.

We can improve the α function by using powers of the lower order primes. Thus:

$$2^5 \times 3^3 \times 5^2 \times 7 \times 11 \times 13 \times 17 \times 19 \times 23 \times 29 \times 31 > 2^{47}.$$

Here $\alpha(> 2^{47})$ is $2^5 = 32$. Thus, finding the minimum α function requires that before increasing the product (in the development of M) by the next larger prime, P_n, we check that there are no lower order primes, P_i, which when raised to their next integer power would not lie between P_{n-1} and P_n. That is for each $i < n - 1$ and x the next integer power of P_i,

$$P_{n-1} < P_i^x < P_n.$$

We use all such qualified P_i^x terms before introducing P_n into the product.

2.2.6 Winograd's Lower Bound on Multiplication

Typical multiplication is simulated by successive add-shifts and takes n addition times, e.g., multiplication of 16-bit numbers (that can be added in 100 ns), takes 1.6 microseconds. Now, Winograd surprises us by saying that multiplication is not necessarily slower than addition! And, if this is not enough, multiplication can be even slightly faster than addition. [BRE 68, WIN 67]

Since multiplication is also a group operation, involving two n-digit d-valued numbers—whose output is dependent on all inputs—the Spira bound applies.

$$t \geq \lceil \log_r 2n \rceil,$$

where

$2n =$ the total number of d-valued input lines.

To see that multiplication can be performed at the same speed as addition, one need only consider multiplication by addition of the log representation of numbers: if $a * b = c$, then $\log a + \log b = \log c$.

Notice that in a log representation fewer significant product bits are required than in the familiar linear weighted system. For example, $\log_2 16 = 4.0$ requiring 4 bits (3 plus one after the binary point) instead of 5 bits as $16.0 = 10000.0$ would require. Of course log representations require subtraction (i.e., negative log) for numbers less than 1.0 and zero is a special case.

Since division in this representation is simply subtraction, the bound applies equally to multiplication and division. Also, for numbers represented with a composite modular base (i.e., A^n where $A^n = A_1 \times A_2 \times \ldots \times A_n$), a set of log representations can be used. This coding of each base A number as an n-tuple; $\{\log Ai; \ i = 1 \text{ to } n\}$ minimizes the length of the carry path by reducing the number of d-valued input lines required to represent a number.

As an analogue to residue representation, numbers can be represented as composite powers of primes and then multiplication is simply the addition of corresponding powers.

Example:

$$12 \times 20$$

$$12 = 2^2 \cdot 3^1 \cdot 5^0$$
$$20 = 2^2 \cdot 3^0 \cdot 5^1$$
$$\text{product} \quad 240 = 2^4 \cdot 3^1 \cdot 5^1$$

$$12 \div 20$$

$$12 = 2^2 \cdot 3^1 \cdot 5^0$$
$$20 = 2^2 \cdot 3^0 \cdot 5^1$$
$$12/20 = 2^0 \cdot 3^1 \cdot 5^{-1} = 3/5$$

Winograd formalizes this by defining $\beta(N)$ akin to the $\alpha(N)$ of addition and shows that for multiplication:

$$\boxed{t \geq \lceil \log_r 2 \lceil \log_d \beta(N) \rceil \rceil,}$$

where

$$\boxed{\beta(N) < \alpha(N).}$$

The exact definition of $\beta(N)$ is more complex than $\alpha(N)$. Three cases are recognized:

Case 1: Binary radix $(N = 2^n)$; $n \geq 3$,

$$\beta(2^n) = 2^{n-2}.$$

Binary radix $(N = 2^n)$; $n < 3$,

$$\beta(4) = 2$$
$$\beta(2) = 1.$$

Case 2: Prime radix $(N = p^n)$; p a prime > 2,

$$\beta(p^n) = p^{n-1}.$$

Case 3: Composite powers of primes $(N = p_1^{n_1} \cdot p_2^{n_2} \ldots p_m^{n_m})$;

$$\beta(N) = \max \left(\beta(p_1^{n_1}), \ldots, \beta(p_i^{n_i}) \ldots \right).$$

Example:

    1. $N = 2^{10} \quad \beta(2^{10}) = 2^8$.

    2. $N = 5^{10} \quad \beta(5^{10}) = 5^9$.

    3. $N = 10^{10} = 5^{10} \cdot 2^{10} = \beta(5^{10}, 2^{10})$;

$$= \max\left(\beta(5^{10}), \beta(2^{10})\right)$$
$$= \max(5^9, 2^8)$$
$$= 5^9.$$

In order to reach the lower bounds of addition or multiplication it is necessary to use data representations which are nonstandard. By optimizing the representation for fast addition or multiplication, a variety of other operations will occur much slower. In particular, performing comparisons or calculating overflow are much more difficult to compute and require additional hardware using this nonstandard representation. Winograd showed that both these functions require at least $\lceil \log_r(2\lceil \log_2 N \rceil) \rceil$ time units to compute [WIN 67]. In conventional binary notation both of these functions can be easily implemented by making minor modifications to the adder. Hence, the type of data representation used must be decided from a broader perspective and not based merely on the addition or multiplication speed.

2.3 MODELING OF ROM SPEED IN GATE DELAYS

As an alternative to computing sums or products each time the arguments were available, one could consider simply storing all possible results in a table. Then we could use the arguments to look up, (address), the answer (as shown on p. 58).

Would such a scheme lead to even faster arithmetic; i.e., better than the (r, d) bound? The answer is probably not since the table size grows rapidly as the number of argument digits, n, increases. For b-based arithmetic there are b^{2n} required entries. Access delay is naturally a function of table size.

Modeling this delay is not the same as finding a lower time bound, however. In ROM's as well as many storage technologies the access delay is a function of many physical parameters. What we present here is a simple model of access delay as an approximation to the access time.

We start by a simple model of 16×1 ROM:

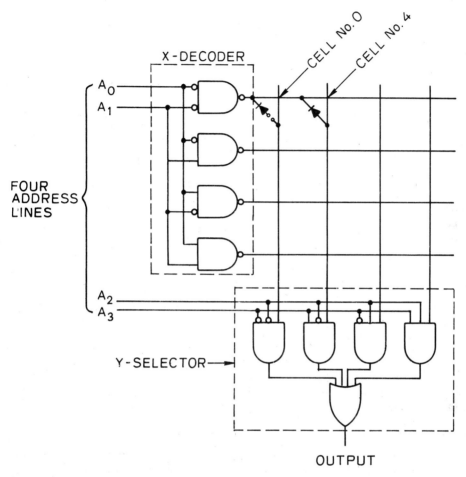

Figure 2–3. ROM model.

This ROM is made of 16 cells which store information by having optional diode connection at each row and column intersection. For example, in the above figure cell #0($A_3A_2A_1A_0 = 0000$) stores one, and cell #4 stores a zero. The delay of the ROM is a combination of the X decoder, the diode matrix and the Y selector. In the above case (for fan-in = 4) the ROM delay is made of four gates (assuming the diode matrix is one gate delay). In general, a ROM with L address lines has the following delays:

$$\text{X-decode} = \left\lceil \log_r \left(\frac{L}{2} \right) \right\rceil,$$

$$\text{diode matrix} = 1,$$

$$\text{Y-selector} = \left\lceil \log_r \left(\frac{L}{2} + 1 \right) \right\rceil + \lceil \log_r 2^{\frac{L}{2}} \rceil.$$

Half of the address lines $(\frac{L}{2})$ are decoded in the X dimension and according to Spira's bound the associated delay is $\lceil \log_r(\frac{L}{2}) \rceil$.

In the Y-selector delay the fan-in to each gate is composed of the $\frac{L}{2}$ address lines plus a single input from the ROM array. These gates must, in turn, be multiplexed to arrive at a final result. As there are $2^{\frac{L}{2}}$ array outputs there are $\lceil \log_r 2^{\frac{L}{2}} \rceil$ stages of delay, again by the Spira argument.

Actually, since only the ROM input to the Y-selector is critical, an improved configuration can be realized. The input to the Y-selector from the ROM, is brought down to a single final gate. The other input to this gate is the Y-selection. Now the Y-selection delay is increased by one gate delay, but this is no worse than the X-decode plus the diode matrix delay. Thus:

$$\text{Unoverlapped Y-selector} = 1 + \left\lceil \log_r 2^{\frac{L}{2}} \right\rceil.$$

Example:
For 1K word ROM L $= 10$, and if we assume $r = 5$ then:

$$\text{X-decode} = 1,$$
$$\text{diode matrix} = 1,$$
$$\text{Y-selector} = 1 + 3 = 4,$$
$$\text{total} = 6 \text{ gate delays.}$$

When the ROM is used as a binary operator on n-bit numbers, the above formula can be expressed as a function of n, where $n = \frac{L}{2}$:

$$\text{ROM delay} = 2 + \lceil \log_r n \rceil + \lceil \log_r 2^n \rceil.$$

In many ways, this ROM delay points out the weakness of the (r, d) circuit model. In practical use of LSI ROM implementations, the delay equation above, is conservative when normalized to the gate delay in the same technology. The (r, d) model gives no "credit" to the ROM for its density, regular implementation structure, limited fan-out requirements, etc.

2.4 ADDITIONAL READINGS

The two classic works in the development of residue arithmetic are by Garner, [GAR 59], and Szabo and Tanaka, [SZA 67]. They are both recommended to the serious student.

A readable, complete proof of Winograd's addition bound is found in Stone, [STO 73], a book that is also valuable for its introduction to residue arithmetic.

2.5 SUMMARY

Alternate representation techniques exist using multiple moduli. These are called residue systems with the principle advantage of allowing the designer use of small independent operands for arithmetic. Thus, a multitude of these smaller arithmetic operations can be performed simultaneously with a potential speed advantage. As we will see in later chapters, the speed advantage is usually limited to about a factor of 2 to 1 over more conventional representations and techniques. Thus, the difficulty in performing operations such as comparison and overflow detection limits the general purpose applicability of the residue representation approach. Of course, where special purpose applications involve only the basic add-multiply, serious consideration could be given to this approach.

Winograd's bound, while limited in applicability by the (r, d) model, is an important and fundamental limitation to arithmetic speed.

2.6 EXERCISES

1. Create an efficient residue system to include the range ± 32. Develop all tables and then perform the operation $-3 \times 2 + 7$.

2. The residue system is used to span the range of 0 to 10,000. What is the best set which includes the smallest maximum prime modulus of residues:

   a. if any integer modulus is permitted;

   b. if moduli only of the form 2^k or $2^k - 1$ are allowed?

3. Repeat the above problem if the range is to be $\pm 8,192$.

4. Analyze the use of an excess code as a method of representing both positive and negative numbers in a residue system.

5. Suppose two numbers to be added are coded in even parity. A parity check on the sum is proposed for error detection.

   a. Show that this scheme cannot be used in general to detect errors in <u>addition</u> (in the sum); i.e., $P(P_A + P_B) = P_S$. The parity on the sum of P_A and P_B is compared against the parity of S.

   $$\begin{array}{ccc} \boxed{A} & & \boxed{P_A} \\ \\ +\quad\boxed{B} & & \boxed{P_B} \\ \hline \\ \boxed{S} & & \boxed{P_S} \end{array}$$

   b. Describe an n-bit check (i.e., P_A, P_B, and P_S each n bits) so that arithmetic errors $(+, -, *)$ can be detected in the above problem.

   c. Find probability of an undetected error in this system, where this probability is defined as:

$$\frac{\text{number of valid representations}}{\text{total number of representations}}$$

6. Devise an alternative scheme which will provide a complete check on the sum using parity. This system may use logic on the individual bit sum and carry signals to complete the check.

7. In Section 2.2.5, the optimum decomposition of prime factors was derived for $M \geq 2^{47}$. Find the next seven factors to be used in enlarging M to form M'. What is the new M' (approximately) and the new $\alpha(M')$?

8. If $r = 4$ and M and M' are defined in Problem 7, find:

    a.   Lower bound on addition;

    b.   Lower bound on multiplication;

    c.   Number of equivalent gate delays in using a ROM implementation of addition or multiplication.

2.7 DESIGN EXERCISES

1. Design a residue adder-multiplier for the 32, 31, 15, 7 residue system using a ROM implementation. Use two 17-bit input registers labeled $\underline{X}$ and $\underline{Y}$ and produce a 17-bit result in the $\underline{R}$ register. Show all chips required. Actually show the ROM contents for add and multiply operations where:

$$\underline{X} = [\underline{18}, \underline{11}, \underline{13}, \underline{4}];$$

$$\underline{Y} = [\underline{27}, \underline{23}, \underline{3}, \underline{6}].$$

2. Design conversion circuits to translate a 16-bit two's complement binary number into the 32, 31, 15, 7, residue system.

3. Design a conversion circuit to convert a number in the 32, 31 15, 7, residue system into a 17-bit binary two's complement integer.

Chapter 3

ADDITION AND SUBTRACTION

3.1 FIXED POINT ALGORITHMS

3.1.1 Historical Review

The first electronic computers used ripple-carry addition. For this scheme the sum at the ith bit is:

$$S_i = A_i \oplus B_i \oplus C_i,$$

where S is the sum bit, A_i and B_i are the ith bits of each operand, and C_i is the carry into the ith stage. The carry to the next stage $(i+1)$ is:

$$C_{i+1} = A_i B_i + C_i(A_i + B_i).$$

Thus, to add two n-bit operands takes at the most $n-1$ carry delays and one sum delay; but, on the average, the carry propagation is about $\log_2 n$ delays (see Problem 2 at the end of this chapter). In the late fifties and early sixties most of the time required for addition was attributable to carry propagation. This observation had resulted in many papers describing faster ways of propagating the carry. In reviewing these papers some confusion may result unless one keeps in mind that there are two different approaches to speeding up addition. The first approach is variable time addition (asynchronous), where the objective is to detect the completion of the addition as soon as possible. The second approach is fixed time addition (synchronous), where the objective is to propagate the carry as fast as possible to the last stage for all operand values. Today most computers are synchronous and as such the second approach is preferred, and that is the only approach we will describe here. However, a good discussion of the variable time adder is given by Wiegel [WIE 66] in his report "Methods of Binary Additions," which also provides one of the best overall summaries of various hardware implementations of binary adders.

Conventional fixed-time adders can be roughly categorized into two classes of algorithms, conditional sum and carry-look-ahead. Conditional sum was invented by Sklansky [SKL 60], and it has been considered by Winograd [WIN 67] to be the fastest addition algorithm, but it never has become a standard integrated circuit building block. In fact, Winograd showed that with (r, d) circuits the lower bound on addition is achievable with the conditional sum algorithm. The carry-look-ahead method was first described by Weinberger and Smith in 1956 [WIE 56], and it has been implemented in standard ICs that have been used to build many different computer systems. A third algorithm described in this chapter, canonic addition, is a generalization of the carry-look-ahead algorithm that is faster than either conditional sum or carry-look-ahead. Canonic addition has implementation limitations, especially for long word length operands. A fourth algorithm, the Ling, [LIN 81], adder uses the ability of certain circuits to perform the OR function by simply wiring together gate outputs. Ling adders provide a very fast sum, performing close to Winograd's bound since the (r, d) circuit premise is no longer valid.

3.1.2 Conditional Sum

The principle in conditional sum is to generate, for each digit position, a sum digit and a carry digit under the assumption that there is a carry into that position, and another sum and carry digit assuming there is no carry input. Then pairs of conditional sums and carries are combined according to whether there is (and is not) a carry into that pair of digits. This process continues until the true sum results. Figure 3–1 illustrates this process for a decimal example.

i →	15	14	13	12	11	10	9	8	7	6	5	4	3	2	1	0	
X_i	2	6	7	7	4	1	0	0	2	6	9	2	4	3	5	8	
Y_i	5	6	0	4	9	7	9	4	1	5	1	7	1	6	4	5	
	08 07	13 12	08 07	12 11	14 13	09 08	10 09	05 04	04 03	12 11	11 10	10 09	06 05	10 09	10 09	13	t_0
	083	082	082	081	139	138	095	094	042	041	110	109	060	059	103		t_1
	08282		08281		13895		13894		04210		04209		06003				t_2
	082823895				082823894				042096003								t_3
	0828238942096003																t_4

Selector bit = The most significant digit of each number.

Figure 3–1. Example of the conditional sum mechanism. The addition performed is:

```
  2 6 7 7 4 1 0 0 2 6 9 2 4 3 5 8
  5 6 0 4 9 7 9 4 1 5 1 7 1 6 4 5
  ───────────────────────────────
  8 2 8 2 3 8 9 4 4 2 0 9 6 0 0 3
```

At any digit position two numbers are shown (at t_0). The right number assumes no carry input, and the number on the left assumes that there is a carry input. During t_1, pairs of digits are combined, and now with each pair of digits two numbers are shown. On the right no carry-in and on the left a carry-in is assumed. This process continues until the true sum results (t_4).

In order to show the hardware implementation of this algorithm the equations for a 4-bit slice can be derived.

The subscripts N and E are used to indicate no carry input and carry input (exists) respectively.

At each bit position the following relations hold:

$$\left.\begin{array}{r} S_{Ni} = A_i \oplus B_i \\ C_{N(i+1)} = A_i B_i \end{array}\right\} \quad \text{when } C_i = 0,$$

$$\left.\begin{array}{r} S_{Ei} = \bar{S}_{Ni} \\ C_{E(i+1)} = A_i + B_i \end{array}\right\} \quad \text{when } C_i = 1.$$

The following is a shorthand notation:

$$G_i = A_i B_i,$$
$$P_i = A_i + B_i,$$
$$T_i = A_i \oplus B_i.$$

For the 4-bit slice $i = 0, 1, 2, 3$.

$$S_{N0} = A_0 \oplus B_0$$
$$S_{E0} = \bar{S}_{N0}$$
$$S_{N1} = A_1 \oplus B_1 \oplus G_0$$
$$S_{E1} = A_1 \oplus B_1 \oplus P_0$$
$$S_{N2} = A_2 \oplus B_2 \oplus (G_1 + T_1 G_0)$$
$$S_{E2} = A_2 \oplus B_2 \oplus (G_1 + T_1 P_0)$$
$$S_{N3} = A_3 \oplus B_3 \oplus (G_2 + T_2 G_1 + T_2 T_1 G_0)$$
$$S_{E3} = A_3 \oplus B_3 \oplus (G_2 + T_2 G_1 + T_2 T_1 P_0)$$
$$C_{N4} = G_3 + T_3 G_2 + T_3 T_2 G_1 + T_3 T_2 T_1 G_0$$
$$C_{E4} = G_3 + T_3 G_2 + T_3 T_2 G_1 + T_3 T_2 T_1 P_0$$

Of course, terms such as $G_1 + T_1 G_0$ could also be written in the more familiar form, $G_1 + P_1 G_0$, which is logically equivalent. Replacing T_i with P_i simplifies the implementation, (Figure 3–2).

Thus, in three gate delays the 4-bit sums that both assume no carry, and carry into the group are generated. The true sum is selected according to the lower-order carry-in; i.e.,

$$S_0 = S_{E0} C_0 + S_{N0} \bar{C}_0$$
$$\vdots \qquad \vdots \qquad \vdots$$
$$S_3 = S_{E3} C_0 + S_{N3} \bar{C}_0.$$

Figure 3–2 shows the logic diagram of a 4-bit slice (conditional sum) adder.

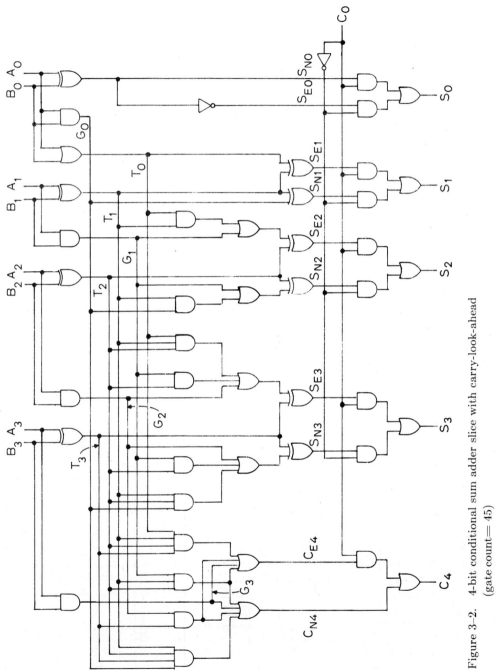

Figure 3–2. 4-bit conditional sum adder slice with carry-look-ahead (gate count= 45)

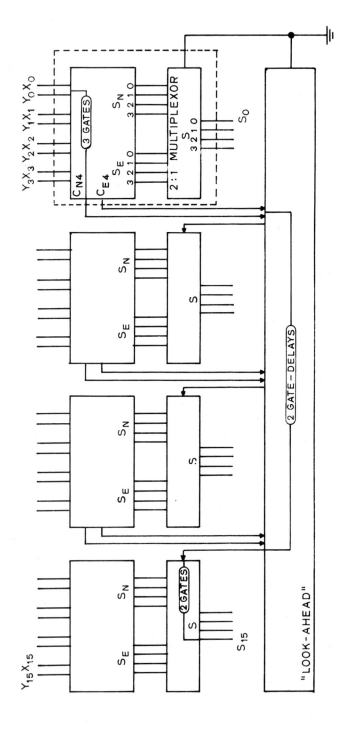

Figure 3–3. 16-bit conditional sum adder. The dotted line encloses a 4-bit slice with internal look-ahead. The rectangular box (on the bottom) accepts conditional carries and generates fast true carries between slices. The worst case path delay is seven gates.

In general, the true carry into a group is formed from the carries of the previous groups. In order to speed up the propagation of the carry to the last stage, look-ahead techniques can be derived assuming a 4-bit adder as a basic block. The carry-out of bit i, C_i, is valid whenever a carry-out is developed within the 4-bit group, C_{Ni}, or whenever there is a conditional carry-out, C_{Ei}, for the group *and* there was a valid carry-in, C_{i-4}. Using this we have:

$$C_4 = C_{N4} + C_{E4}C_0,$$
$$C_8 = C_{N8} + C_{E8}C_4,$$
$$C_8 = C_{N8} + C_{E8}C_{N4} + C_{E8}C_{E4}C_0,$$
$$C_{12} = C_{N12} + C_{E12}C_8,$$
$$C_{12} = C_{N12} + C_{E12}C_{N8} + C_{E12}C_{E8}C_{N4} + C_{E12}C_{E8}C_{E4}C_0,$$
$$C_{16} = C_{N16} + C_{E16}C_{12},$$
$$C_{16} = C_{N16} + C_{E16}C_{N12} + C_{E16}C_{E12}C_{N8} + C_{E16}C_{E12}C_{E8}C_{N4} +$$
$$C_{E16}C_{E12}C_{E8}C_{E4}C_0.$$

With a fan-in of 5, the above equations can propagate the carry across 16 bits in two gate delays. Thus, 16-bit addition (Figure 3–3) can be completed in seven gate delays (three to generate conditional sum, two to propagate the carry, and two gate delays to select the correct sum bit). This delay can be generalized for n bits and r fan-in as

$$t = 5 + 2\lceil \log_{r-1}(\lceil n/r \rceil - 1) \rceil.$$

If $r \gg 1$, then $r \simeq r - 1$; and if $r \ll n$,

then $t \simeq 3 + 2\lceil \log_r n \rceil$.

3.1.3 Carry-Look-Ahead Addition

In the last decade the carry-look-ahead has become the most popular method of addition, due to a simplicity and modularity that make it particularly adaptable to integrated circuit implementation. To see this modularity we derive the equations for a 4-bit slice.

The sum equations for each bit position are:

$$\left.\begin{array}{l} S_0 = A_0 \oplus B_0 \oplus C_0 \\ S_1 = A_1 \oplus B_1 \oplus C_1 \\ S_2 = A_2 \oplus B_2 \oplus C_2 \\ S_3 = A_3 \oplus B_3 \oplus C_3 \end{array}\right\}$$
in general:
$$S_i = A_i \oplus B_i \oplus C_i.$$

The carry equations are as follows:

$$\left.\begin{array}{l} C_1 = A_0B_0 + C_0(A_0 + B_0) \\ C_2 = A_1B_1 + C_1(A_1 + B_1) \\ C_3 = A_2B_2 + C_2(A_2 + B_2) \\ C_4 = A_3B_3 + C_3(A_3 + B_3) \end{array}\right\}$$
in general:
$$C_{i+1} = A_iB_i + C_i(A_i + B_i).$$

The general equations for the carry can be verbalized as follows: there is a carry into the $(i + 1)^{\text{th}}$ stage if a carry is generated locally at the ith stage or if a carry is propagated through the ith stage from the $(i - 1)^{\text{th}}$ stage. Carry is generated locally if both A_i and B_i are ones, and it is expressed by the generate equation $G_i = A_i B_i$. A carry is propagated only if either A_i or B_i is one, and the equation for the propagate term is: $P_i = A_i + B_i$.

We now proceed to derive the carry equations, and show that they are functions only of the previous generate and propagate terms:

$$C_1 = G_0 + P_0 C_0,$$
$$C_2 = G_1 + P_1 C_1.$$

Substitute C_1 into the C_2 equation (in general substitute C_i in the C_{i+1} equation):

$$C_2 = G_1 + P_1 G_0 + P_1 P_0 C_0,$$
$$C_3 = G_2 + P_2 C_2 = G_2 + P_2 G_1 + P_2 P_1 G_0 + P_2 P_1 P_0 C_0,$$
$$C_4 = G_3 + P_3 G_2 + P_3 P_2 G_1 + P_3 P_2 P_1 G_0 + P_3 P_2 P_1 P_0 C_0;$$

we can now generalize the carry-look-ahead equation.

$$C_{i+1} = G_i + P_i G_{i-1} + P_i P_{i-1} G_{i-2} + \cdots + P_i P_{i-1} \ldots P_0 C_0.$$

This equation implies that a carry to any bit position could be computed in two gate delays, if it were not limited by fan-in and modularity. But the fan-in is a serious limitation since for n-bit look-ahead the required fan-in is n, and modularity requires a somewhat regular implementation structure so that similar parts can be used to build adders of differing operand sizes. This latter modularity requirement, in fact, is what distinguishes the CLA algorithm from the canonic algorithm discussed in the next section.

The solution of the fan-in and modularity problems is to have several levels of carry-look-ahead. This concept is illustrated by rewriting the equation for C_4 (assuming fan-in of 4, or 5 if a C_0 term is required):

$$C_4 = \underbrace{G_3 + P_3 G_2 + P_3 P_2 G_1 + P_3 P_2 P_1 G_0}_{\text{Group generate} = G'_0} + \underbrace{P_3 P_2 P_1 P_0}_{\text{Group propagate} = P'_0} C_0$$

$$C_4 = G'_0 + P'_0 C_0.$$

Notice the similarity between C_4 in the last equation to that of C_1. Similarly, the equations for C_5 and C_6 resemble those for C_2 and C_3.

With a fan-in of 4, one level of carry-look-ahead (CLA) is sufficient for 16 bits. CLA across 17 to 64 bits requires a second level of carry generator. In general, the number of CLA levels is:

$$\lceil \log_r n \rceil,$$

where r is the fan-in, and n is the number of bits to be added.

We now describe the hardware implementation of a carry-look-ahead addition. It is assumed that the fan-in is 4, consequently, the building blocks are 4-bit slices. Two building blocks are necessary. The first one is a 4-bit adder with internal carry-look-ahead across 4 bits, and the second one is 4-group carry generator. Figure 3–4 shows the gate level implementation of the 4-bit CLA adder, according to the equations for S_0 through S_3, and C_1 through C_3.

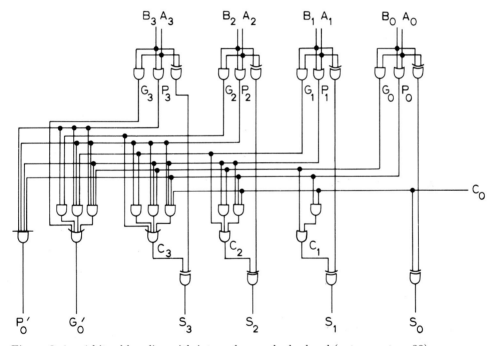

Figure 3–4.   4-bit adder slice with internal carry-look-ahead (gate count = 30).

Figure 3–5 is the gate implementation of the 4- group CLA generator. The equations for this generator are as follows:

$$C_4 = G'_0 + P'_0 C_0,$$

where G'_0 and P'_0 are the (0–3) *group* generate and propagate terms (to distinguish them from G_0 and P_0, which are *bit* generate and propagate terms).

$$C_8 = G'_1 + P'_1 G'_0 + P'_1 P'_0 C_0,$$
$$C_{12} = G'_2 + P'_2 G'_1 + P'_2 P'_1 G'_0 + P'_2 P'_1 P'_0 C_0,$$

and the second level generate (G″) and propagate (P″) terms are:

$$G'' = G'_3 + P'_3 G'_2 + P'_3 P'_2 G'_1 + P'_3 P'_2 P'_1 G'_0,$$
$$P'' = P'_3 P'_2 P'_1 P'_0.$$

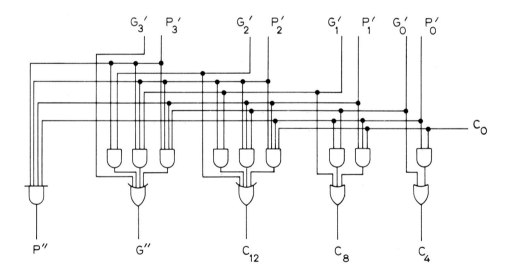

Figure 3–5.   Four group carry-look-ahead generator (gate count = 14).

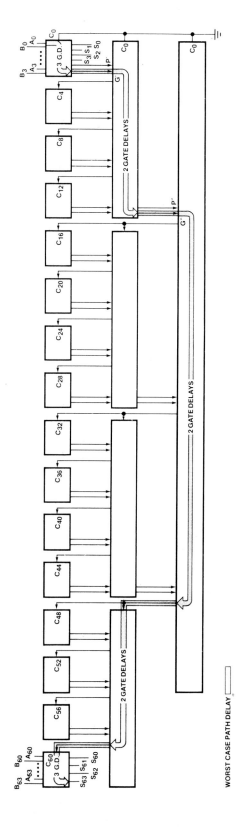

Figure 3–6. 64-bit addition using full carry-look-ahead. The first row is made of 4-bit adder slice with internal carry-look-ahead (see Figure 3–4). The rest are look-ahead-carry generators (see Figure 3–5). The worst case path delay is 12 gates.

WORST CASE PATH DELAY

87

The implementation of a 64-bit addition from the above building blocks is shown in Figure 3–6. From this figure we can derive the general equation for worst case path delay (in gates) as a function of fan-in and number of bits.

The longest path in the 64-bit addition consists of the following delays:

• initial generate term	per bit	1 gate delay
• generate term	across 4 bits	2 gate delays
• generate term	across 16 bits	2 gate delays
• C_{48} generation		2 gate delays
• C_{60} generation		2 gate delays
• C_{63} generation		2 gate delays
• S_{63} generation		1 gate delays
	Total =	12 gate delays.

In general for n-bit addition limited by fan-in of r:

• generate term	per bit	1 gate delay
• generate C_n		$2 \times (2(\text{number of CLA levels}) - 1)$ gate delays
• generate S_n		1 gate delay

$$\text{CLA delays} = 2 + 4 \, (\text{number of CLA levels}) - 2.$$

$$\text{CLA delays} = 4 \, (\text{number of CLA levels}).$$

The number of CLA levels is: $\lceil \log_r n \rceil$.

$$\boxed{\text{CLA gate delays} = 4 \lceil \log_r n \rceil.}$$

Before we conclude the discussion on carry-look-ahead, it is interesting to survey the actual integrated circuit implementations of the adder slice and the carry-look-ahead generator. The TTL 74181 [TI 81] is a 4-bit slice that can perform addition, subtraction, and several Boolean operations such as AND, OR, XOR, etc. Therefore, it is called an ALU (Arithmetic Logic Unit) slice. The slice depicted in Figure 3–4 is a subset of the 74181. The 74182 [TI 81] is a 4-group carry-look-ahead generator which is very similar in implementation to Figure 3–5. The only difference is in the opposite polarity of the carries, due to an additional buffer on the input carry (inspection of Figure 3–6 shows that the generate and propagate signals drive only one package regardless of the number of levels, whereas the carries' driving requirement increases directly with the number of levels). For more details on integrated circuit implementation of adders, see [WAS 78a].

3.1.4 Canonic Addition: Very Fast Addition and Incrementation

So far, we have examined the delay in practical implementation algorithms—conditional sum and CLA—as well as reviewing Winograd's theoretic delay limit. Now Winograd shows [WIN 65] that his bound of binary addition is achievable using (r, d) circuits with a conditional sum algorithm. The question remaining is what is the fastest known binary addition algorithm using conventional AND-OR circuits (fan-in limited without use of a wired OR).

Before developing such fast adders, called canonic adders, consider the problem of incrementation—simply adding one to X, an n-bit binary number. Winograd's approach would yield a bound on an increment of:

$$\text{Increment } (r, d) \text{ delays} = \lceil \log_r (n + 1) \rceil.$$

Such a bound is largely realizable by AND circuits since the longest path delay, the highest order sum bit, S_n, depends simply on the configuration of the old value of X. Thus if we designate I as the increment function:

$$
\begin{array}{r}
X_{n-1} X_{n-2} \ldots X_0 \\
+ \qquad\qquad\qquad I \\
\hline
C_n \, S_{n-1} \, S_{n-2} \ldots S_0
\end{array}
$$

Then C_n, the overflow carry, is determined by

$$C_n = \prod_{i=0}^{n-1} X_i \cdot I; \quad \text{i.e., the AND of all elements in X,}$$

and intermediate carries, C_j:

$$C_j = \prod_{i=0}^{j-1} X_i \cdot I.$$

C_n is implementable as a fan-in limited tree of AND circuits in

$$C_n \text{ gate delays} = \lceil \log_r (n + 1) \rceil.$$

Each output, S_j-bit in the increment would have an AND tree:

$$S_0 = X_0 \oplus I,$$
$$S_j = X_j \oplus C_{j-1}.$$

Thus the delay in realizing S_{n-1} (the nth sum bit) is:

$$\text{Increment gate delays} = \lceil \log_r n \rceil + 1,$$

that is, the gate delays in C_{n-2} plus the final exclusive OR.

Example:
A 15-bit incrementer, (bits 0–14), might have the following high-order configuration for S_{14} and C_{15}.

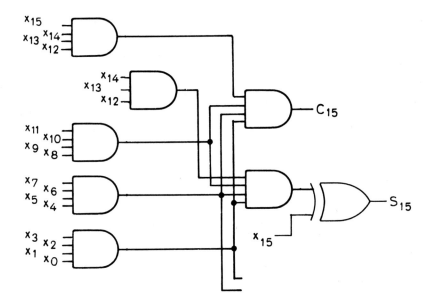

The amount of hardware required to implement this approach is not as significant as it first appears. The carry-out circuitry requires:

$$\left\lceil \frac{n}{r} \right\rceil + \left\lceil \frac{n}{r} \cdot \frac{1}{r} \right\rceil + \ldots \text{ gates},$$

or approximately

$$\left\lceil \frac{n}{r} \right\rceil \left(1 + \frac{1}{r} + \frac{1}{r^2} \cdots \right),$$

where the series consists of only a few terms, as it terminates for the lowest k that satisfies:

$$\left\lceil \frac{n}{r^k} \right\rceil = 1.$$

The familiar geometric series $(1 + \frac{1}{r} + \frac{1}{r^2} + \cdots)$ can conservatively be replaced by its infinite sum $\frac{r}{r-1}$. Thus:

the number of increment gates in $C_n \leq \left\lceil \dfrac{n}{r} \right\rceil \left(\dfrac{r}{r-1} \right)$,

and summing over the carry terms and adding the n exclusive ORs for the sums,

$$\text{total increment gates } \leq \sum_{i=1}^{n} \left\lceil \dfrac{i}{r} \right\rceil \left(\dfrac{r}{r-1} \right) + n.$$

Or, ignoring effects of the ceiling,

$$\text{total increment gates } \simeq \dfrac{n(n+1)}{2(r-1)} + n.$$

Now most of these gates can be shared by lower-order sum terms (fan-out permitting). Thus for lower-order terms, e.g., S_{n-2}:

$$S_{n-2} = (P_{n-1} \cdot P_{n-2} \cdots P_{n-1-r}) \cdot (\text{existing terms from } S_n).$$

Thus only two additional circuits per lower-order sum bit are required. The total number of increment gates is then approximately:

$$\text{increment gates } \simeq \left\lceil \dfrac{n}{r} \right\rceil + 2(n-1) + n \simeq \left\lceil \dfrac{n}{r} \right\rceil + 3n;$$

e.g., for $r = 4$ and $n = 32$, the total number of gates is 104 gates.

The same technique can be applied to the problem of n-bit binary addition. Here in order to add two n-bit binary numbers:

$$\begin{array}{r} X_{n-1} X_{n-2} \ldots X_0 \\ + Y_{n-1} Y_{n-2} \ldots Y_0 \\ \hline S_{n-1}\, S_{n-2}\, \ldots S_0. \end{array}$$

We have:

$$
\begin{aligned}
C_n =\ & G_{n-1} \\
& + P_{n-1} \cdot G_{n-2} \\
& + P_{n-1} \cdot P_{n-2} \cdot G_{n-3} \\
& + \\
& \ \ \vdots \\
& + \prod_{i=1}^{n-1} P_i \cdot G_0
\end{aligned}
\qquad \text{designated as} \qquad
\begin{aligned}
C_n =\ & C_n^{n-1} \\
& + C_n^{n-2} \\
& + C_n^{n-3} \\
& + \\
& \ \ \vdots \\
& + C_n^0
\end{aligned}
$$

and for each sum bit $S_j, ((n-1) \geq j > 0)$,

$$S_j = X_j \oplus Y_j \oplus C_{j-1}$$
$$\text{and} \quad S_0 = X_0 \oplus Y_0.$$

In the above $G_i = X_i \cdot Y_i$, $P_i = X_i + Y_i$ and C_n^i designates the term which generates a carry-out of bit i and propagates it to a bit n. This is simply an AND-OR expansion of the required carry, hence the term "canonic addition."

The C_n term consists of an n-way OR, the longest of whose input paths is an n-way AND which generates in bit 0 and propagates elsewhere. Note that since $G_i = X_i \cdot Y_i$, a separate level to form G_i is not required, but each P_i requires an OR level.

Thus the number of gate delays is $\lceil \log_r n \rceil$ for the AND tree and a similar number for the OR tree, plus one for the initial P_i:

$$\text{gate delays in } C_n = 2\lceil \log_r n \rceil + 1.$$

The formation of the highest order sum, S_{n-1}, requires the formation of C_{n-1} and a final exclusive OR. Thus,

$$\text{gate delays in } S_n = 2\lceil \log_r (n-1) \rceil + 2.$$

Actually the delay bound can be slightly improved in a number of cases by arranging the inputs to the OR tree so that short paths such as G_{n-1} or $P_{n-1} \cdot G_{n-1}$ are assigned to higher nodal inputs while long paths such as $\prod_{i=1}^{n-1} P_i \cdot G_i$ are assigned to a lower node.

This prioritization of the inputs to the OR tree provides a benefit in a number of cases—where the number of inputs n exceeds an integer tree boundary by a limited amount. In our case of a fan-in limited tree, the limit is twice the possible number of inputs to the next lower level of the OR tree: $2 \times r^{\lceil \log_r n \rceil - 1}$.

Therefore, the exact delay is:

$$\boxed{\text{Canonic addition gate delays} = 2\lceil \log_r (n-1) \rceil + 2 - \delta,}$$

where δ is the Kronecker δ and is equal to 1 whenever $\lceil \log_r n \rceil > 1$ and the above integer boundary condition is satisfied.

Consider the example: $r = 4$ and $n = 20$.

$$\text{Now } \lceil \log_4 20 \rceil = 3$$

and

$$r^{\lceil \log_r n \rceil - 1} = r^{3-1} = 16.$$

Since

$$n = 20 \leq 32,$$

then

$$\delta = 1,$$

$$\text{gate delays} = 2\lceil \log_4 19 \rceil + 2 - 1,$$

$$= 7.$$

Whereas

$$\text{Winograd's bound} = \lceil \log_4 2 \cdot 20 \rceil = \lceil \log_4 40 \rceil,$$

$$= 3.$$

Example:
The AND tree for the *generate* in bit 0 and propagate to bit 19, C_{19}^0 is:

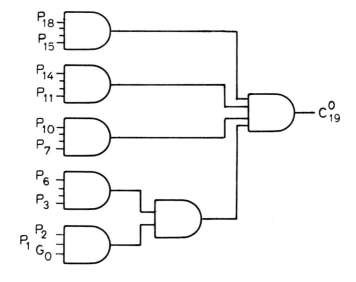

Terms C_{19}^1, C_{19}^2, and C_{19}^3 will have similar structures, (i.e., three stages of delay), however, higher stages C_{19}^i for i between 4 and 14 have two stages of delay, while C_{19}^{15} through G_{19} have one stage.

Thus in the OR tree we must insure that terms C_{19}^0 through C_{19}^3 are preferentially situated ($\delta = 1$).

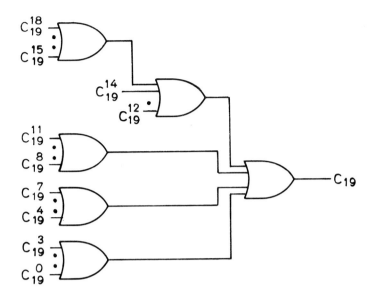

The amount of hardware required is not determinable in a straightforward way, especially for the AND networks. For the OR networks, we have:

$$4 \text{ bits at 6 gates,}$$
$$4 \text{ bits at 5 gates,}$$
$$8 \text{ bits at 4 gates,}$$
$$\text{and} \quad 4 \text{ bits at 1 gate.}$$

or 80 gates total. To this must be added 20×2 gates for initial propagate and generate terms. The AND gates required for bit 19 include the six gates in the AND tree used to form C_{19}^0 plus the AND circuits required to form all other C_{19}^i (i from 1 to 18), terms. Since many of the AND network terms have been formed in C_{19}^0, only two additional gates are required for each i in C_{19}^i; one to create an initial term and one to collect all terms. Actually we ignore a number of cases where only one additional gate is required. Then the C_{19} AND network consists of $6 + 2 \cdot 18 = 42$ gates. So far we have ignored fan-out limitations, and it is worth noting that many terms are heavily used—up to 20 times. However, careful design using consolidated terms (gates) where appropriate, can keep the fan-out down to about ten—probably a practical maximum. Thus, fan-out limits the use of C_{19} terms in C_{18}, etc. But the size of the AND trees decreases for intermediate bits C_j; e.g., for C_9 about 13 gates are required. As a conservative estimate, assume that $(1/2)(42)$ gates are required as an average for the AND networks. The total number of gates is then:

$$\begin{array}{lrl} \text{AND networks:} & (1/2)(42)(20)= & 420 \\ \text{OR networks:} & = & 80 \\ \text{initial terms:} & 2 \times 20= & 40 \\ \text{Exclusive ORs:} & 2 \times 20= & 40 \\ \hline \text{total:} & = & 580 \text{ gates.} \end{array}$$

While 580 gates (closer to 450 with a more detailed count), is high compared with a 20-bit CLA addition, the biggest drawbacks to canonic addition are fan-out and topology, not cost. The high average gate fan-out coupled with relatively congested layout problems load to an almost three-dimensional communication structure within the AND trees. Both serve to significantly increase average gate delay. Still, canonic addition is an interesting algorithm with practical significance in those cases where at least one operand is limited in size.

3.1.5 Ling Adders

Adders can be developed to recognize the ability of certain circuit families to perform special logic functions very rapidly. The classic case of this is the ability to "DOT" gates together. Here the output of AND gates (usually) can simply be wired together giving an OR function. This wired OR or DOT OR has no additional gate delay (although a small additional loading delay is experienced per wired output, due to a line capacitance). Another circuit family feature of interest is complementary outputs: each gate has both the expected (true) output and another complemented output. The widely used current switching (sometimes called emitter coupled or current mode), circuit family incorporates both features. Of course, using the DOT feature invalidates the premise of the (r, d) circuit model—that all logic decisions have unit delay. Ling [LIN 81] has carefully developed adder structures to capitalize on the DOT OR ability of these circuits. By encoding pairs of digit positions $(A_i, B_i, A_{i-1}, B_{i-1})$, Ling redefines our notion of sum and carry. To somewhat over simplify Ling's approach we attribute the local (lower neighbor) carry-enable terms (P_{i-1}), to the definition of the sum, S_i, leaving a reduced synthetic carry (designated H_i) for nonlocal carry propagation. Ling finds that the sum, S_i, at bit i can be written as

$$S_i = (H_i \oplus P_i) + G_i \cdot H_{i-1} \cdot P_{i-1},$$
$$= (G_i + P_{i-1} \cdot H_{i-1}) \oplus P_i + G_i \cdot H_{i-1} \cdot P_{i-1},$$

where H_i is defined by the recursion

$$H_i = G_i + H_{i-1} \cdot P_{i-1}.$$

While the combinatorics of the derivation are formidable, the validity of the above can be seen from the following table.

Function	Inputs			Outputs	
$f(n)$	A_i	B_i	H_{i-1}	S_i	H_i
0	0	0	0	0	0
1	0	0	1	P_{i-1}	P_{i-1}
2	0	1	0	1	0
3	0	1	1	$\overline{P}_{i-1}$	P_{i-1}
4	1	0	0	1	0
5	1	0	1	$\overline{P}_{i-1}$	P_{i-1}
6	1	1	0	0	1
7	1	1	1	P_{i-1}	1

H_{i-1} is conditioned by P_{i-1} in determining the equivalent of C_{i-1}. If a term in the table has $H_{i-1} = 0$, the equivalent C_{i-1} must be zero and the S_i determination can be directly made, (as in the cases: $f(0)$, $f(2)$, $f(4)$, $f(6)$). Now whenever $H_{i-1} = 1$ determines the sum outcome, the P_{i-1} dependency must be introduced. For $f(1)$ and $f(7)$, the $S_i = 1$ if $P_{i-1} = 1$, for $f(3)$ and $f(5)$, the $S_i = 0$ if $P_{i-1} = 1$; (i.e., $f(3)$ and $f(5)$ are conditioned by $\overline{P}_{i-1}$). A direct expansion of the minterms of

$$S_i = (G_i + P_{i-1} \cdot H_{i-1}) \oplus P_i + G_i \cdot H_{i-1} \cdot P_{i-1},$$

produces the S_i output in the above table;

$$S_i = P_{i-1} \cdot (f(1) + f(7)) + \overline{P}_{i-1} \cdot (f(3) + f(5)) + f(2) + f(4).$$

The synthetic carry, H_i, has similar dependency on P_{i-1}; for $f(3)$ and $f(5)$, $H_i = 1$ occurs if $P_{i-1} = 1$. For $f(6)$ and $f(7)$, $H_i = 1$ regardless of the $H_{i-1} \cdot P_{i-1}$, since $G_i = 1$. The $f(1)$ term is an interesting "don't care" term introduced to simplify the H_i structure. This $f(4)$ term in H_i does not affect S_i since S_i depends on H_{i-1}. Now S_{i+1} cannot be affected by $H_i(f(1))$, since $P_i(f(1)) = 0$. Similarly H_{i+1} also contains the term H_iP_i, which for $f(1)$ is zero by action of P_i.

To understand the advantage of the Ling adder consider the conventional C_3, (carry-out of bit 3) as contrasted with H_3:

$$C_3 = G_3 + P_3G_2 + P_3P_2G_1 + P_3P_2P_1G_0,$$

$$H_3 = G_3 + P_2G_2 + P_2P_1G_1 + P_2P_1P_0G_0.$$

Without the DOT function C_3 is implementable, $r = 4$, in three gate delays (two shown plus one for either P or G). C_3 can be expanded in terms of the input arguments:

$$C_3 = A_3B_3 + (A_3 + B_3)A_2B_2 + (A_3 + B_3)(A_2 + B_2)A_1B_1,$$
$$+ (A_3 + B_3)(A_2 + B_2)(A_1 + B_1)A_0B_0.$$

$$C_3 = A_3B_3 + A_3A_2B_2 + B_3A_2B_2 + A_3A_2A_1B_1$$
$$+ A_3B_2A_1B_1 + B_3A_2A_1B_1 + B_3B_2A_1B_1$$
$$+ A_3A_2A_1A_0B_0 + A_3A_2B_1A_0B_0 + A_3B_2A_1A_0B_0$$
$$+ A_3B_2B_1A_0B_0 + B_3A_2A_1A_0B_0 + B_3A_2B_1A_0B_0$$
$$+ B_3B_2A_1A_0B_0 + B_3B_2B_1A_0B_0.$$

If we designate s as the maximum number of lines that can be dotted, then we see that to perform C_3 in one dotted gate delay requires $r = 5$ and $s = 15$.
Now consider the expansion of H_3:

$$H_3 = A_3B_3 + (A_2 + B_2)A_2B_2 + (A_2 + B_2)(A_1 + B_1)A_1B_1$$
$$+ (A_2 + B_2)(A_1 + B_1)(A_0 + B_0)A_0B_0.$$

$$H_3 = A_3B_3 + A_2B_2 + A_2A_1B_1 + B_2A_1B_1$$
$$+ A_2A_1A_0B_0 + A_2B_1A_0B_0$$
$$+ B_2A_1A_0B_0 + B_2B_1A_0B_0.$$

Thus, the Ling structure provides one dotted gate delay with $r = 4$ and $s = 8$.

Higher-order H-look-ahead can be derived in a similar fashion by defining a fan-in limited I term as the conjunction of P_i's; e.g.,

$$I_7 = P_6P_5P_4P_3,$$

Rather than dot ORing the summands to form the P_i term, the bipolar nature of the ECL circuit can be used to form the OR in one gate delay;

$$P_i = A_i + B_i,$$

and the P_i terms can be dot ANDed to form the I terms. Thus, I_7, I_{11}, and I_{15} can be found with one gate delay. The second level synthetic carry (out of bit 15), H', can then be determined in two gate delays as follows:

$$H' = H_{15} + I_{15}H_{11} + I_{15}I_{11}H_7 + I_{15}I_{11}I_7H_3.$$

Now, Ling suggests that the conditional sum algorithm be used in forming the final result. Thus S_{31} through S_{16} is found for both $H' = 0$ and $H' = 1$. These results are gated with the appropriate true value of H' or $\overline{H}'$ and dot ORed in one gate delay. Thus, the Ling adder can realize a sum delay in:

$$\boxed{\text{Ling gate delays} = \lceil \log_r \tfrac{n}{2} \rceil + 1,}$$

so long as the gates can be dotted with capability

$$2^{r-1} \leq s.$$

3.1.6 Addition Using Residue Number Systems

The discussion of the residue number system in Chapter 2 pointed out that the "carry-free" operation of this number system can provide more speed than the conventional binary operation. In this section we describe the hardware implementation of residue number addition using ROM look-up tables. But before we go into the detailed description of the ROM implementation, we briefly survey other techniques.

Szabo and Tanaka [SZA 67] have summarized, in their book, three implementation techniques:

1. Magnetic matrix implementation—look-up table;

2. Direct implementation of Boolean function;

3. Modulus substitution—generalization of the end-around-carry adder; (e.g. moduli of the form $2^k - 1$ using mod 2^n arithmetic units).

A fourth implementation technique which uses combinatorial rotate logic is described by Banerji [BAN 74]. Figure 3–7 shows a modulo 7 addition table, and Figure 3–8 shows the process of computing the sum $(5 + 4) \bmod 7$. Figure 3–9 is a realization of a modulo 3 adder using combinatorial rotate logic (the last two figures are taken from Banerji).

	0	1	2	3	4	5	6
0	0	1	2	3	4	5	6
1	1	2	3	4	5	6	0
2	2	3	4	5	6	0	1
3	3	4	5	6	0	1	2
4	4	5	6	0	1	2	3
5	5	6	0	1	2	3	4
6	6	0	1	2	3	4	5

Figure 3–7.   Modulo 7 addition table.

Position # $\longrightarrow$ 0 1 2 3 4 5 6

	0	1	2	3	4	5	6
a.	0	1	2	3	4	5	6
b.	5	6	0	1	2	3	4

c. Final Sum $= (5 + 4) \bmod 7 = 2$.

Figure 3–8.   Computing the sum $(5 + 4) \bmod 7$:
  a.   Initial contents of register;
  b.   Contents of register after rotating left by 5;
  c.   Final sum modulo 7 from position 4.

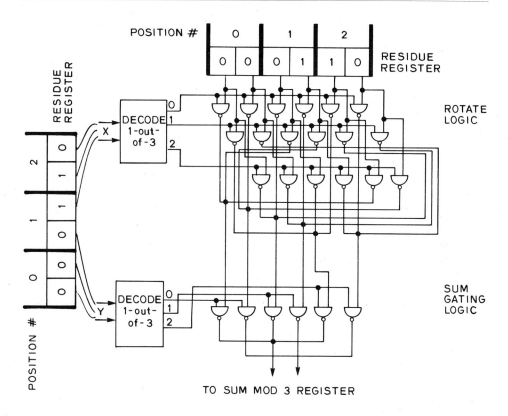

Figure 3–9.   Modulo 3 adder realization using rotate logic.

The remainder of this section is devoted to a ROM implementation of residue addition. The discussion is based on an article by Jullien [JUL 78], but the original idea of using a look-up table for residue addition was suggested as a "magnetic matrix" in Szabo, [SZA 67].

The original "magnetic matrix" was not acceptable due to the slow access time of the core memories in the 1960's. However, in the 1970's the ROM had made great improvement in speed and density, and the look-up table is probably the best approach for implementing residue addition (and other residue operations). For example, the truth table of Figure 3–7 can be stored in 64×3 ROM, as shown:

The state of the art in access time to a fast large ROM (at this time) is 50 ns for $1K \times 8$ ROM [MMI 82]. With such an organization the ROM has ten inputs and it can store the truth table for two 5-bit operands; i.e., the $1K \times 8$ can be programmed as a modulo 32 adder (note: only five of the eight outputs are used). In order to have maximum speed (only one package delay), the maximum modulus is 32. The largest representable number under this restriction is the product of all the relative prime moduli that are equal to or less than 32 as shown below.

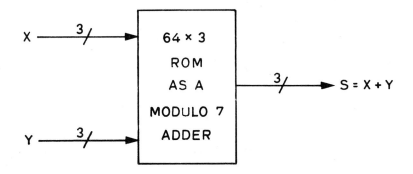

Maximum range is:
$$32 \times 31 \times 29 \times 27 \times 25 \times 23 \times 19 \times 17 \times 13 \times 11 \times 7 \cong 1.03 \times 2^{47}.$$

This range is equivalent to the range of 47 binary bits. The addition speed is the access time of one ROM which is seven gate delays (see Chapter 2), and 11 ROMs are required to implement the entire addition. Of course, subtraction is also accomplished in one ROM access time, but eleven different ROMs are required to implement the subtraction look-up table for each modulus.

To obtain larger range with the same $1K \times 8$ building block, additional moduli are required. Each of these moduli is larger than 32, therefore it requires two more inputs to its look-up table. Thus, the look-up table is $4K \times 8$, and it can be built from four $1K \times 8$ ROMs whose outputs are multiplexed by an AND-OR arrangement; i.e., two gate delays are added. To get a range of 64 binary bits, the following 3 moduli are added to the previous 11 moduli: 61, 59, 53.

Maximum range is: $1.03 \times 2^{47} \times 61 \times 59 \times 53 \simeq 1.52 \times 2^{64}.$

Figure 3–10 lists the various ROMs required for the residue implementation of 64-bit addition. The same amount of ROMs is required for subtraction and multiplication, and the delay is made up of nine gates (seven gates for ROM access time and two gates for multiplexing).

3.1.7 Hardware Realization Versus Winograd's Bounds

Figure 3–11 summarizes the speed performance of each algorithm and compares it with Winograd's lower bound. When fixed radix is used (conventional binary number system), the conditional sum and canonic algorithms are closer to the theoretical limit than the carry-look-ahead algorithm. Nevertheless, all the integrated circuit implementations of the 1970's use the latter algorithm, because of

Modulus	Bits/Package	Package Count
61	8K (1K × 8)	4
59	8K	4
53	8K	4
32	8K	1
31	8K	1
29	8K	1
27	8K	1
25	8K	1
23	8K	1
19	8K	1
17	8K	1
13	1K (256 × 4)	1
11	1K	1
7	1K	1
		TOTAL: 23 ROMs

Figure 3–10. Twenty-three ROMs are required to implement addition in the 2^{64} range using residue number system. (It is assumed that 1K × 8 is the largest available fast ROM.)

its simpler modular structure and lower gate count. For example, the conditional sum 4-bit slice is made of 45 gates (Figure 3–2) while the carry-look-ahead slice is made of 30 gates (Figure 3–4).

Using variable radix (residue) seems to achieve the best possible speed, both in theory (Figure 3–11) and in practice (Figure 3–12). However, there are two problems. The first problem is the speed loss in the conversion from binary to residue, and vice versa. The second problem is the difficulty in implementing certain operations such as divide, scaling, and overflow detection. Nevertheless, the residue number system implementation is quite attractive for a class of problems that uses only addition, subtraction, and multiplication; for example, a digital correlator [CHE 61]. Another speed advantage can be realized if some of the operands in a chain of binary operations are fixed [JUL 78], e.g., the following equation can be computed with one ROM look-up table:

$$X_3 = K_3 * [(K_1 * X_1) + (K_2 * X_2)],$$

(X_i is a variable and K_i is a constant, $i = 1, 2, 3$).

Fixed Radix (Binary)

	Winograd's lower bound	Conditional sum	Carry-look-ahead	Canonic	Ling
Formula	$\lceil \log_r 2n \rceil$	$5 + 2\lceil \log_{r-1}(\lceil \frac{n}{r} \rceil - 1) \rceil$	$4\lceil \log_r n \rceil$	$2\lceil \log_r n - 1 \rceil + 2 - \delta$	$\lceil \log_r \frac{n}{2} + 1 \rceil$
gate delays $n = 64$ bits $r = \text{fan-in} = 5$	4	9	12	7	4*

Variable Radix (Residue)

	Winograd's lower bound	ROM look-up table
Formula	$\lceil \log_r 2\lceil \log_d \alpha(n) \rceil \rceil$	$2 + \lceil \log_r m \rceil + \lceil \log_r 2^m \rceil$
gate delays $n = 64$ bits $r = \text{fan-in} = 5$	$d = 2, \quad \alpha(> 2^{64}) = 61; \quad m = \lceil \log_d \alpha(n) \rceil = 6$	
	2	7

Figure 3–11. Comparison of addition speed (in gate delay) of the various hardware realizations and the lower bounds of Winograd.

* The Ling adder requires dot OR of 16 terms and assumes no additional delay for such dotting.

	Carry-look-ahead 74S181 and 74S182	Residue number system 1K $\times$ 8 ROM (6281)
Speed	51 ns	50 ns
Package count	21	23

Figure 3–12.   Comparison of integrated circuit implementation (1978) of carry-look-ahead in binary number system (64 bits) versus the residue number system.

3.1.8 Simultaneous Addition of Multiple Operands: Carry-Save Adders.

Frequently more than two operands (positive or negative) are to be summed in the minimum time. In fact, this is the basic requirement of multiplication. Clearly one can do better than simply summing a pair and then adding each additional operand to the previous sum. Consider the following decimal example:

Carry-	176	
Saving	324	
Addition	<u>558</u>	
Carry-	948	Column sum
Propagating	<u>11</u>	Column carry
Addition	1058	Total

Regardless of the number of entries to be summed, summation can proceed simultaneously on all columns generating a pair of numbers: column sum and column carry. These numbers must be added with carry propagation. Thus it should be possible to reduce the addition of any number of operands to a *carry-propagating addition* of only two: Column sum and Column carry. Of course the generation of these two column operands may take some time but this should be significantly less than the serial operand by operand-propagating addition.

Consider the addition of three n-bit binary numbers. We refer to the structure that sums a column as a *carry-save adder* (CSA). That is, the CSA will take 3 bits of the same significance and produce the sum (same significance) and the carry (1-bit higher significance). Note that this is exactly what a 1-bit position of a *binary-full adder* does. But the input connections are different between CSA and binary-full adder. Suppose we wish to add X, Y, and Z. Let X_i, Y_i, and Z_i represent the ith bit position.

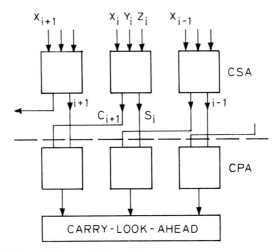

Figure 3–13.   Addition of three n-bit numbers.

Thus we have the desired structure: the binary-full adder. However, instead of chaining the carry-out signal from a lower-order position to the carry-in input, the third operand is introduced to the "carry-in" and the output produces two operands which must now be summed by a propagating adder. Binary full adders when used in this way are simply called carry-save adders (CSA). Thus to add three numbers we require only two additional gate delays, (the CSA delay), in excess of the carry-propagate adder delay.

The same technique can be extended to more than 3-operand addition by cascading CSAs.

Suppose we wish to add W, X, Y, Z. The ith bit position might be implemented as follows:

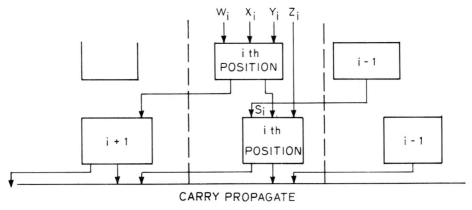

Figure 3–14.   Addition of four n-bit numbers.

High-speed multiplication depends on rapid addition of multiples of the multiplicand and, as we shall see in the next chapter, uses a generalization of the carry-save adder technique.

3.2 FLOATING POINT ADDITION AND SUBTRACTION

In this section we start with the algorithm for floating point addition and subtraction, then we show a simplified hardware implementation, then we describe in detail each of the building blocks used in the implementation. Finally, we discuss overflows, underflows, and zeros.

3.2.1 An Illustrative Format

For illustrative purposes the following floating point format will be used (it is similar to PDP-11 long format).

63	62	55	54	0		
Sign	8 bits of binary exponent excess 128		55 bits of mantissa		G_1	G_2

The mantissa is represented by a sign-magnitude notation. The 55 bits of the mantissa magnitude have 56 bits of precision (16 decimal digits) due to the implied 1 (hidden 1) as its most significant bit. The binary point is to the left of the hidden 1, thus the mantissa magnitude has the range of $0.5 \leq M < 1.0$.

The 8-bit exponent is represented by the excess 128 (2^7) code:

Characteristic	True Exponent
0	*
1	−127
2	−126
.	.
.	.
.	.
128	0
129	1
.	.
.	.
.	.
255	127

Thus the approximate range of this representation is $\pm 2^{-127}$ to 2^{127}; i.e., 10^{-38} to 10^{38}. All floating point numbers are assumed to be normalized. The number zero has a special representation which is all 64 bits of zero; this explains the lack of a true exponent for the characteristics of 0 (see above table).

Finally, two guard bits are appended to the right of the LSB of the mantissa. Recall from Chapter 1 that two guard digits are always sufficient to preserve maximum accuracy.

3.2.2 Algorithm and Block Diagram

1. ALIGN (prenormalize) the two operands by shifting the mantissa of the smaller operand to the right. The shift amount is equal to the difference between the two exponents. The larger exponent is the common exponent.

2. ADD/SUBTRACT the two mantissas.

3. POSTNORMALIZE
   Case A: If the result of Step 2 overflows, then shift right one place and increment the common exponent;
   OTHERWISE
   Case B: Shift left the result of Step 2 and subtract the shift amount from the common exponent. The shift amount is equal to the number of leading zeros.

4. ROUND the result of Step 3 by adding 1 at the position of the first guard bit. If the mantissa overflows as a result of the rounding, then shift right one place and increment the common exponent.

5. CHECK for exponent overflow and underflow.

It is assumed that the floating point adder/subtractor operates on two operands A and B, and the result of $A + B$ or $A - B$ is delivered as operand R; i.e., $A \pm B \rightarrow R$. Figure 3–15 shows the hardware implementation of the above algorithm. The block diagram is made up of three major portions. The alignment section is a combinatorial shifter that receives the shift amount from the exponent difference unit. The add section is a sign-magnitude adder/subtractor that receives instruction from the sign unit. The last section performs the postnormalization and consists of a leading zero detector, a combinatorial shifter, an incrementer (for rounding), and an exponent update unit.

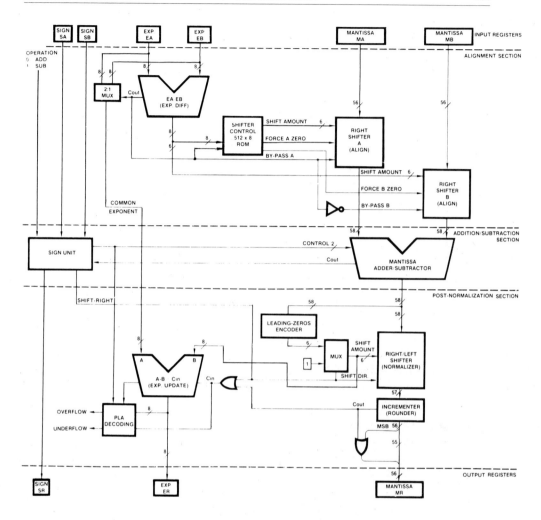

Figure 3–15.   Block diagram of a floating point adder/subtractor.

3.2.3 Combinatorial Shifter

This type of shifter is used in alignment (right shifts) and in postnormalization (right or left shifts). The diagram below illustrates such a shifter.

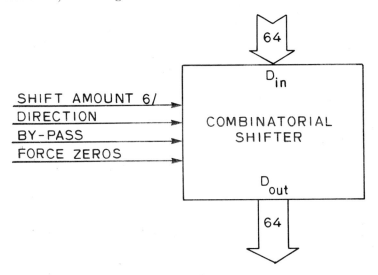

We selected 64 bits, even though only 58 bits ($56 + 2$ guard bits) are necessary, since it will be easier to partition a 64-bit unit to smaller, modular subunits. The shifter has the following capabilities:

- Shift right or left 0–63 bit positions, inserting zeros into the vacant positions;

- Pass the data input unshifted to the data outputs;

- Force the data outputs to be all zeros.

Shifting right is used during the alignment while shifting left is used during postnormalization. The by-pass capability is used on the larger operand during the alignment process (see the top right of Figure 3–15). The forced zero capability is used when the exponent difference is greater then 63, and when a zero result is produced.

The design of such a combinatorial shifter is discussed mostly in the patent literature and in some application notes of the semiconductor manufacturers. These sources are given in the reference list of an article by Davis [DAV 74].

An excellent overview of combinatorial shifters with interesting notes on their history is given in an article by Hastings [HAS 79].

The remainder of this section is divided into two parts. In the first one we describe the partitioning of the 64-bit shifter into modular 16-bit units; while the second part is a detailed description of the design of a 16-bit modular unit, similar to an existing integrated circuit from Motorola [MOT 78].

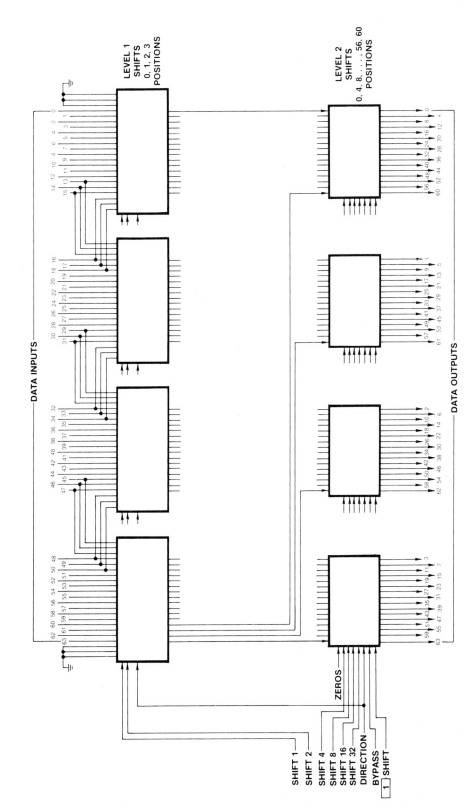

Figure 3–16.   64-bit combinatorial right/left shifter capable of shifting 0-63 bit positions.

Figure 3–16 shows the implementation of the 64-bit shifter from eight 16-bit modules. The design uses a two-level approach. The first level shifts 0, 1, 2, or 3 places; whereas the second level shifts 0, 4, 8, … $4i$, …, 52, 56, 60 ($i = 0$ to 15). For example, to shift 35 places the first level shifts 3 places and the second level shifts 32 places. Thus, the first level shifts 0–3 places, and the second, 0–60 places.

Figure 3–17 gives the fairly simple truth table of Level 1 shifter, while Figure 3–18 shows its hardware implementation. This shifter is made of 16 identical cells, where each cell is a 7 to 1 multiplexer. The seven inputs are made of three inputs to be shifted left (one, two or three positions), three inputs to be shifted right, and one input for zero shift or the by-pass case. The control of the multiplexers comes from a gate generator which decodes (as a PLA) the shift amount, the shift direction, and the by-pass case. For example, the equation for G_3 (which enables shifting right 3 positions) is as follows:

$$G_3 = S_1 \cdot S_2 \cdot \overline{\text{DIR}} \cdot \overline{\text{BY-PASS}};$$

where: **DIR**ection $= \text{DIR} = 0$ for right shift,

$$S_1 = \text{shift 1 positions},$$
$$S_2 = \text{shift 2 positions}.$$

By-Pass	Dir	Shift Amt	15	14	13	12	11	10	9	8	7	6	5	4	3	2	1	0	Notes
									OUTPUTS										
0	X	0 0	15	14	13	12	11	10	9	8	7	6	5	4	3	2	1	0	Zero Shift
0	0	0 1	16	15	14	13	12	11	10	9	8	7	6	5	4	3	2	1	
0	0	1 0	17	16	15	14	13	12	11	10	9	8	7	6	5	4	3	2	
0	0	1 1	18	17	16	15	14	13	12	11	10	9	8	7	6	5	4	3	Right Shift
0	1	0 1	14	13	12	11	10	9	8	7	6	5	4	3	2	1	0	−1	
0	1	1 0	13	12	11	10	9	8	7	6	5	4	3	2	1	0	−1	−2	
0	1	1 1	12	11	10	9	8	7	6	5	4	3	2	1	0	−1	−2	−3	Left Shift
1	X	X X	15	14	13	12	11	10	9	8	7	6	5	4	3	2	1	0	No Shift

Figure 3–17.   Truth table for 16-bit shifter capable of shifting/rotating 0–3 bit positions right or left.

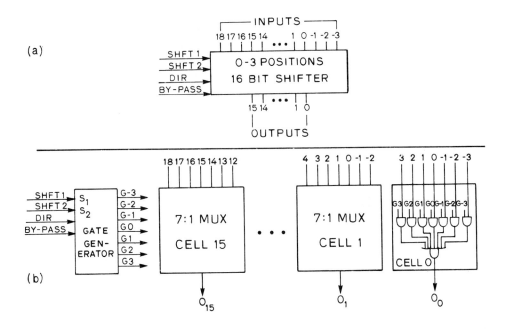

Figure 3–18.

a.   Block diagram of a 16-bit shifter capable of shifting/rotating 0–3
bit positions right or left.

b.   The shifter is made of 16 cellular multiplexers.

The interconnections between these shifters are shown in the upper part of
Figure 3–16. Notice that the extension inputs of the two extreme units are tied to
ground in order to insert zeros into the vacant positions.

By contrast with the simple design of the first-level shifter, the design of the
second-level shifter is much more complex. This 16-bit shifter has to shift the data
input 0–15 places right or left while inserting zeros into the vacant positions. The
design of this module is made of two stages; the first stage is a rotator (barrel
shifter) while the second stage is a mask that inserts the zeros into the proper
places. Figure 3–18 is the truth table for such a shifter. The upper part is the
rotator truth table and the lower parts are the truth tables for the right and left
shifts (where Z indicates zeros). It is obvious that each of the two lower tables
is the rotation truth table masked with the proper Z's. The rotation truth table
illustrates the interesting property of the two's complement relation between right
and left rotations. For example, left rotation of two positions is identical to right
rotation of 14 positions (14 is the two's complement of 2). Figure 3–20 shows the
block diagram of a Level 2 shifter.

ZEROS	BYPASS	ROTATE	DIRECTION	SHIFT AMOUNT LEFT	SHIFT AMOUNT RIGHT	Ø15	Ø14	Ø13	Ø12	Ø11	Ø10	Ø09	Ø08	Ø07	Ø06	Ø05	Ø04	Ø03	Ø02	Ø01	Ø00	
0	0	0		0	0	I15	I14	I13	I12	I11	I10	I09	I08	I07	I06	I05	I04	I03	I02	I01	I00	ROTATE
				15	1	I00	I15	I14	I13	I12	I11	I10	I09	I08	I07	I06	I05	I04	I03	I02	I01	
				14	2	I01	I00	I15	I14	I13	I12	I11	I10	I09	I08	I07	I06	I05	I04	I03	I02	
				13	3	I02	I01	I00	I15	I14	I13	I12	I11	I10	I09	I08	I07	I06	I05	I04	I03	
				12	4	I03	I02	I01	I00	I15	I14	I13	I12	I11	I10	I09	I08	I07	I06	I05	I04	
				11	5	I04	I03	I02	I01	I00	I15	I14	I13	I12	I11	I10	I09	I08	I07	I06	I05	
				10	6	I05	I04	I03	I02	I01	I00	I15	I14	I13	I12	I11	I10	I09	I08	I07	I06	
				9	7	I06	I05	I04	I03	I02	I01	I00	I15	I14	I13	I12	I11	I10	I09	I08	I07	
				8	8	I07	I06	I05	I04	I03	I02	I01	I00	I15	I14	I13	I12	I11	I10	I09	I08	
				7	9	I08	I07	I06	I05	I04	I03	I02	I01	I00	I15	I14	I13	I12	I11	I10	I09	
				6	10	I09	I08	I07	I06	I05	I04	I03	I02	I01	I00	I15	I14	I13	I12	I11	I10	
				5	11	I10	I09	I08	I07	I06	I05	I04	I03	I02	I01	I00	I15	I14	I13	I12	I11	
				4	12	I11	I10	I09	I08	I07	I06	I05	I04	I03	I02	I01	I00	I15	I14	I13	I12	
				3	13	I12	I11	I10	I09	I08	I07	I06	I05	I04	I03	I02	I01	I00	I15	I14	I13	
				2	14	I13	I12	I11	I10	I09	I08	I07	I06	I05	I04	I03	I02	I01	I00	I15	I14	
		0		1	15	I14	I13	I12	I11	I10	I09	I08	I07	I06	I05	I04	I03	I02	I01	I00	I15	
		1	0		0	I15	I14	I13	I12	I11	I10	I09	I08	I07	I06	I05	I04	I03	I02	I01	I00	SHIFT RIGHT
					1	Z	I15	I14	I13	I12	I11	I10	I09	I08	I07	I06	I05	I04	I03	I02	I01	
					2	Z	Z	I15	I14	I13	I12	I11	I10	I09	I08	I07	I06	I05	I04	I03	I02	
					3	Z	Z	Z	I15	I14	I13	I12	I11	I10	I09	I08	I07	I06	I05	I04	I03	
					4	Z	Z	Z	Z	I15	I14	I13	I12	I11	I10	I09	I08	I07	I06	I05	I04	
					5	Z	Z	Z	Z	Z	I15	I14	I13	I12	I11	I10	I09	I08	I07	I06	I05	
					6	Z	Z	Z	Z	Z	Z	I15	I14	I13	I12	I11	I10	I09	I08	I07	I06	
					7	Z	Z	Z	Z	Z	Z	Z	I15	I14	I13	I12	I11	I10	I09	I08	I07	
					8	Z	Z	Z	Z	Z	Z	Z	Z	I15	I14	I13	I12	I11	I10	I09	I08	
					9	Z	Z	Z	Z	Z	Z	Z	Z	Z	I15	I14	I13	I12	I11	I10	I09	
					10	Z	Z	Z	Z	Z	Z	Z	Z	Z	Z	I15	I14	I13	I12	I11	I10	
					11	Z	Z	Z	Z	Z	Z	Z	Z	Z	Z	Z	I15	I14	I13	I12	I11	
					12	Z	Z	Z	Z	Z	Z	Z	Z	Z	Z	Z	Z	I15	I14	I13	I12	
					13	Z	Z	Z	Z	Z	Z	Z	Z	Z	Z	Z	Z	Z	I15	I14	I13	
					14	Z	Z	Z	Z	Z	Z	Z	Z	Z	Z	Z	Z	Z	Z	I15	I14	
			0		15	Z	Z	Z	Z	Z	Z	Z	Z	Z	Z	Z	Z	Z	Z	Z	I15	
			1	0		I15	I14	I13	I12	I11	I10	I09	I08	I07	I06	I05	I04	I03	I02	I01	I00	SHIFT LEFT
				1		I14	I13	I12	I11	I10	I09	I08	I07	I06	I05	I04	I03	I02	I01	I00	Z	
				2		I13	I12	I11	I10	I09	I08	I07	I06	I05	I04	I03	I02	I01	I00	Z	Z	
				3		I12	I11	I10	I09	I08	I07	I06	I05	I04	I03	I02	I01	I00	Z	Z	Z	
				4		I11	I10	I09	I08	I07	I06	I05	I04	I03	I02	I01	I00	Z	Z	Z	Z	
				5		I10	I09	I08	I07	I06	I05	I04	I03	I02	I01	I00	Z	Z	Z	Z	Z	
				6		I09	I08	I07	I06	I05	I04	I03	I02	I01	I00	Z	Z	Z	Z	Z	Z	
				7		I08	I07	I06	I05	I04	I03	I02	I01	I00	Z	Z	Z	Z	Z	Z	Z	
				8		I07	I06	I05	I04	I03	I02	I01	I00	Z	Z	Z	Z	Z	Z	Z	Z	
				9		I06	I05	I04	I03	I02	I01	I00	Z	Z	Z	Z	Z	Z	Z	Z	Z	
				10		I05	I04	I03	I02	I01	I00	Z	Z	Z	Z	Z	Z	Z	Z	Z	Z	
				11		I04	I03	I02	I01	I00	Z	Z	Z	Z	Z	Z	Z	Z	Z	Z	Z	
				12		I03	I02	I01	I00	Z	Z	Z	Z	Z	Z	Z	Z	Z	Z	Z	Z	
				13		I02	I01	I00	Z	Z	Z	Z	Z	Z	Z	Z	Z	Z	Z	Z	Z	
				14		I01	I00	Z	Z	Z	Z	Z	Z	Z	Z	Z	Z	Z	Z	Z	Z	
	0	1	1	15		I00	Z	Z	Z	Z	Z	Z	Z	Z	Z	Z	Z	Z	Z	Z	Z	
0	1	X	X	X		I15	I14	I13	I12	I11	I10	I09	I08	I07	I06	I05	I04	I03	I02	I01	I00	
1	X	X	X	X		Z	Z	Z	Z	Z	Z	Z	Z	Z	Z	Z	Z	Z	Z	Z	Z	

Figure 3–19.   Truth table of a 16-bit combinatorial shifter capable of shifting/rotating 0–15 bit positions right or left.

For Example: the second entry of the table is 1-bit right-shift. In this case the LSB of the output (000) will take on the value of the second LSB of the input (I01).

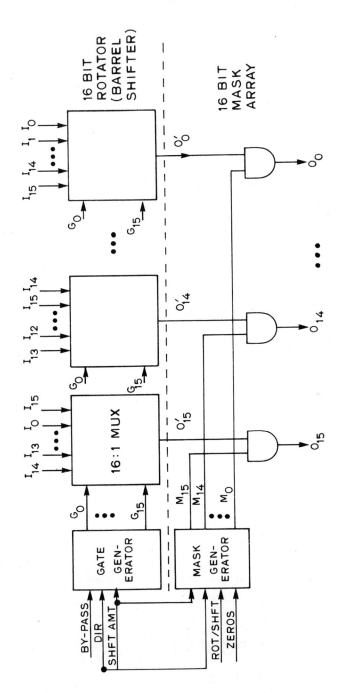

Figure 3–20. Block diagram of a 16-bit combinatorial shifter.

The rotation section is made of 16 identical cells, each of which is a 16 to 1 multiplexer. Each cell is controlled by 16 gating signals, only one of which is active at a time, selecting the proper input. For example, G1 is active if the rotation amount is 1 right or 15 left and the by-pass (BP) signal is not active. Thus, the G1 equation is:

$$G1 = \overline{BP} \cdot \overline{DIR} \cdot \overline{S8} \cdot \overline{S4} \cdot \overline{S2} \cdot S1 + \overline{BP} \cdot DIR \cdot S8 \cdot S4 \cdot S2 \cdot S1;$$

and the entire gate generator is a simple PLA with 16 product terms. The lower section of Figure 3–20 is made of 16 input AND gates, which are used to mask the rotator outputs. There are four masking conditions: rotation, forcing zeros, shifting right, and shifting left. If rotation is desired, all the mask terms are ones. If forcing zeros is required, the mask is set to all zeros. For shifting right or left, say six positions, the masks are set as follows:

	MASK															
	15	14	13	12	11	10	9	8	7	6	5	4	3	2	1	0
Shift right 6	0	0	0	0	0	0	1	1	1	1	1	1	1	1	1	1
Shift left 6	1	1	1	1	1	1	1	1	1	1	0	0	0	0	0	0

Figure 3–21.   Example of mask setting for 6-bit shift.

The mask generator is also a PLA, but this time it has twice as many product terms, since the logical shift (right and left) cannot be ORed like the right and left rotations.

Before we conclude the discussion on the combinatorial shifter it is interesting to note that for a hexadecimal floating point format (like IBM 360/370), the alignment and normalization are done in shifts which are multiples of four. Thus a hexadecimal shifter can be simply implemented by just four modules (the lower portion of Figure 3–16).

3.2.4 Exponent Difference and Alignment

The controls over the combinatorial shifters are generated by the exponent difference, which is a simple subtractor, that always executes EA−EB (Figure 3–15). Four cases need to be considered (Figure 3–22):

$$\begin{aligned}
\text{Case 1:} & \quad (EA - EB) < -63 \\
\text{Case 2:} & \quad -63 \leq (EA - EB) < 0 \\
\text{Case 3:} & \quad 0 \leq (EA - EB) \leq 63 \\
\text{Case 4:} & \quad 63 < (EA - EB)
\end{aligned}$$

In the first case the A operand is so small relative to the B operand, that A is shifted right (out of range) leaving all zeros. Thus the A shifter is forced to all zeros, while the B shifter passes the input data unshifted. Similarly in the fourth case zeros are forced to the outputs of the B shifter (since the B operand is so small), and the A shifter is by-passed. In the third case, where B is smaller than A (by less then 64) the B operand is shifted right according to 6 LSBs of the exponent difference. In the second case where A is smaller than B, the exponent difference is actually the two's complement of the amount to be shifted right (since we always execute $EA - EB$). Thus, the A shifter has to be shifted by the two's complement of the exponent difference. This is implemented by a 512×8 ROM which decodes the 8 bits of the exponent difference and the carry-out according to the truth table of Figure 3–22. The same ROM also controls forcing zeros for either the A or the B shifter (Cases 1 and 4), as can be seen in Figure 3–23. Since the carry-out indicates whether $A \geq B(C_{out} = 0)$ or $A < B(C_{out} = 1)$, it is used to provide the by-pass control for the appropriate shifter, and it also selects the larger exponent as the new common exponent.

3.2.5 Mantissa Adder and a Sign Unit

After the two operands are aligned (by proper right shifting), they are sent to the mantissa adder/subtractor. This unit has to perform sign-magnitude addition/subtraction, which is a little more complicated than the equivalent two's complement operations. The reason for the complication is due to the case of a negative result which is expressed in two's complement representation but has to be converted to sign-magnitude representation. Figure 3–24 shows the two-level implementation of a sign-magnitude adder/subtractor, which corrects (if necessary) on the second level. Thus, the first level performs $A + B$ or $A - B$. The second level takes the two's complement of the first level or else passes it unchanged.

It was stated earlier that the only two instructions the floating point adder accepts are $A + B$ and $A - B$. However, since A may have a negative sign the operation $A+B$ is effectively $B-A$, but since the second level can be used to compute the negative of the first level result, we can let the first level do $R' = A - B$, and then correct in the second level by doing $R = -R' = -(A-B) = B-A$. Similarly, there is a case of an instruction $A + B$ where both operands have negative signs, so the effective operation is $-A - B$. Again, we let the first level do $A + B$, and we let the second level do $R = -R' = -(A + B) = -A - B$.

CASE	Cout	7	6	5	4	3	2	1	0	Decimal	Force Zeros A	Force Zeros B	By-pass A	By-pass B	DIR A	DIR B	Shift Amount A	Shift Amount B	Condition
1	1	0	X	X	X	X	X	X	X	−256 to −129	1	0	X	1	X	X	X	X	$(EA - EB) < -63$
	1	1	0	X	X	X	X	X	X	−128 to −65	1	0	X	1	X	X	X	X	
	1	1	1	0	0	0	0	0	0	−64	1	0	X	1	X	X	X	X	
2	1	1	1	0	0	0	0	0	1	−63	0	0	0	1	0	X	63	X	$-63 \le (EA - EB) < 0$
	.	.	.	.	.	.	.	.	.	.	.	.	.	.	.	.	.	.	
	.	.	.	.	.	.	.	.	.	.	.	.	.	.	.	.	.	.	
	1	1	1	1	1	1	1	1	1	−1	0	0	0	1	0	X	1	X	
3	0	0	0	X	X	X	X	X	X	0 to +63	0	0	1	0	X	0	X	0 − 63	$0 \le (EA - EB) \le 63$
4	0	0	1	X	X	X	X	X	X	+64 to +127	0	1	1	X	X	X	X	X	$63 < (EA - EB)$
	0	1	X	X	X	X	X	X	X	+128 to +255	0	1	1	X	X	X	X	X	

Figure 3–22. Tabulation of all possible exponent differences, and the corresponding shifter controls. Since there are nine inputs, a 512×8 ROM provides the controls for both shifters and the shift amount for the A-shifter.

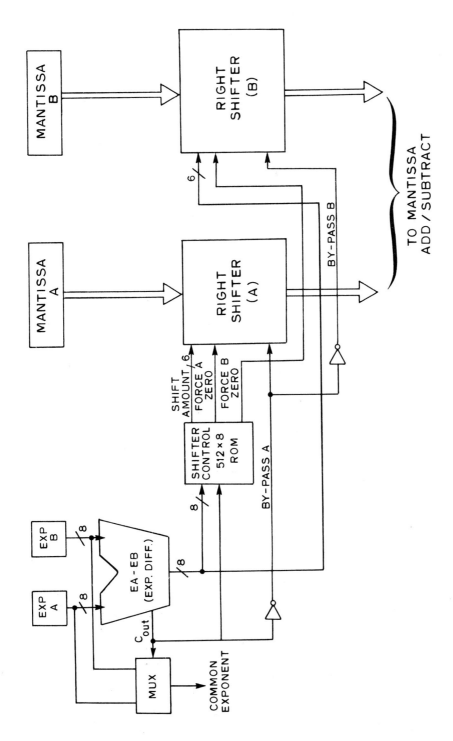

Figure 3–23. Block diagram of the alignment section.

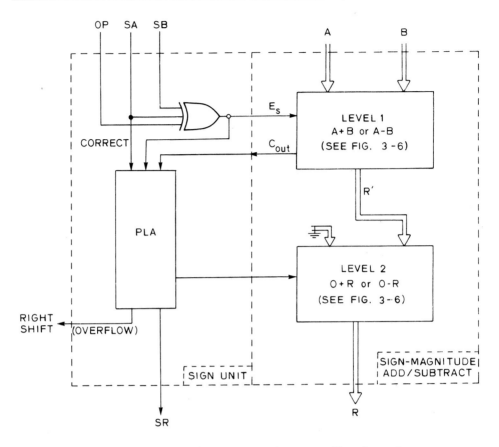

Figure 3–24.   The mantissa adder/subtractor and its controlling sign unit.

The table below lists all eight combinations of signs and operations (OP $= 0$ implies A+B and OP $= 1$ implies A−B). The effective sign (ES) is the Exclusive-OR of the operation and the signs of A and B.

OP	SA	SB	Effective Operation	Level 1 Operation	ES
0	0	0	A + B	A + B	0
0	0	1	A − B	A − B	1
0	1	0	−A + B	$(A - B)^*$	1
0	1	1	−A − B	$(A + B)^*$	0
1	0	0	A − B	A − B	1
1	0	1	A + B	A + B	0
1	1	0	−A − B	$(A + B)^*$	0
1	1	1	−A + B	$(A - B)^*$	1

∗ The starred entries are those that need a correction in Level 2.

The next table analyzes the four effective operations and the carry-out from the first level. It determines whether the effective operation of Level 2 is to compute the two's complement of the result from the first level or to just pass it unchanged. It also shows the final sign, and the two overflow cases. These cases occur when none of the operands were shifted in the alignment section; i.e., both operands had the same exponent. Since the magnitude is larger than or equal to 0.5, adding two such mantissas will result in a number greater than one (but less than two). Thus, an overflow requires the resultant mantissa to be shifted right one place while incrementing the common exponent.

Level 1 Operation	C_{out}	Level 2 Operation	Final Sign	Over-flow
A + B	0	$0 + R'$	0	0
A + B	1	$0 + R'$	0	1^*
A − B	0	$0 - R'$	1	0
A − B	1	$0 + R'$	0	0
$(A + B)^*$	0	$0 + R'$	1	0
$(A + B)^*$	1	$0 + R'$	1	1^*
$(A - B)^*$	0	$0 - R'$	0	0
$(A - B)^*$	1	$0 + R'$	1	0

∗ The starred entries are those that need a correction in Level 2.

3.2.6 Leading Zeros Encoder

This encoder is used in postnormalization to provide the left-shifter with the shift amount needed to normalize the output of the mantissa adder/subtractor. For example, if the output has the form:

$$0.000001XXX\ldots XX,$$

then the shift amount is the 6-bit binary code for five (000101) since there are five leading zeros. Figure 3–25 gives the truth table for a 32-bit leading zero encoder; notice that the truth table is the same as that of a priority encoder, where bit 31 has the highest priority and bit 0 has the lowest. Indeed, most present-day hardware floating point processors implement a leading zero encoder from a commercially available 8-bit priority encoder IC, like 74LS348 [TI 81]. However, with the increased availability of larger PLAs, it is possible to implement a 32-bit expandable leading zeros encoder as shown in Figure 3–26.

A 64-bit encoder is made of two such PLAs (Figure 3–27). The expansion mechanism is quite straightforward since only three cases need to be considered:

Case	Number of Leading Zeros (N)
1	$0 \leq N < 32$
2	$32 \leq N < 64$
3	$N = 64$

In the first case encoder 1 will provide the shift amount on $A_0 - A_4$, while disabling (via E_0) the three state outputs of the second encoder. In the second case the first encoder will detect 32 zeros and it will turn off its own three-state drivers while enabling the second encoder to provide the shift amount, which together with $A_5 = 1$ will give a number between 32 and 63. In case 3 all 64 bits are zeros so both encoders turn off their three-state outputs, but E_0 of the second encoder indicates an all-zero word.

Input Enable	Data Inputs																																Count of Leading Zeros					Output Enable
Ei	31	30	29	28	27	26	25	24	23	22	21	20	19	18	17	16	15	14	13	12	11	10	9	8	7	6	5	4	3	2	1	0	A_4	A_3	A_2	A_1	A_0	E_0
1	1	X	X	X	X	X	X	X	X	X	X	X	X	X	X	X	X	X	X	X	X	X	X	X	X	X	X	X	X	X	X	X	0	0	0	0	0	0
	0	1	X	X	X	X	X	X	X	X	X	X	X	X	X	X	X	X	X	X	X	X	X	X	X	X	X	X	X	X	X	X	0	0	0	0	1	
	0	0	1	X	X	X	X	X	X	X	X	X	X	X	X	X	X	X	X	X	X	X	X	X	X	X	X	X	X	X	X	X	0	0	0	1	0	
	0	0	0	1	X	X	X	X	X	X	X	X	X	X	X	X	X	X	X	X	X	X	X	X	X	X	X	X	X	X	X	X	0	0	0	1	1	
	0	0	0	0	1	X	X	X	X	X	X	X	X	X	X	X	X	X	X	X	X	X	X	X	X	X	X	X	X	X	X	X	0	0	1	0	0	
	0	0	0	0	0	1	X	X	X	X	X	X	X	X	X	X	X	X	X	X	X	X	X	X	X	X	X	X	X	X	X	X	0	0	1	0	1	
	0	0	0	0	0	0	1	X	X	X	X	X	X	X	X	X	X	X	X	X	X	X	X	X	X	X	X	X	X	X	X	X	0	0	1	1	0	
	0	0	0	0	0	0	0	1	X	X	X	X	X	X	X	X	X	X	X	X	X	X	X	X	X	X	X	X	X	X	X	X	0	0	1	1	1	
	0	0	0	0	0	0	0	0	1	X	X	X	X	X	X	X	X	X	X	X	X	X	X	X	X	X	X	X	X	X	X	X	0	1	0	0	0	
	0	0	0	0	0	0	0	0	0	1	X	X	X	X	X	X	X	X	X	X	X	X	X	X	X	X	X	X	X	X	X	X	0	1	0	0	1	
	0	0	0	0	0	0	0	0	0	0	1	X	X	X	X	X	X	X	X	X	X	X	X	X	X	X	X	X	X	X	X	X	0	1	0	1	0	
	0	0	0	0	0	0	0	0	0	0	0	1	X	X	X	X	X	X	X	X	X	X	X	X	X	X	X	X	X	X	X	X	0	1	0	1	1	
	0	0	0	0	0	0	0	0	0	0	0	0	1	X	X	X	X	X	X	X	X	X	X	X	X	X	X	X	X	X	X	X	0	1	1	0	0	
	0	0	0	0	0	0	0	0	0	0	0	0	0	1	X	X	X	X	X	X	X	X	X	X	X	X	X	X	X	X	X	X	0	1	1	0	1	
	0	0	0	0	0	0	0	0	0	0	0	0	0	0	1	X	X	X	X	X	X	X	X	X	X	X	X	X	X	X	X	X	0	1	1	1	0	
	0	0	0	0	0	0	0	0	0	0	0	0	0	0	0	1	X	X	X	X	X	X	X	X	X	X	X	X	X	X	X	X	0	1	1	1	1	
	0	0	0	0	0	0	0	0	0	0	0	0	0	0	0	0	1	X	X	X	X	X	X	X	X	X	X	X	X	X	X	X	1	0	0	0	0	
	0	0	0	0	0	0	0	0	0	0	0	0	0	0	0	0	0	1	X	X	X	X	X	X	X	X	X	X	X	X	X	X	1	0	0	0	1	
	0	0	0	0	0	0	0	0	0	0	0	0	0	0	0	0	0	0	1	X	X	X	X	X	X	X	X	X	X	X	X	X	1	0	0	1	0	
	0	0	0	0	0	0	0	0	0	0	0	0	0	0	0	0	0	0	0	1	X	X	X	X	X	X	X	X	X	X	X	X	1	0	0	1	1	
	0	0	0	0	0	0	0	0	0	0	0	0	0	0	0	0	0	0	0	0	1	X	X	X	X	X	X	X	X	X	X	X	1	0	1	0	0	
	0	0	0	0	0	0	0	0	0	0	0	0	0	0	0	0	0	0	0	0	0	1	X	X	X	X	X	X	X	X	X	X	1	0	1	0	1	
	0	0	0	0	0	0	0	0	0	0	0	0	0	0	0	0	0	0	0	0	0	0	1	X	X	X	X	X	X	X	X	X	1	0	1	1	0	
	0	0	0	0	0	0	0	0	0	0	0	0	0	0	0	0	0	0	0	0	0	0	0	1	X	X	X	X	X	X	X	X	1	0	1	1	1	
	0	0	0	0	0	0	0	0	0	0	0	0	0	0	0	0	0	0	0	0	0	0	0	0	1	X	X	X	X	X	X	X	1	1	0	0	0	
	0	0	0	0	0	0	0	0	0	0	0	0	0	0	0	0	0	0	0	0	0	0	0	0	0	1	X	X	X	X	X	X	1	1	0	0	1	
	0	0	0	0	0	0	0	0	0	0	0	0	0	0	0	0	0	0	0	0	0	0	0	0	0	0	1	X	X	X	X	X	1	1	0	1	0	
	0	0	0	0	0	0	0	0	0	0	0	0	0	0	0	0	0	0	0	0	0	0	0	0	0	0	0	1	X	X	X	X	1	1	0	1	1	
	0	0	0	0	0	0	0	0	0	0	0	0	0	0	0	0	0	0	0	0	0	0	0	0	0	0	0	0	1	X	X	X	1	1	1	0	0	
	0	0	0	0	0	0	0	0	0	0	0	0	0	0	0	0	0	0	0	0	0	0	0	0	0	0	0	0	0	1	X	X	1	1	1	0	1	
	0	0	0	0	0	0	0	0	0	0	0	0	0	0	0	0	0	0	0	0	0	0	0	0	0	0	0	0	0	0	1	X	1	1	1	1	0	
	0	0	0	0	0	0	0	0	0	0	0	0	0	0	0	0	0	0	0	0	0	0	0	0	0	0	0	0	0	0	0	1	1	1	1	1	1	0
1	0	0	0	0	0	0	0	0	0	0	0	0	0	0	0	0	0	0	0	0	0	0	0	0	0	0	0	0	0	0	0	0	Z	Z	Z	Z	Z	1
0	X	X	X	X	X	X	X	X	X	X	X	X	X	X	X	X	X	X	X	X	X	X	X	X	X	X	X	X	X	X	X	X	Z	Z	Z	Z	Z	0

Figure 3–25. Truth table of a 32-bit leading zeros encoder

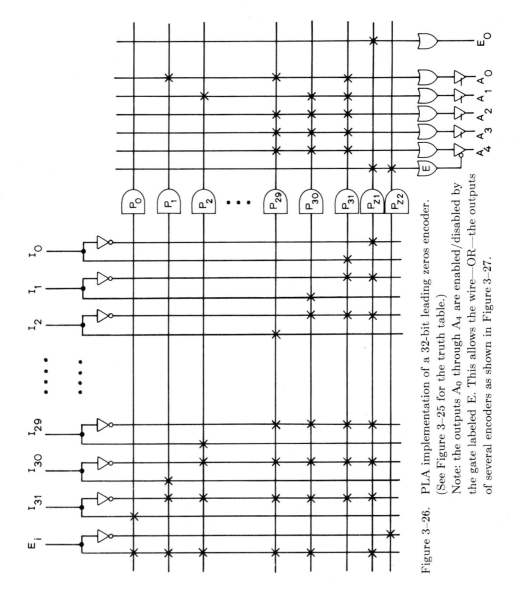

Figure 3-26. PLA implementation of a 32-bit leading zeros encoder.
(See Figure 3-25 for the truth table.)
Note: the outputs A_0 through A_4 are enabled/disabled by
the gate labeled E. This allows the wire—OR—the outputs
of several encoders as shown in Figure 3-27.

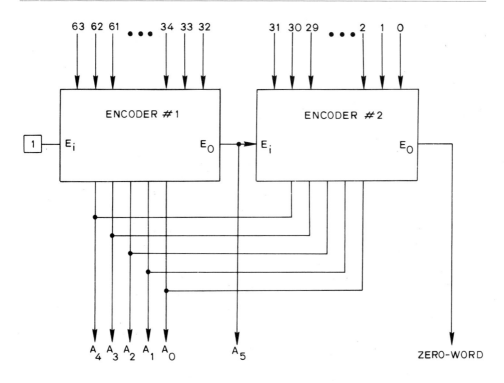

Figure 3–27.   Expanding two 32-bit encoders to provide leading zeros encoding across 64
bits. (Note that the outputs A_0 through A_4 are wired, ORed.)

3.2.7 Postnormalization

As was indicated by the floating point algorithm, two cases need to be considered. In the first case the output of the mantissa adder may overflow, and a
one place right shift is necessary to normalize the result. Therefore the common
exponent has to be incremented by one by activating the carry-in to the exponent
update unit. In the second case the result of the mantissa adder may contain leading
zeros, in which case a left shift is necessary. Of course, the shift amount is provided
by the leading zeros encoder just described. The same shift amount is sent also to
an exponent update unit, which subtracts this amount from the common exponent.

3.3 ROUNDING

Rounding is accomplished by adding one to the first guard bit of the normalized
result. The rounding circuit is a simple incrementer which is a subset of a binary
adder (see Figure 3–6). There is one special case that requires an exponent update;
this happens when all the bits of the normalized word are one, and so is the

guard bit. Thus, adding one to the guard bit will cause a local overflow, so the common exponent is incremented by activating the carry-in to the exponent update unit. Fortunately, this overflow case is mutually exclusive with the overflow mantissa case so both of these cases can be simply ORed to drive the carry-in of the exponent update (Figure 3–15). To see that they are indeed mutually exclusive consider the following simple example:

$$
\begin{array}{r|l}
 & \text{G1} \\
A = 0.11 & 0 \\
B = 0.11 & 0 \\
\overline{A + B = 1.10} & 0 \\
\text{Right shift} \quad A + B = 0.11 & 0
\end{array}
$$

Thus, if a mantissa overflow occurs, then at least the guard bit (G1) will be zero, in which case the rounding will not cause overflow. By the way, a design "trick" to accomplish the required right shift, if the rounder overflows, is to use a simple OR gate as shown below.

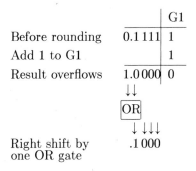

		G1
Before rounding	0.1 111	1
Add 1 to G1		1
Result overflows	1.0 000	0
	OR	
Right shift by one OR gate	.1 000	

Before we conclude this section let us look at the exceptional conditions: overflows, underflows, and zeros.

3.3.1 Overflows

Overflow can occur only if the common exponent has the largest possible value (+127) and the exponent update unit is incremented by one, due to mantissa overflow or rounding overflow. Thus, the overflow flag is the result of ANDing the carry-out with the carry-in of the exponent unit. The overflow can be handled in two ways; the common way is simply to stop computation at once and interrupt the CPU. The second way would be to reset the result to the largest representable value, and the computation continues without interrupting the CPU.

3.3.2 Underflows

Underflow happens only when the effective operation is subtraction, and the number of leading zeros subtracted from the common exponent causes the final exponent value to be less than -127. Intuitively, this happens when the two operands are very close, and their difference is very small.

Example:

$$
\begin{aligned}
& 2^{-127} \times 0.10010\ldots00 \\
-\ & 2^{-127} \times 0.10000\ldots00 \\
\hline
\end{aligned}
$$

Before normalization $\quad 2^{-127} \times 0.00010\ldots00$

After normalization $\quad\quad 2^{-130} \times 0.10000\ldots00$

Since $-130 < -127$ then the normalized result underflows

Recall that the hardware operates on a characteristic which is an exponent biased by 128. Thus, if the common exponent is -127, then the common characteristic is 1.

$$
\begin{array}{l}
\text{Bit Number} \\
\underline{7\,6\,5\,4\,3\,2\,1\,0}
\end{array}
$$

Common characteristics (CC)$=0\,0\,0\,0\,0\,0\,0\,1$

Subtract 3

i.e., add TC(3) $\quad\quad\quad\quad =\underline{1\,1\,1\,1\,1\,1\,0\,1}$

Updated characteristics (UC) $=1\,1\,1\,1\,1\,1\,1\,0$

To summarize: underflow happens when the Effective Sign (ES $= 1$) is subtraction, and the MSB of the characteristic changes (bit 7 in the example) from 0 to 1; it also happens if the Updated Characteristic is zero (all 8 bits equal to zero). Thus, the logic equation is:

$$\text{UNDERFLOW} = \text{ES} \cdot \overline{\text{CC7}} \cdot \text{UC7} + (\text{UC} = \text{ZERO}).$$

The common way to handle underflows is to reset the result to a normalized zero. However, numerical analysts such as Kahan [COO 78] have suggested a gradual underflow (see Chapter 1), and this has been recently implemented by Intel Corp. [PAL 77]. In a gradual underflow more range for small numbers is obtained by allowing denormalizing numbers. Thus, in our format instead of having the smallest number be

$$2^{-127} \times .10000\ldots00 = 2^{-128},$$

we let it be:

$$2^{-127} \times .00000\ldots01 = 2^{-127} \times 2^{-56} = 2^{-183}.$$

Only numbers smaller than 2^{-183} will generate UNDERFLOW and be set to zero. The difficulty in implementing the gradual underflow is in the need to handle both normalized and unnormalized input operands. For detailed discussion of handling underflow and other exceptional conditions see Section 1.8.

3.3.3 Handling Zeros

When one of the input operands is a zero, the only exception needed is not to insert the 'hidden 1' into the MSB, but rather leave it as a zero. This way the zero operand, which will always be smaller than the other operands, will be shifted right. But right shifting a string of zeros any number of positions will still result in a string of zeros as an input to the mantissa. Thus, the other operand will be unchanged through the mantissa adder   and the left shifter (since it is already normalized). Therefore, the zero operand will act as the additive identity.

If the output operand is zero due to $X - X$, then the leading zeros encoder will activate the "zero word" signal which can be used to clear the output registers and, thereby, generate a normalized zero.

3.4 ADDITIONAL READINGS

Much interesting earlier work on asynchronous adders (carry-completion detection) is covered in [WIE 56] and in [HWA 78]. A good treatment of the early addition algorithm literature is found in [MAC 61]. Residue adders are covered in [SZA 67] with improvements covered by [JUL 78] and [TAY 82].

3.5 SUMMARY

Addition is the fundamental transformation in computer systems. It is required in address computation and internal state control as well as in execution.

Several techniques are in current use especially CLA— carry-look-ahead—which realizes a sum in $4\lceil \log_r n \rceil$ gate delays, as contrasted with Winograd's bound of $\lceil \log_r 2n \rceil$.

Both conditional sum and canonic addition provide faster approaches—the latter realizing the sum in about $2\lceil \log_r n \rceil + 2$. Ling realizes addition in $\lceil \log_r \frac{n}{2} \rceil + 1$ by use of dotted logic on the gate outputs.

Floating point addition/subtraction requires two serial add operations: one for the exponent arithmetic prior to the alignment of fraction, the other for the addition of the fractions. Practical realizations require careful integration of these two adds with shift and rounding requirements.

3.6 EXERCISES

1. Consider the following full-adder slice of an n-bit binary adder:

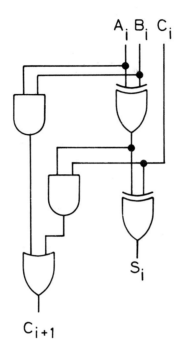

Show that the delay from inputs valid to S_n valid is at worst $2n$ gate delays.

2. Most additions in a ripple-carry adder will have short carry-propagation sequences relative to the length of the numbers.

For the addition of two randomly chosen n-bit binary numbers let $P_n(v)$, $v = 0, 1, \ldots n - 1$ be the probability that a carry-propagate sequence of length at least v occurs. Consider that a carry propagate of at least v occurs in either of two mutually exclusive ways:

   a.   The first $n - 1$ bits have a carry sequence of length at least v;

   b.   The first $n - 1$ bits do not have a carry sequence of length at least v but the last v bits, including the nth bit, have a sequence of exactly v.

Hence derive the recurrence relation:

$$P_n(v) = P_{n-1}(v) + \frac{(1 - P_{n-v}(v))}{2^{v+1}},$$

and show that:

$$P_n(v) - P_{n-1}(v) \leq 2^{-(v+1)}.$$

Since $P_n(v) = \sum_{i-1}^{n} [P_i(v) - P_{i-1}(v)]$ (where $P_0(v) = 0$ for $v > 0$). Show that if $v = \lceil \log_2 n \rceil$ than $P_n(v) \leq \frac{1}{2}$. Thus the probability is less than or equal $1/2$ that an addition of two randomly chosen n-bit numbers will have a carry-propagation sequence of more than $\log_2 n$ positions.

For a complete proof that the expected longest carry-proposition sequence is bonded by $\log_2 n$ see [BUR 46], by Bellard Newel, pp. 98–99.

3. Design a "borrow-look-ahead" subtractor 4-bit slice and a fan-in 4 borrow generator.

4. Design a "conditional difference" 4-bit subtractor slice and a fan-in 5 borrow-look-ahead generator to be used with the subtractor slice.

5. Design a canonic adder for adding/subtracting an unsigned 6-bit increment field to a 24-bit address. Fan-in is limited to 5, fan-out to 10.

6. Design an adder/subtractor for the IBM System 370 floating point short format, without rounding.

7. The System/370 effective address computation involves the addition of three unsigned numbers, two of 24 bits and one of 12 low-order bits.

   a. Design a fast adder for this address computation (an overflow is an invalid address)

   b. Extend your adder to accommodate a fast comparison of the effective address with a 24-bit upper bound address.

8. Design a circuit which can be connected to a 4-bit ALU to detect two's complement arithmetic overflow. The ALU takes two 4-bit input operands and provides a 4-bit output result defined by 3 function bits. The ALU can perform eight functions defined by $F_2F_1F_0$. The object is to make the circuit as fast as possible. Use as many gates as you like.

For gate timing use the following:

NAND, NOR, NOT: 5 ns
        OR, AND: 7 ns
            XOR: 10 ns

| Note: Assume delay through ALU $\gg$ single gate delay |

F_2	F_1	F_0	Function
0	0	0	0
0	0	1	$B - A$
0	1	0	$A - B$
0	1	1	$A + B$
1	0	0	$A \oplus B$
1	0	1	A OR B
1	1	0	A AND B
1	1	1	-1

A_0
A_1
A_2
A_3
B_0
B_1
B_2
B_3
F_0
F_1
F_2

ALU

S_0
S_1
S_2
S_3

9. Design a Ling subtractor bit slice.

10. Show a full realization of a Ling adder of $n = 16$, $r = 4$, $s = 9$.

3.7 DESIGN EXERCISES

1. Use the following assumptions to design a floating point adder.

   - Use 74S381 and 74S182 for ALU's.

   - Use the imaginary 16-bit shifter in the text. Assume max delay $= 25$ ns.

   - Use leading zero encoder from the text: max delay $= 25$ ns from I_i to A_i and E_o

   - Max ROM (PROM) size $= 1K \times 8$; max delay $= 50$ ns.

   - For random logic use PLA (or PAL); max delay $= 25$ ns.

     a. Design the floating point adder/subtractor for maximum speed using IBM/370 short (32-bit) format (without rounding).

     b. Calculate worst-case add/subtract time.

     c. Calculate the number of IC's required.

Chapter 4

MULTIPLICATION

In this chapter the hardware implementations of parallel multipliers are described. The basis for all of these implementations is the add-and-shift algorithm, which is similar to the way one multiplies using pencil and paper. For example, in multiplying two numbers each bit of the multiplier requires a corresponding add-and-shift operation.

multiplicand	110	(6)
multiplier	$\times 101$	$\times$ (5)
	110	(6×2^0)
partial products	000	(0×2^1)
	110	(6×2^2)
final product	11110	(30)

Figure 4–1a illustrates the concept for multiplication of two 8-bit operands, and Figure 4–1b introduces a convenient dot representation of the same multiplication. In this chapter we will describe the three major categories of parallel multiplier implementation:

- Simultaneous generation of partial products and simultaneous reduction;
- Simultaneous generation of partial products and iterative reduction;
- Iterative arrays of cells.

We will conclude the chapter by comparing the speed of each implementation with Winograd's theoretic lower bound.

a.

$$
\begin{array}{rl}
X_7X_6X_5X_4X_3\ X_2\ X_1X_0\leftarrow & \text{MULTIPLICAND} \\
Y_7Y_6Y_5Y_4Y_3\ Y_2\ Y_1Y_0\leftarrow & \text{MULTIPLIER} \\
\hline
A_7A_6A_5A_4A_3\ A_2\ A_1A_0\leftarrow & \text{A PARTIAL PRODUCT} \\
B_7B_6B_5B_4B_3B_2\ B_1\ B_0 & \\
C_7C_6C_5C_4C_3C_2C_1\ C_0 & \\
D_7\ D_6D_5D_4D_3D_2D_1D_0 & \\
E_7\ E_6\ E_5E_4E_3E_2E_1E_0 & \\
F_7\ F_6\ F_5\ F_4F_3F_2F_1F_0 & \\
G_7\ G_6\ G_5\ G_4\ G_3G_2G_1G_0 & \\
H_7\ H_6\ H_5\ H_4\ H_3\ H_2H_1H_0 & \\
\hline
S_{15}S_{14}S_{13}S_{12}S_{11}S_{10}S_9\ S_8\ S_7\ S_6\ S_5\ S_4\ S_3\ \ S_2\ \ S_1\ S_0\leftarrow & \text{FINAL PRODUCT}
\end{array}
$$

b.

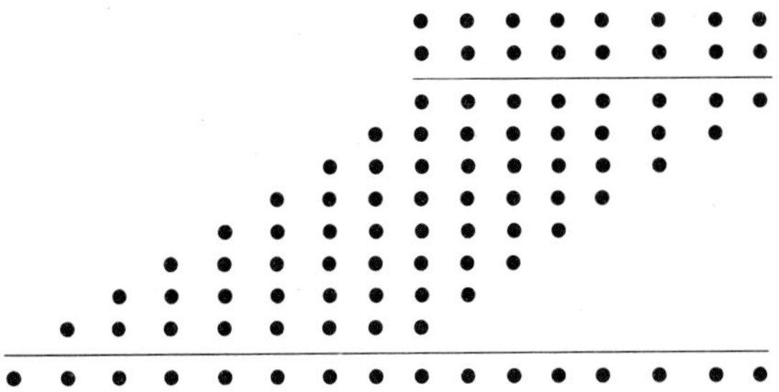

Figure 4–1.

a. Multiplying two 8-bit operands results in eight partial products which are added to form a 16-bit final product.

b. Convenient dot representation of the same multiplication.

4.1 SIMULTANEOUS MATRIX GENERATION AND REDUCTION

This scheme is made of two distinct steps. In the first step the partial products are generated simultaneously and in the second step the resultant matrix is reduced to the final product. Since the algorithms for each step are mostly independent of each other, we will describe them separately.

4.1.1 Partial Products Generation: Booth's Algorithm

The simplest way to generate partial products is to use AND gates as 1-by-1 multipliers. For example, in Figure 4–1a,

$$A_0 = Y_0X_0, A_1 = Y_0X_1, B_0 = Y_1X_0,$$

and so on. In this manner an n-bit multiplier generates n partial products. However, it is possible to use encoding techniques that will reduce the number of partial products. The modified Booth's algorithm is such an encoding technique which reduces the number of partial products by half.

The original Booth's algorithm [BOO 51] allows the multiplication operation to skip over any contiguous string of all 1's and all 0's in the multiplier, rather than form a partial product for each bit. Skipping a string of 0's is straightforward, but in skipping over a string of 1's, the following property is put to use: a string of 1's can be evaluated by subtracting the weight of the rightmost 1 from the modulus. A string of n 1's is the same as 1 followed by n 0's less 1. For example, the value of the binary string 11100 computes to $2^5 - 2^2 = 28$ (i.e., $100,000 - 100$).

A modified version of Booth's algorithm is more commonly used. The difference between the Booth's and the modified Booth's algorithm is as follows: the latter always generates $n/2$ independent partial products, whereas the former generates a varying (at most $n/2$) number dependent of partial products, depending on the bit pattern of the multiplier. Of course, parallel hardware implementation lends itself only to the fixed independent number of partial products. The modified multiplier encoding scheme encodes 2-bit groups and produces five partial products from an 8-bit multiplier, the fifth partial product being a consequence of the fact that the algorithm only handles two's complement numbers (only four partial products are generated if only two's complement representation is used).

Each multiplier is divided into substrings of 3 bits, with adjacent groups sharing a common bit. Booth's algorithm can be used with either unsigned or two's complement numbers, (the most significant bit of which has a weight of -2^n), and requires that the multiplier be padded with a 0 to the right to form four complete groups of 3 bits each. To work with unsigned numbers, the n-bit multiplier must also be padded with one or two zeros in the multipliers to the left. Figure 4–2 [AND 67] is the encoding table of the eight permutations of the 3 multiplier bits.

Bit			Operation	
2^1	2^0	2^{-1}		
Y_{i+1}	Y_i	Y_{i-1}		
0	0	0	add zero (no string)	$+0$
0	0	1	add multiplicand (end of string)	$+X$
0	1	0	add multiplicand (a string)	$+X$
0	1	1	add twice the multiplicand (end of string)	$+2X$
1	0	0	subtract twice the multiplicand (beginning of string)	$-2X$
1	0	1	subtract the multiplicand ($-2X$ and $+X$)	$-X$
1	1	0	subtract the multiplicand (beginning of string)	$-X$
1	1	1	subtract zero (center of string)	-0

Figure 4–2. Encoding the 3 multiplier bits, in the modified Booth's algorithm.

In using the table, (Figure 4–2), the multiplier is partitioned into 3-bit groups with one bit shared between groups. If this shared bit is a 1, subtraction is indicated since we prepare for a string of 1's. Consider the case of unsigned (i.e., positive) numbers; let X represent the multiplicand (all bits), and $Y = Y_{n-1}, Y_{n-2}, \ldots Y_1, Y_0$ an integer multiplier—the binary point following Y_0. (The placement of the point is arbitrary, but all actions are taken with respect to it.) The lowest order action is derived from multiplier bits $Y_1 Y_0.0$—the LSB has been padded with a zero. Only four actions are possible, $Y_1 Y_0.0$ may be either $00.0, 01.0, 10.0$, or 11.0. The first two cases are straightforward; for 00.0 the partial product is 0, for 01.0 the partial products is $+X$. The other two cases are perceived as the beginning of a string of 1's. Thus, we subtract $2X$, (i.e., add $-2X$), for the case 10.0 and subtract X for the case 11.0. Higher order actions must recognize that this subtraction has occurred. The next higher action is found from multiplier bits $Y_3 Y_2 Y_1$, (remember Y_1 is the shared bit). Its action on the multiplicand has 4 times the significance of $Y_1 Y_0.0$. Thus it uses the table as $Y_3 Y_2 Y_1$, but resulting actions are shifted by 2 (multiplied by 4). Thus, suppose the multiplier was 0010.0, the first action (10.0) would detect the start of a string of 1's and subtract $2X$ while the second action (00.1) would detect the end of a string of 1's and add X. But the second action has a scale or significance point 2 bits higher than the first action (4 times more significant). Thus $4 \times X - 2X = 2X$, the value of the multiplier, 0010.0. This may seem to the reader to be a lot of work to simply find $2X$ and indeed in this case two actions were required rather than one. By inspection of the table, however, only one action (addition or subtraction) is required for each <u>two</u> multiplier bits. Thus use of the algorithm insures that for an n-bit multiplier only $n/2$ actions will be required for any multiplier bit pattern.

For the highest order action with an unsigned multiplier, the action must be derived with a leading or padded zero. For an odd number of multiplier bits, the last action will be defined by $0Y_{n-1}.Y_{n-2}$. For an even number of multiplier bits, $\frac{n}{2} + 1$ actions are required; the last action being defined by $00.Y_{n-1}$.

Multipliers in two's complement form may be used directly in the algorithm. In this case the highest order action is determined by $Y_{n-1} Y_{n-2} Y_{n-3}$ (no padding) for an even number of multiplier bits and $Y_{n-1} Y_{n-1}.Y_{n-2}$, a sign extended group for odd sized multipliers. E.g., suppose $Y = -1$; in two's complement $Y = 1111 \ldots 11$. The lowest order action (11.0), is $-X$, all other actions (11.1), are -0, producing the desired result, $(-X)$.

In implementing the actions the $2X$ term is simply a 1-bit left shift of X. Thus, multiplicands must be arranged to be gated directly with respect to a scale point or shifted 1 bit. Subtraction is implemented by gating the complement of X (i.e., the one's complement) as the and then adding a 1 with respect to the scale point. In implementing this, the Y_{i+1} can be used as a subtractor indicator that will be added to the LSB of the partial product. If bit $Y_{i+1} = 0$, no subtraction is called for and adding 0 changes nothing. On the other hand, if bit $Y_{i+1} = 1$, then subtraction is called for and the proper two's complement is performed by adding 1 to the LSB. Of course, in the two's complement, the sign bit must be extended to the full width of the final result, as shown by the repetitive terms in Figure 4–3.

In Figure 4–3, if X and Y are 8-bit unsigned numbers then $A_8 - A_0$ are determined by the $Y_2 Y_1.0$ action on X. Since $2X$ is a possible action, A_8 may be affected and A_9 is the sign and extension. If a $\pm X$ action is determined, then A_8 will be the sign and $A_8 = A_9$.

$$
\begin{array}{cccccccccccccccc}
A_9 & A_9 & A_9 & A_9 & A_9 & A_9 & A_9 & A_8 & A_7 & A_6 & A_5 & A_4 & A_3 & A_2 & A_1 & A_0 \\
B_9 & B_9 & B_9 & B_9 & B_9 & B_8 & B_7 & B_6 & B_5 & B_4 & B_3 & B_2 & B_1 & B_0 & & Y_1 \\
C_9 & C_9 & C_9 & C_8 & C_7 & C_6 & C_5 & C_4 & C_3 & C_2 & C_1 & C_0 & & Y_3 & & \\
D_9 & D_8 & D_7 & D_6 & D_5 & D_4 & D_3 & D_2 & D_1 & D_0 & & Y_5 & & & & \\
E_7 & E_6 & E_5 & E_4 & E_3 & E_2 & E_1 & E_0 & & Y_7 & & & & & & \\
\hline
S_{15} & S_{14} & S_{13} & S_{12} & S_{11} & S_{10} & S_9 & S_8 & S_7 & S_6 & S_5 & S_4 & S_3 & S_2 & S_1 & S_0
\end{array}
$$

Figure 4–3. Generation of five partial products in 8×8 multiplication using modified Booth's algorithm (only four partial products are generated if the representation is restricted to two's complement).

The fifth action is determined by $00.Y_7$—always a positive, unshifted action ($+X$ or $+0$). If X and Y are 8-bit two's complement numbers, then $A_8 = A_9$, the sign and extension. Also no fifth action, $(E_7 - E_0)$, is required.

The A_9, B_9, C_9, D_9 terms appear to significantly increase the hardware required for partial product addition. There are 15 such terms. While the full addition of these terms results in the correct product formations, $S_{15} - S_0$, simpler implementations are possible. By recognizing the $A_9, B_9, \ldots$ terms are sign identifiers and generating the sign logic separately, the additional summing hardware for such terms can be eliminated.

The additional gate delay in implementing the modified Booth's algorithm consists of four gates: two gates for decoding the 3-bit multiplier and two gates for selecting X or 2X.

2^2	2^1	2^0	2^{-1}	
Y_{i+2}	Y_{i+1}	Y_i	Y_{i-1}	Operation
0	0	0	0	$+0$
0	0	0	1	$+X$
0	0	1	0	$+X$
0	0	1	1	$+2X$
0	1	0	0	$+2X$
0	1	0	1	$+3X$
0	1	1	0	$+3X$
0	1	1	1	$+4X$
1	0	0	0	$-4X$
1	0	0	1	$-3X$
1	0	1	0	$-3X$
1	0	1	1	$-2X$
1	1	0	0	$-2X$
1	1	0	1	$-X$
1	1	1	0	$-X$
1	1	1	1	-0

Figure 4–4. Extension of the modified Booth's algorithm to 3-bit multiplier group encoding. This requires generation of $\pm 3X$, which is not as trivial as the operations in the 2-bit multiplier encoding. (Compare with Figure 4–2.)

An extension of the modified Booth's algorithm involves an encoding of 3 bits at a time while examining 4 multiplier bits. This scheme would generate only $n/3$ partial products. However, the encoding truth table in Figure 4–4 requires the generation of a three times multiplicand term, which is not as trivial as generating twice the multiplicand. Thus, most hardware implementations use only the 2-bit encoding.

Example:
Suppose the multiplicand, X, is to be multiplied by an unsigned Y:

$$0011101011.$$

That is, decimal 235.

We use modified Booth's algorithm (Figure 4–2) and assume that this multiplier is a binary integer with point indicated by (.). Now the multiplier must be decomposed into overlapping 3-bit segments and actions determined for each segment. Note that the first segment has an implied "0" to the right of the binary point. Thus, we can label each segment as follows:

$$
\begin{array}{c}
\underline{(5)} \quad \underline{(3)} \quad \underline{(1)} \\
0\ 0\ \underline{1\ 1}\ 1\ \underline{0\ 1}\ 0\ \underline{1\ 1}\ .0 \\
\quad (4) \quad\quad (2)
\end{array}
$$

While segment (1) is referenced to the original binary point, segment (2) is *four times more significant*. Thus, any segment (2) action on X (the multiplicand) must be scaled by a factor of 4. Similarly, segment (3) is four times more significant than 2 and 16 times more significant than 1.

Now, by using the table and scaling as appropriate, we get the following actions:

segment number	bits	action	scale factor	result
(1)	110	−X	1	−X
(2)	101	−X	4	−4X
(3)	101	−X	16	−16X
(4)	111	0	64	0
(5)	001	+X	256	+256X
	total action			235X

Note that the table of actions can be simplified for the first segment (Y_{i-1} always 0) and the last segment (depending on whether there is an even or odd number of bits in the multiplier).

Also note that the actions specified in the table are independent of one another. Thus the five result actions in the example may be summed simultaneously using the carry-save addition techniques discussed in the last chapter.

4.1.2 Using ROMs to Generate Partial Products

Another way to generate partial products is to use ROMs. For example, the 8×8 multiplication of Figure 4–1 can be implemented using four 256×8 ROMs where each ROM performs 4×4 multiplication, as shown in Figure 4–5a.

In Figure 4–5a, each 4-bit value of each element of the pair (Y_A, X_A) (Y_B, X_A) (Y_A, X_B) and (Y_B, X_B) is concatenated to form an 8-bit address into the 256 entry ROM table. The entry contains the corresponding 8-bit product. Thus four tables are required to simultaneously form the products: $Y_A \cdot X_A$, $Y_B \cdot X_A$, $Y_A \cdot X_B$, and $Y_B \cdot X_B$. Note that the $Y_A \cdot X_A$ and the $Y_B \cdot X_B$ terms have disjoint significance; thus only three terms must be added to form the product. The number of rearranged partial products which must be summed is referred to as the matrix height—the number of initial inputs to the CSA tree.

A generalization of the ROM scheme is shown is Figure 4–5b [TI 76] for various multiplier arrays of up to 64×64. In the latter case, 256 partial products are generated. But upon rearranging, the maximum column height of the matrix is 31.

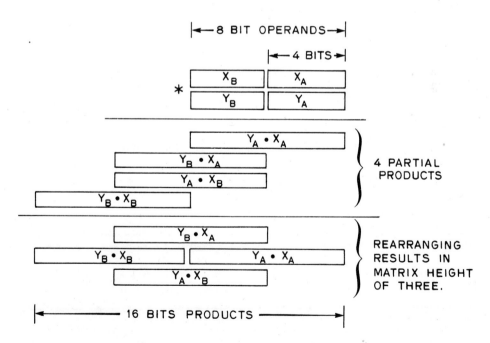

Figure 4–5a.   Implementation of 8×8 multiplication using four 256×8 ROMs where each ROM performs 4×4 multiplication.

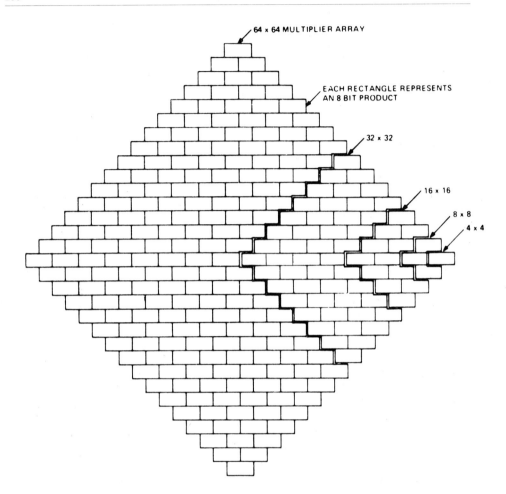

Figure 4–5b.   Using ROMs for various multiplier arrays for up to 64 × 64 multiplication.
Each ROM is a 4 × 4 multiplier with 8-bit product. Each rectangle represents the 8-bit partial products.

The table below summarizes the maximum height of the partial products matrix for the various partial generation schemes:

	GENERAL FORMULA	MAX HEIGHT OF THE MATRIX							
SCHEME		Number of Bits							
		8	16	24	32	40	48	56	64
1×1 multiplier (AND gate)	n	8	16	24	32	40	48	56	64
4×4 multiplier (ROM)	$(n/2) - 1$	3	7	11	15	19	23	27	31
8×8 multiplier (ROM)	$(n/4) - 1$	1	3	4	7	9	11	13	15
Modified Booth's algorithm	$(n/2)$	4	8	12	16	20	24	28	32

These partial products can be viewed as adjacent columns of height h. Now we are ready to discuss the implementations of column reductions.

4.1.3 Partial Products Reduction

As mentioned in the last chapter the common approach in all of the summand reduction techniques is to reduce the n partial products to two partial products. A carry-look-ahead is then used to add these two products. One of the first reduction implementations was the Wallace tree [WAL 64], where carry-save adders are used to reduce 3 bits of column height to 2 bits (Figure 4–6). In general, the number of the required carry-save adder levels (L) in a Wallace tree to reduce height h to 2 is:

$$L = \left\lceil \log_{3/2}\left(\frac{h}{2}\right) \right\rceil = \left\lceil \log_{1.5}\left(\frac{h}{2}\right) \right\rceil,$$

where h is the number of operands (actions) to be summed and L is the number of CSA stages of delay required to produce the pair of column operands. For 8×8 multiplication $h = 8$, and four levels of carry-save adders are required as illustrated in Figure 4–7. Below we show the number of levels versus various column heights.

Column Height (h)	Number of Levels (L)
3	1
4	2
$4 < n \leq 6$	3
$6 < n \leq 9$	4
$9 < n \leq 13$	5
$13 < n \leq 19$	6
$19 < n \leq 28$	7
$28 < n \leq 42$	8
$42 < n \leq 63$	9

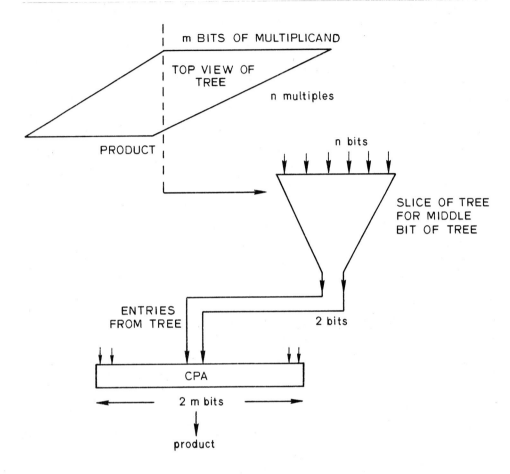

Figure 4–6.   Wallace tree

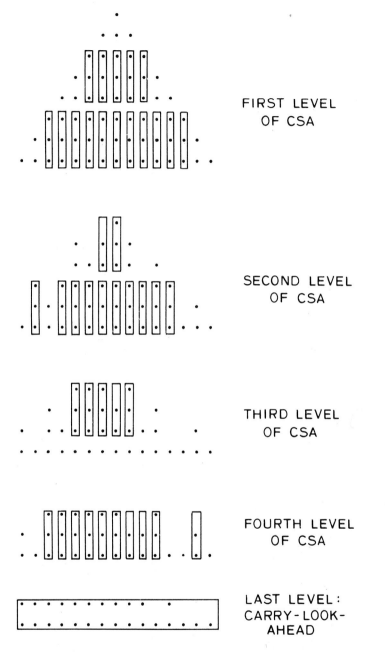

FIRST LEVEL
OF CSA

SECOND LEVEL
OF CSA

THIRD LEVEL
OF CSA

FOURTH LEVEL
OF CSA

LAST LEVEL:
CARRY-LOOK-
AHEAD

Figure 4–7.   Wallace tree reduction of 8×8 multiplication, using carry-save adders, (CSA).

Dadda [DAD 65] coined the term "parallel (n, m) counter." This counter is a combinatorial network with m outputs and $n(\leq 2^m)$ inputs. The m outputs represent a binary number encoding the number of ones present at the inputs. The carry-save adder in the above Wallace tree is a $(3, 2)$ counter.

This class of counters has been extended in an excellent article [STE 77] that shows the Wallace tree and the Dadda scheme to be special cases. The generalized counters take several successively weighted input columns and produce their weighted sum. Counters of this type are denoted as:

$$(C_{R-1}, C_{R-2}, \ldots, C_0, d)$$

counters, where R is the number of input columns, C_i is the number of input bits in the column of weight 2^i, and d is the number of bits in the output word. The suggested implementation for such counters is a ROM. For example, a $(5,5,4)$ counter can be programmed in $1K \times 4$ ROM, where the ten address lines are treated as two adjacent columns of 5 bits each. Note that the maximum sum of the two columns is 15, which requires exactly 4 bits for its binary representation. Figure 4–8a and 4–8b illustrate the ROM implementation of the $(5,5,4)$ counter and Figure 4–8c shows several generalized counters. The use of the $(5,5,4)$ counter to reduce the partial products in a 12×12 multiplication is shown in Figure 4–9, where the partial products are generated by 4×4 multipliers.

Parallel compressors, which are a subclass of parallel counters, have been introduced by Gajski [GAJ 80]. These compressors are distinctively characterized by the set of inputs and outputs that serves as an interconnection between different packages in a one-dimensional array of compressors. These compressors are said to be more efficient than parallel counters. For more details on this interesting approach the reader is referred to Gajski's article [GAJ 80].

(a)

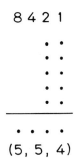

(b)

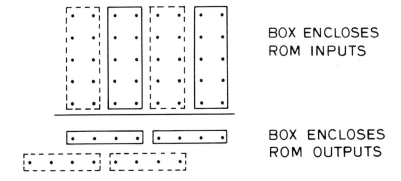

BOX ENCLOSES
ROM INPUTS

BOX ENCLOSES
ROM OUTPUTS

Figure 4-8.   The 1K × 4 ROM reduces the five input operands to one operand.
    a. Adding two columns, each 5 bits in height, gives maximum result
       of 15 which is representable by 4 bits (the ROM outputs).
    b. Four ROMs are used to reduce the five operands (each 8 bits wide)
       to two operands, which can be added using carry-look-ahead. Note
       that regardless of the operand width, five operands are always
       reduced to no more than two operands.

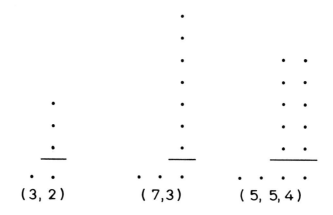

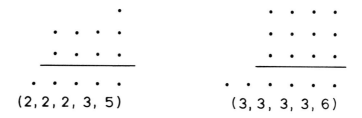

Figure 4–8c.   Some generalized counters [STE 77].

(a)

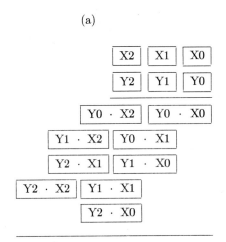

(b)

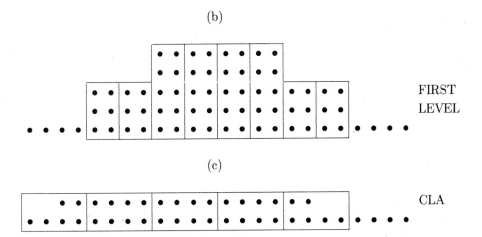

Figure 4–9. 12×12 bit partial reduction using $(5, 5, 4)$ counters. The X0, Y0, X1, etc.
terms each represent 4 bits of the argument. Thus, the product X0Y0 is an
8-bit summand.

a. Partial products are generated by 4×4 multipliers [STE 77].

b. Eight $1K \times 4$ ROMs are used to compress the column height from
five to two. Each dot represents a bit of a summand (partial
product) in (a).

c. Five 4-bit CLA adders are used to add the last two operands. The
output of each counter in (b) produces a 4-bit result—2 bits of the
same significnce and 2 of higher. These are combined in (c).

4.2 ITERATION AND PARTIAL PRODUCTS REDUCTION

4.2.1 A Tale of Three Trees

The Wallace tree can be coupled with iterative techniques to provide cost effective implementations. A basic requirement for such implementation is a good latch to store intermediate results. In this case "good" means that it does not add additional delay to the computation. As we shall see in more detail later, the Earle latch (Figure 4–10), accomplishes this by simply providing a feed-back path from the output of an existing canonic circuit pair to an additional input.

Thus, an existing path delay is not increased (but fan-in requirements are increased by one). In a given logic path, an existing "AND-OR" pair is replaced by the latch which also performs the "AND-OR" function.

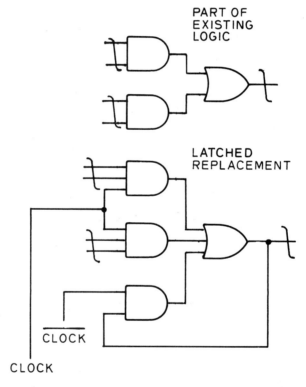

Figure 4–10.   Earle latch

Use of this latch can significantly reduce implementation costs if appropriate care is taken in design (see Chapter 6).

Consider the operation of an n-bit multiplier on an m-bit multiplicand; that is, we reduce n partial products, each of m bits, to two partial products, then propagate the carries to form a single (product) result. Trees of size L actually have some bits of their partial product tree for which L CSA stages are required. Note that for both low-order and high-order product bits the tree size is less.

Now in the case of the simple Wallace tree the time required for multiplication is:

$$\tau \leq L \cdot 2 + \text{CLA}(2m \text{ bits}),$$

where τ is in unit gate delays. Each CSA stage has 2 serial gates (an AND-OR in both sum and carry). The CLA $(2m)$ term represents the number of unit gate delays for a carry-look-ahead structure with operand size $2m$ bits. Actually since the tree height at the less significant bits is smaller than the middle bits, entry into the CLA from these positions arrives early. Thus the CLA term is somewhat conservative.

The full Wallace tree is "expensive" and, perhaps more important, is topologically difficult to implement. That is, large trees are difficult to map onto planes (printed wire boards) since each CSA communicates with its own slice, transmits carries to the higher order slice, and receives carries from a lower order. This "solid" topology creates both I/0 pin difficulty (if the implementation "spills" over a single board) and wire length (routing) problems.

Iterating on smaller trees has been proposed [AND 67] as a solution. Instead of entering n multiples of the multiplicand we use an n/I tree and perform I iterations on this smaller tree.

Consider three types of tree iterations:

1. Simple iteration: in this case the n/I multiples of the m-bit multiplicand are reduced and added to form a single partial product. This is latched and fed back into the top of the tree for assimilation on the next iteration.

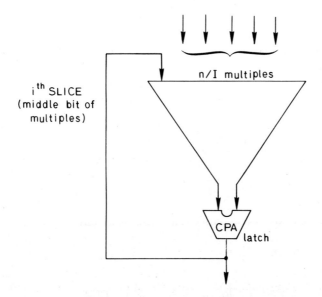

Figure 4–11.   Slice of a simple iteration tree showing one product bit.

The multiplication time is now the number of iterations, I, times the sum of the delay in the CSA tree height (two delays per CSA) and the CLA delay. The CSA tree is approximately $\log_{3/2}$ of the number of inputs $\lceil \frac{n}{I} + 1 \rceil$ divided by 2 since the tree is reduced to *two* outputs, not *one*. The maximum size of the operands entering the CLA on any iteration is $m + \lceil \frac{n}{I} + 1 \rceil$;

$$\tau \approx I\left(2\left\lceil \log_{3/2}\left\lceil \frac{n}{I} + 1 \right\rceil / 2 \right\rceil + \text{CLA}\left(m + \left\lceil \frac{n}{I} + 1 \right\rceil \right) \right)$$

unit gate delays.

2. Iterate on tree only: the above scheme can be improved by avoiding the use of the CPA until the partial products are reduced to two. This requires that the (shifted) two partial results be fed back into the tree *before* entering the CLA, (Figure 4–12). The "shifting" is required since the new $\frac{n}{I}$ input multiples are at least (could be more, depending on multiplier encoding) $\frac{n}{I}$ bits more significant than the previous iteration. Thus, each pair of reduced results is returned to the top of the tree and shifted to the correct significance. Therefore, we require only one CLA and I iterations on the CSA tree.

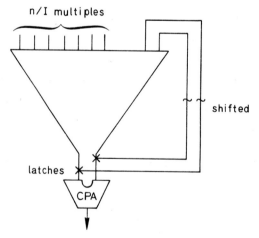

n/I multiples

shifted

latches

CPA

Figure 4–12.   Slice of tree iteration showing one product bit.

The time for multiplication is now:

$$\tau \approx I\left(2\left\lceil \log_{3/2}\left\lceil \frac{n}{I} + 2 \right\rceil / 2 \right\rceil \right) + \text{CLA}\,(2m).$$

3.   Iterate on lowest level of tree: In this case the partial products
are assimilated by returning them to the lowest level of the
tree. When they are assimilated to two partial products again
a single CLA is used, (Figure 4–13). Thus:

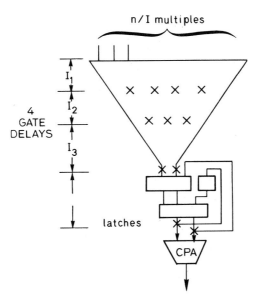

Figure 4–13.   Slice of low level tree iteration.

As the Earle latch requires (approximately) a minimum of four gate
delays for a pipeline stage, returning the CSA output one level back
into the tree provides an optimum implementation (Chapter 6 provides
more detailed discussion). The tree height is increased; but only the
initial set of multiples sees the delay of the total tree. Subsequent sets
are introduced at intervals of four gate delays, (Figure 4–13). Thus,
the time for multiplication is now:

$$\tau \approx 2\left(\left\lceil \log_{\frac{3}{2}} \left\lceil \frac{n}{I} \right\rceil / 2 \right\rceil\right) + I \cdot 4 + \text{CLA}(2m).$$

Note that while the cost of the tree has been significantly reduced, only the $I \cdot 4$
term differs from the full tree time. So long as I is chosen so that this term does
not dominate the total time, attractive implementations are possible using a tree
of size L′ instead of L levels.

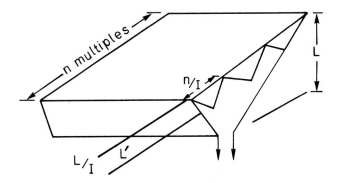

Figure 4–14.   Iteration.

In all of these approaches we are reducing the height of the tree by inputing significantly fewer terms, about $\frac{n}{I}$, instead of n. These fewer input terms mean a much smaller tree—fewer components (cost) and quicker generation of a partial result but now I iterations are needed for a complete result instead of a single pass.

4.3 ITERATIVE ARRAY OF CELLS

The matrix generation/reduction scheme, (Wallace tree), is the fastest way to perform parallel multiplication, however, it also requires the most hardware. The iterative array of cells requires less hardware but it is slower. The hardware required in the iterative approach can be calculated from the following formula:

$$\text{number of building blocks} = \left\lceil \frac{N \times M}{n \times m} \right\rceil,$$

where N, M are the number of bits in the final multiplication, and n, m are the number of bits in each building block. For example, nine 4×4 multipliers are required to perform 12×12 multiplication in the iterative approach (since $(12 \times 12)/(4 \times 4) = 9$). By contrast, using the matrix generation technique to do 12×12 multiplication requires 13 adders in addition to the nine 4×4 multipliers (see Figure 4–9). In general, the iterative array of cells is more attractive for shorter operand lengths since their delay increases linearly with operand length, whereas the delay of the matrix-generation approach increases with the log of the operand length.

The simplest way to construct an iterative array of cells is to use 1-bit cells, which are simply full adders. Figure 4–15a depicts the construction of a 5×5 unsigned multiplication from such cells.

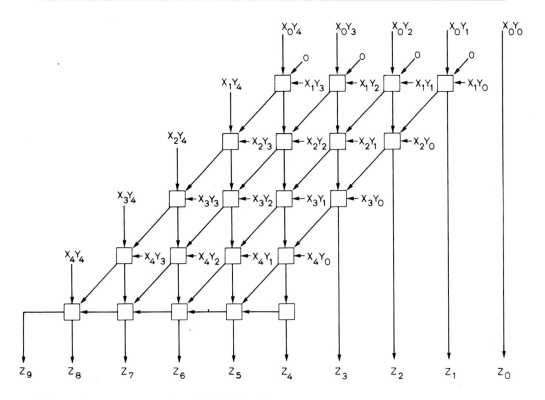

Figure 4–15a. 5×5 unsigned multiplication.

This scheme with a minor variation is implemented as a series of integrated circuits that perform 8×8, 12×12, 16×16, and 24×24 multiplication, in 100–200 ns [TRW 81].

To perform signed (two's complement) multiplication the scheme is slightly more complex, as described in [PEZ 70]. Pezaris illustrates his scheme by building 5×5 multipliers from two types of circuits, using the following 1-bit adder cell (Figure 4–15b.):

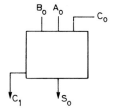

Figure 4–15b.   1-bit adder cell.

$$
\begin{array}{ccccc}
& \mathrm{A_0} & \mathrm{B_0} & \mathrm{C_0} & \mathrm{C_1} & \mathrm{S_0} \\
\text{TYPE I:} & (0,1) + (0,1) + & (0,1) & = (0,2) + (0,1). \\
\text{TYPE II:} & (0,-1) + (0,1) + & (0,1) & = (0,2) + (0,-1). \\
\text{TYPE II}': & (0,1) + (0,-1) + & (0,-1) & = (0,-2) + (0,1). \\
\text{TYPE I}': & (0,-1) + (0,-1) + & (0,-1) & = (0,-2) + (0,-1).
\end{array}
$$

Type I is the conventional carry-save adder, and it is the only type used in Figure 4–15 for the unsigned multiplication. Types I and I$'$ correspond to identical truth tables (because if $x + y + z = u + v$, then $-x - y - z = -u - v$) and, therefore, to identical circuits. Similarly, types II and II$'$ correspond to identical circuits. Figure 4–16a shows the entire 5×5 multiplication.

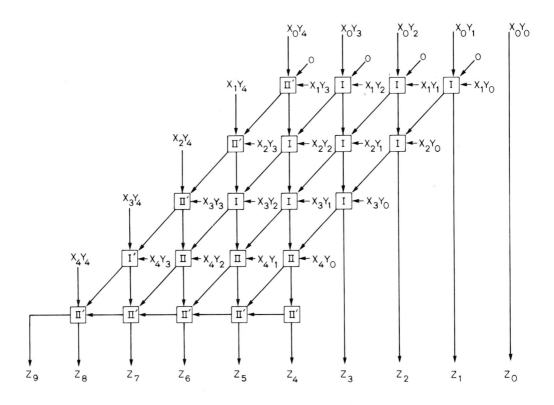

Figure 4–16a. 5×5 two's complement multiplication [PEZ 70].

Pezaris extends the 1-bit adder cell to a 2-bit adder cell, as shown below:

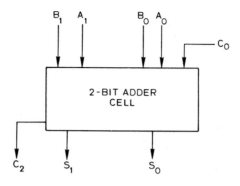

Figure 4–16b.   2-bit adder cell.

Implementation of this method with 2-bit adders requires *three* types of circuits, (the L101, L102, L103). The arithmetic operations performed by these three types are given below:

$$
\begin{array}{ccccccccc}
& A_1 & B_1 & A_0 & B_0 & C_0 & C_2 & S_1 & S_0 \\
\text{L101} : & (0,2)+ & (0,2) & +(0,1)+ & (0,1) & +(0,1)= & (0,4)+ & (0,2) & +(0,1); \\
\text{L102} : & (0,2)+ & (0,-2) & +(0,1)+ & (0,1) & +(0,1)= & (0,4)+ & (0,-2) & +(0,1); \\
\text{L103} : & (0,2)+ & (0,-2) & +(0,1)+ & (0,-1)+ & (0,1)= & (0,4)+ & (0,-2) & +(0,1).
\end{array}
$$

These cells implemented in ECL technology were used at MIT to construct a 40 ns 17×17 two's complement multiplier. This was quite a respectable achievement for 1970.

In the world of TTL-MSI one of the most popular multipliers in the early 1970's was a 2×4 iterative multiplier (25S05). This device is described in an excellent application note [GHE 71] which is available from AMD. The 25S05, like all iterative multipliers, performs the operation

$$ S = X \cdot Y + K; $$

(whereas the matrix-generation schemes perform only $S = X \cdot Y$). The device uses the (3-bit) modified Booth's algorithm to halve the number of partial products generated. Figure 4–17 shows the block diagram of the iterative cell. The X_{-1} input is needed in expanding horizontally since the Booth encoder may call for 2X, which is implemented by a left shift. The Y_{-1} is used as the overlap bit during multiplier encoding. Note that outputs S_4 and S_5 are needed only on the most significant portion of each partial product (these 2 bits are used for sign correction). Figure 4–18 shows the implementation of a 12×12 two's complement multiplier, using the 25S05 iterative cells. This scheme can be extended to larger cells. For example, in Figure 4–18, the dotted line encloses an 8×8 iterative cell.

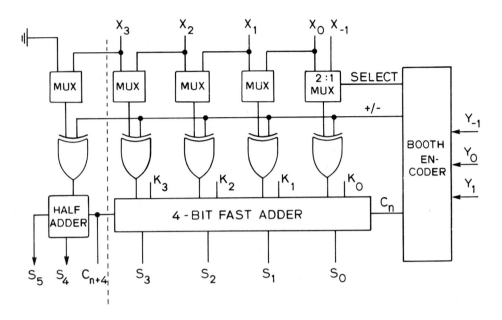

Figure 4–17.   Block diagram of 2×4 iterative multiplier.

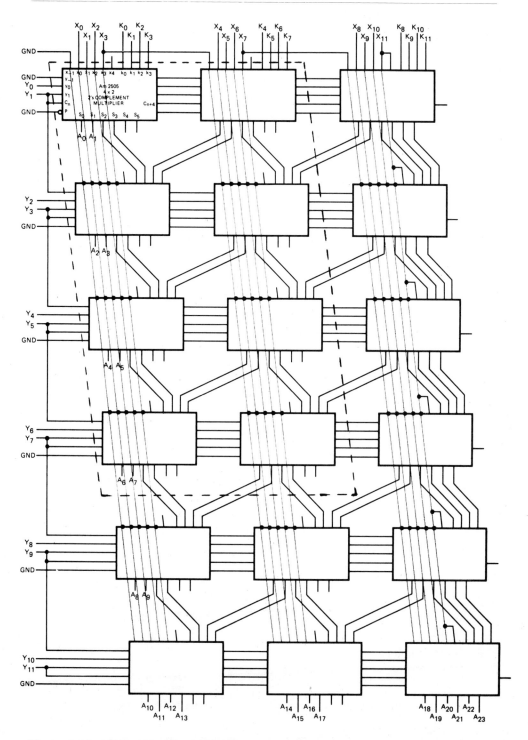

Figure 4–18. 12×12 two's complement multiplication $A = X \cdot Y + K$. Adapted from [GHE 71].

4.4 DETAILED DESIGN OF LARGE MULTIPLIERS

4.4.1 Design Details of a 64×64 Multiplier

In this section we describe the design of a 64×64 multiplier using the technique of simultaneous generation of partial products. The design uses standard LSI/MSI devices that are commonly available. For a complete list of the many variations of monolithic multipliers consult [WAS 78b]. Actually, only four types of ICs are needed to implement the three steps of a parallel multiplier.

1. Simultaneous generation of partial products—using 125 ns 8×8 multiplier (MMI 67558).

2. Reduction of the partial products to two operands — using 50 ns $1K \times 4$ ROM (MMI 63S441).

3. Adding the two operands — using MSI adders and carry-look-ahead units (TI 74S181/2).

Figure 4–19 depicts the generation of the partial products in a 64×64 multiplication, using 8×8 multipliers. Each of the two 64-bit operands is made of 8 bytes (byte = 8 bits), which are numbered 0, 1, 2, ... 7 from the least to the most significant byte. Thus, 64-bit multiplication involves multiplying each byte of the multiplicand (X) by all 8 bytes of the multiplier (Y). For example, in Figure 4–19 the eight rectangles marked with a dot are those generated from multiplying byte 0 of X, by each of the 8 bytes of Y. Note that the product "01" is shifted 8 bits with respect to product "00," and so is "02" with respect to "01" and so on. These 8-bit shifts are due to shifted position of each byte within the 64-bit operand. Also, note that for each $Xi \cdot Yj (i \neq j)$ byte multiplication there is a corresponding product $XjYi$ with the same weight. Thus, product "01" corresponds to product "10" and product "12" corresponds to product "21." As before, for $N \times M$ multiplication the number of $n \times m$ multipliers required is:

$$\frac{N \times M}{n \times m}$$

and in our specific case:

$$\text{number of multipliers} = \frac{64 \times 64}{8 \times 8} = 64 \text{ multipliers.}$$

X7	X6	X5	X4	X3	X2	X1	X0
Y7	Y6	Y5	Y4	Y3	Y2	Y1	Y0

$$
\begin{array}{c}
Y0 \cdot X0 \\
Y0 \cdot X1 \\
Y0 \cdot X2 \\
Y0 \cdot X3 \quad\quad Y1 \cdot X0 \\
Y0 \cdot X4 \quad\quad Y1 \cdot X1 \\
Y0 \cdot X5 \quad\quad Y1 \cdot X2 \\
Y0 \cdot X6 \quad\quad Y1 \cdot X3 \\
Y0 \cdot X7 \quad\quad Y1 \cdot X4 \\
Y1 \cdot X5 \\
Y1 \cdot X6 \\
Y1 \cdot X7
\end{array}
$$

Figure 4–19a.   A 64×64 multiplier using 8×8 multipliers. Only 16 of the 64 partial products are shown. Each 8×8 multiplier produces a 16–bit result.

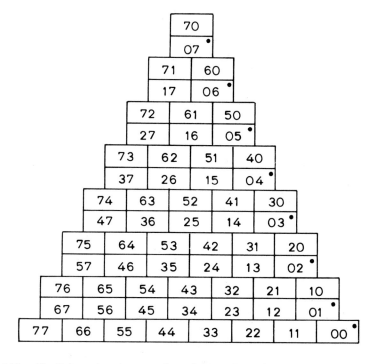

Figure 4–19b.   Partial products generation of 64×64 multiplication using 8×8 multipliers. Each rectangle represents the 16–bit product of each 8×8 multiplier. These partial products are reduced later on to two operands, which are then added by a CLA adder. Each box entry above corresponds to a partial product index pair; e.g., the 70 corresponds to the term Y7·X0.

The next step is to reduce the partial products to two operands. As was shown in Figure 4–9, a 1K $\times$ 4 ROM can reduce two columns, each 5 bits high, to two operands. The matrix of the partial products in Figure 4–19 can be viewed as eight groups of 16 columns each. The height of the eight groups is equal to: 1, 3, 5, 7, 9, 11, 13 and 15. Figure 4–20 illustrates with a dot representation the use of 1K $\times$ 4 ROMs to reduce the various column heights to 2 bits high. Now we can compute the total number of ROMs required to reduce the partial product matrix of a 64 $\times$ 64 multiplication to two operands.

Number of Columns	Height of Columns	Number of ROMs per two Columns	Number of ROMs for all Columns of same height
16	15	5	$8 \times 5 = 40$
16	13	4	$8 \times 4 = 32$
16	11	3	$8 \times 3 = 24$
16	9	3	$8 \times 3 = 24$
16	7	2	$8 \times 2 = 16$
16	5	1	$8 \times 1 = 8$
16	3	1	$8 \times 1 = 8$
16	1	–	—
Total number of ROMs			152

The last step in the 64 $\times$ 64 multiplication is to add the two operands using 4-bit adders and carry-look-ahead units, as was described earlier. Since the double length product is 128 bits long, 32 adders are required for the final addition. The carry-look-ahead (CLA) is implemented in three levels using eight, two, and one unit for the first, second, and third level, respectively.

The total IC count of this 64 $\times$ 64 implementation is as follows:

Multipliers	64
ROMs	152
Adders	32
CLA units	11
Total ICs	259

The total delay in getting a double length product is made of the following delays:

Multiplier delay	125 ns
Three ROM delays	150 ns
Addition	55 ns
Total Delay	330 ns

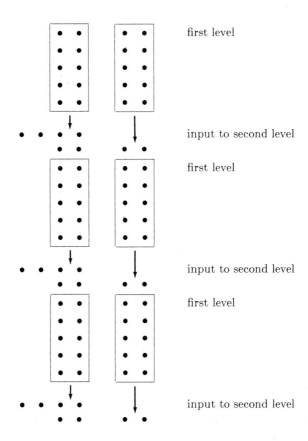

Figure 4–20a.   Using 1K × 4 ROM (5,5,4 counters) to implement the reduction of the partial products of height 15, showing only the first level and its output. This maximum height occurs (Figure 4–19b) when partial products 70 (Y7·X0) through 44 (or 33) are to be summed. For example, the top 5,5,4 counter above would have inputs from 70, 07, 71, 17, 61; the middle counter inputs form 16, 62, 26, 52, 25; the lowest from 53, 35, 43, 34, and 44. The three counters above provide three 4-bit outputs (2 bits of the same significance, 2 of higher). Thus, six outputs must be summed in the second level, three form the three shown counters, and three from the three lower order counters.

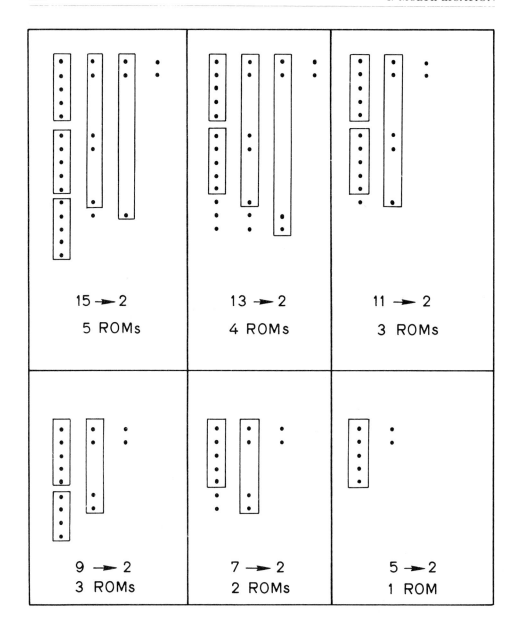

Figure 4–20b. Using 1K × 4 ROM to reduce various column heights to 2 bits high. The 15 → 2 shows the summation as required in Figure 4–20a (height 15). Each other height required in Figure 4–19b is shown in 5,5,4 implementation.

4.4.2 Design Details of a 56×56 Single-Length Multiplier

The last section described a 64×64 multiplier with double-length precision. In this section we illustrate the implementation of single-length multiplication and the hardware reduction associated with it, as contrasted with double-length multiplication. We selected 56×56 multiplication because 56 bits is a commonly used mantissa length in long floating point formats.

A single-length multiplier is used in fractional multiplication, where the precision of the product is equal to that of each of the operands. For example, in implementing the mantissa multiplier in a hardware floating point processor, input operands and the output product have the range and the precision of:

$$0.5 \leq \text{mantissa range} \leq 1 - 2^{-n},$$

$$\text{mantissa precision} = 2^{-n},$$

where n is the number of bits in each operand.

Figure 4–21 shows the partial products generated by using 8×8 multipliers. The double-length product is made of 49 multipliers since

$$\text{number of multipliers} = \frac{56 \times 56}{8 \times 8} = 49.$$

However, for single precision a substantial saving in the number of multipliers can be realized by "chopping" away all the multipliers to the right of the 64 MSBs (shaded area). But we need to make sure that this chopping does not affect the precision of the 56 MSBs. Assume a worst case contribution from the "chopped" area that is, all ones. The MSB of the discarded part has the weight of 2^{-65}, and the column height at this bit position is 11. Thus, the first few terms of the "chopped" area are:

$$\text{Max error} = 11 * (2^{-65} + 2^{-66} + 2^{-67} + \dots).$$
$$\text{But:} \quad 11 < 2^4.$$
$$\text{Therefore:} \quad \text{Max error} < (2^{-61} + 2^{-62} + 2^{-63} + \dots).$$

From the last equation it is obvious that "chopping" right of the 64 MSBs, will give us 60 correct MSBs which is more than enough to handle the required 56 bits plus the 2 guard bits.

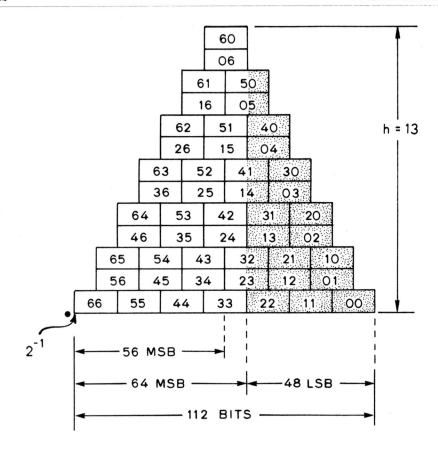

Figure 4–21.   Partial products generation in a 56 × 56 multiplication, using 8 × 8 multi-
              pliers. The shaded multipliers can be removed when a single-length product
              (56 MSBs) is required.

Now we can compute hardware saving of the single-length multiplication. From
Figure 4–21, we count 15 fully shaded multipliers. We cannot remove the half-
shaded multipliers, since their most significant half is needed for the 58-bit precision. Thus, a total of 34 instead of 49 multipliers are used for the partial product
generation.

Using the technique outlined previously, the number of ROMs needed for column
reduction is easily computed for double and single-length.

Number of Columns		Height of Columns	Number of ROMs per Two Columns	Number of ROMs for All Columns of Same Height	
Double Length	Single Length			Double Length	Single Length
16	16	13	4	32	32
16	8	11	3	24	12
16	8	9	3	24	12
16	8	7	2	16	8
16	8	5	1	8	4
16	8	3	1	8	4
16	8	1	–	–	–
Total Number of ROMs				112	72

Finally, adding the resulting two operands in the double-length case (112 bits) requires 28 4-bit adders and ten carry-look-ahead (CLA) units. For the single-length case, the addition of the two 64-bit operands is accomplished by 16 adders and five CLA units.

The total IC count of the single and double-length multiplication is as follows:

	Double Length	Single Length
Multipliers	49	34
ROMs	112	72
Adders	28	16
CLA Units	10	5
TOTAL	199	127

From the above table, we see that there is a 34% hardware savings using the single-length multiplication. However, there is no speed improvement assuming the component delay mentioned earlier, that is, ROM delay of 50 ns, and 64-bit addition in 55 ns. This is because the 48 LSBs are reduced in two ROM delays, (their maximum column height is 11), while the 64 MSBs are reduced in three ROM delays (maximum column height is 13). Thus adding the 48 LSBs overlaps the third ROM delay. So both single and double-length multiplication are executed in 330 ns.

	FIXED RADIX (BINARY)			VARIABLE RADIX (RESIDUE)	
	Winograd's Lower Bound	Matrix Generation and Reduction (Note 1)	Iterative Array of Cells (Note 2)	Winograd's Lower Bound	ROM Look-Up Table (Note 3)
Gate Delay	8	40	140	4	8
Speed	–	330 ns	1000 ns	–	50 ns
Package Count	–	259	64	–	23

Note 1: Matrix generation is accomplished by 125 ns 8 × 8 multiplier [MMI 82]. Column reduction is accomplished by 50 ns 1K × 4 PROM = (5, 5, 4) counter. Final two operands are added by CLA units 74S181 and 74S182.

Note 2: Iterative cell is a hypothetical 125 ns 8 × 8 multiplier.

Note 3: Look-up table is a 50 ns 1K × 8 ROM.

Figure 4–22.   64 × 64 multiplication comparison between the various hardware realizations and the Winograd lower bounds (whose gate delays are multiplied by 2 to account for AND-OR realization). Fan-in is assumed to be 5.

4.5 HARDWARE REALIZATION VERSUS WINOGRAD'S LOWER BOUNDS

Figure 4–22 compares the speed obtained from the various multiplication hardware realizations with the speed predicted by Winograd's lower bounds. These results show that in a fixed-radix number system, the multiplication hardware is not nearly as close to the bounds as is the addition. However, the fixed residue number system implementation (which performs addition and multiplication at the same speed) is now much closer to the bounds than any other conventional implementation. In addition to the higher speed, the residue number system uses fewer packages. Thus, for multiplication, the variable-radix (residue number) system is a very attractive alternative that should be considered seriously in spite of the difficulties of conversion, scaling, and overflow detection.

4.6 ADDITIONAL READINGS

One of the very first papers to address the technique of high-speed multiplication using a modified Booth's algorithm was written in 1964 by MacSorley, [MAC 61]. Many of MacSorley's ideas were implemented in the floating point units of the IBM 360/91, [AND 67]. These two papers, plus a few other classic papers on computer arithmetic were reprinted in a book by Swartzlander, [SWA 76].

An excellent review of many multiplication techniques is presented in an article by Gordon and Hastings, [GOR 82]. The authors address optimizing ROM sizes for column compression in high-speed multipliers plus an economic approach for multiplication using a serial parallel approach. Serial parallel techniques are used in LSI circuits such as in 74S516, which is a 16-bit multiplier/divider, [MMI 82a].

4.7 SUMMARY

Three hardware implementations of parallel multipliers have been shown. These implementations are based on a two step approach: the first step is generation of partial products and the second step is adding the partial products to one final product. Booth's algorithm was applied to halve the number of the partial products while ROM look-up tables were used as an LSI solution to adding these products. The detailed design of a 56-bit multiplier has also been developed in this chapter. This multiplier is an important building block in the design of a fast floating point processor, as will be shown in the next chapter.

4.8 EXERCISES

1. Design a modified Booth's encoder for a 4-bit multiplier.

2. Find the delay of the encoder in Problem 1.

3. Construct an action table for modified Booth's algorithm (2-bit multiplier encoded) for sign and magnitude numbers (be careful about the sign bit).

4. Design a modified Booth's encoder for sign and magnitude numbers (4-bit multiplier encoded).

5. Construct the middle bit section of the CSA tree for 48×48 multiplication for:

    a.   full Wallace tree;

    b.   simple iteration;

    c.   iterate on tree;

    d.   iterate on lowest level of tree;

6. Compute the number of CSA's required for 48×48 multiplication for a full Wallace tree.

7. Derive an improved delay formula (taking into account the skewed significance of the partial products) for:

    a.   full Wallace tree;

    b.   simple iteration;

    c.   iterate on tree;

    d.   iterate on lowest level of tree.

8. Suppose 256×8 ROMs are used to implement 12-bit $\times$ 12-bit multiplication. Find the partial products, the rearranged product matrix, and the delay required to form a 24-bit product.

9. If (5,5,4) counters are used for partial product reduction, compute the number of counter levels required for column heights of 8, 16, 32, and 64 bits. How many such counters are required for each height?

10. Suppose (5,5,4) counters are being used to implement an iterative multiplication with a column height of 32 bits. Iteration on the tree only is to be used. Compare the tree delay and number of counters required for one, two, and four iterations.

11. Refer to Figure 4–3. Develop the logic on the A_9, B_9, C_9, D_9 terms to eliminate the required summing of these terms to form the required product. Assume X and Y are 8-bit unsigned integers.

12. Refer to Figure 4–2. Show that this table is valid for the two's complement form of the multiplier.

13. We wish to design a unit to multiply two unsigned 31-bit numbers using a modified Booth scheme. Suppose that all partial products are available, and are arranged in a triangular structure. For a 1 pass (no iterations) (5,5,4) counter tree;

    a.   How many partial products are required?

    b.   What is the tree height?

    c.   How many dots are in the tree?

    d.   For product col 30–33 (LSB is identified col 0) show all counters and connections in tree. Explicitly show carries at each level of tree.

    e.   For $r = 5$ and ROM implementation of the 5,5,4 counter what is the number of gate delays in the above? Use CLA and ROM gate delay model. Do <u>not</u> use actual MSI part delays as presented in text.

4.9 DESIGN EXERCISES

1. There are several ways to design a 56×56 single-length multiplier. In the text we used a fully parallel approach to obtain maximum speed. The following two problems ask you to trade-off speed in order to reduce chip count. Compute for each of the following:

- fastest cycle;

- final result (in μ sec);

- chip count.

    a.   Design a 56×56 bit multiplier using seven 8×8 multiplier chips that will perform 8×56 multiplication in one cycle. Use 74S381 and 74S182 for ALU. Use 74S374 register combined with the ALU to perform accumulation. <u>HINT</u>: it takes *seven* cycles to get the final result.

    b.   Design a poor man's 56×56 bit multiplier using only ALU, Registers, and PLAs (don't use LSI multipliers). Design it with the modified Booth's algorithm; i.e., shift 2 bits at a time so in 28 cycles you get the final result.

Note: in both problems use PLA (or PAL) at 25 ns for miscellaneous logic.

2. Design a synchronous microprogrammable 32-bit arithmetic processor (data paths and control).

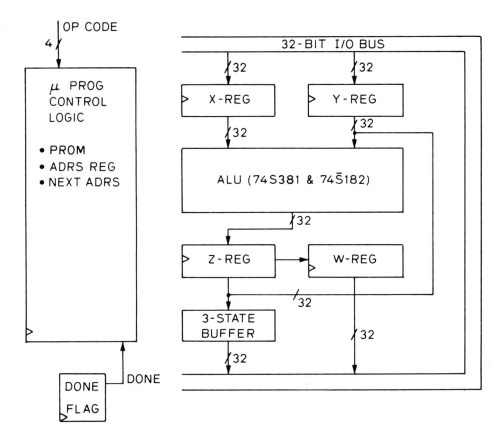

Note: opcode is ignored if done flag is not set.
Use 74S374 registers; setup = 5 ns, clk → out 17 ns.
Use output registered PAL; setup = 25 ns, clk → out 15 ns.
Maximum PROM size is 1K × 8. Access time = 50 ns.

The processor can execute the following instructions:

opcode	Instruction
0	NOP
1	$Z \leftarrow X + Y$
2	$Z \leftarrow X - Y$
3	$Z, W \leftarrow X * Y$ (multiply)
4	$Z, W \leftarrow KZ, KW + X * Y$ (multiply and accumulate)

Hints:

To execute X + Y:

> Cycle 1: X ← BUS, CLR Z, CLR W, Reset done;
> Cycle 2: Y ← BUS;
> Cycle 3: Z ← X + Y;
> Cycle 4: BUS ← Z, set done flag.

To do X * Y:

> Cycle 1:   X ← BUS, CLR Z, CLR W, Reset done;
> Cycle 2:   Y ← BUS;
> Cycle $3 - n$: X * Y using Booth's algorithm;
> Cycle $n + 1$: BUS ← Z;
> Cycle $n + 2$: BUS ← W, set done flag.

a. Show the logic diagram and microprogram.

b. Determine maximum clock frequency of processor (assume fixed cycle time).

c. Determine execution time for all operations.

d. Calculate total chip count.

Chapter 5

DIVISION

Division algorithms can be grouped into two classes according to their iterative operator. The first class, where subtraction is the iterative operator, contains many familiar algorithms, such as nonrestoring division, which are relatively slow as their execution time is proportional to the operand (divisor) length. Then we examine a higher speed class of algorithm where multiplication is the iterative operator. Here the algorithm converges quadratically; its execution time is proportional to $\log_2$ of the divisor length.

5.1 SUBTRACTIVE ALGORITHMS: GENERAL DISCUSSION

5.1.1 Restoring and Nonrestoring Binary Division

Most existing descriptions of nonrestoring division are from one of two distinct viewpoints. The first is mathematical in nature and describes the quotient digit selection as being -1 or $+1$, but it does not show the translation from the set $\{-1, +1\}$ to the standard binary representation $\{0, 1\}$. The second is found mostly in application notes of semiconductor manufacturers, where the algorithm is given without any explanation of what makes it work. The following section ties together these two viewpoints. We start by reviewing the familiar pencil and paper division, then show the similarities and differences between this and restoring and nonrestoring division. After this we examine nonrestoring division, from the mathematical concepts of the signed digit representation to the problem of conversion to the standard binary representation. This is followed by an example of hardware implementation. Special attention is given to two exceptional conditions: the case of a zero partial remainder, and the case of overflow.

5.1.2 Pencil and Paper Division

Let's perform the division $4537/3$ using the method we learned in elementary school:

$$\begin{array}{r} 1512 \\ 3\overline{)4537} \\ 3 \\ \hline 15 \\ 15 \\ \hline 3 \\ 3 \\ \hline 7 \\ 6 \\ \hline 1 \end{array}$$

The above is an acceptable shorthand; for example, in the first step a 3 is shown subtracted from 4, but mathematically the number 3000 is actually subtracted from 4537, yielding a partial remainder of 1537. The above division is now repeated showing the actual steps more explicitly:

$$\begin{array}{l} 1512 \leftarrow \text{Quotient} \\ 3\overline{)4537} \leftarrow \text{Dividend} \\ 3000 \leftarrow \text{Divisor} * q(\text{MSD}) * 10^3 \\ \overline{1537} \leftarrow \text{Partial remainder} \\ 1500 \\ \overline{0037} \\ 0030 \\ \overline{0007} \\ 0006 \\ \overline{0001} \leftarrow \text{Remainder} \end{array}$$

Let us represent the remainder as R, the divisor as D, and the quotient as Q. We will indicate the ith digit of the quotient as q_i and the value of the partial remainder after subtraction of the jth radix power, trial product; $(q_j * D * B^j)$ as R(j); i.e., R(0) is the final remainder. Then the process of obtaining the quotient and the final remainder can be shown as follows:

$$\begin{array}{lll} 4537 - 1 * 3 * 10^3 = 1537 & \text{or} & R(4) - q_3 * D * 10^3 = R(3), \\ 1537 - 5 * 3 * 10^2 = 0037 & \text{or} & R(3) - q_2 * D * 10^2 = R(2), \\ 0037 - 1 * 3 * 10^1 = 0007 & \text{or} & R(2) - q_1 * D * 10^1 = R(1), \\ 0007 - 2 * 3 * 10^0 = 0001 & \text{or} & R(1) - q_0 * D * 10^0 = R(0); \end{array}$$

or in general at any step:

$$\boxed{R(i) = R(i+1) - q_i * D * 10^i}$$

where

$$i = n - 1, n - 2, \ldots, 1, 0.$$

How did we determine at every step the value q_i? Well, we did it by a mental trial and error; for example, for q_3 we may have guessed 2, which would have given $q_3 \cdot D \cdot 10^3 = 2 \cdot 3 \cdot 1000 = 6000$, but that is larger than the dividend so we mentally realized that $q_3 = 1$, and so on. Now a machine would have to go explicitly through the above steps, that is, it would have to subtract until the partial remainder became negative, which means it was subtracted one time too many and it would have to be restored to a positive partial remainder. This brings us to restoring division: algorithms, which restore the partial remainder to a positive condition before beginning the next quotient digit iteration.

5.1.3 Restoring Division

The equations below illustrate the restoring division process for the previous decimal example:

$$4537 - 3 * 10^3 = +1537 \qquad\qquad q_3 = 1$$
$$1537 - 3 * 10^3 = -1463 \qquad\qquad q_3 = 2$$
$$-1463 + 3 * 10^3 = +1537 \quad \text{restore} \quad \boxed{q_3 = 1}$$

$$+1537 - 3 * 10^2 = +1237 \qquad\qquad q_2 = 1$$
$$+1237 - 3 * 10^2 = + 937 \qquad\qquad q_2 = 2$$
$$+ 937 - 3 * 10^2 = + 637 \qquad\qquad q_2 = 3$$
$$+ 637 - 3 * 10^2 = + 337 \qquad\qquad q_2 = 4$$
$$+ 337 - 3 * 10^2 = + 37 \qquad\qquad q_2 = 5$$
$$+ 37 - 3 * 10^2 = - 263 \qquad\qquad q_2 = 6$$
$$- 263 + 3 * 10^2 = + 37 \quad \text{restore} \quad \boxed{q_2 = 5}$$

$$+ 37 - 3 * 10^1 = + 7 \qquad\qquad q_1 = 1$$
$$+ 7 - 3 * 10^1 = - 23 \qquad\qquad q_1 = 2$$
$$- 23 + 3 * 10^1 = + 7 \quad \text{restore} \quad \boxed{q_1 = 1}$$

$$+ 7 - 3 * 10^0 = + 4 \qquad\qquad q_0 = 1$$
$$+ 4 - 3 * 10^0 = + 1 \qquad\qquad q_0 = 2$$
$$+ 1 - 3 * 10^0 = - 2 \qquad\qquad q_0 = 3$$
$$- 2 + 3 * 10^0 = + 1 \quad \text{restore} \quad \boxed{q_0 = 2}$$

For binary representation the restoring division is simply a process of quotient digit selection from the set $\{0, 1\}$. The selection is performed according to the following recursive relation:

$$R(i + 1) - q_i * D * 2^i = R(i).$$

We start by assuming $q_i = 1$, therefore, subtraction is performed:

$$R(i + 1) - D * 2^i = R(i).$$

Consider the following two cases (for simplicity assume that dividend and divisor are positive numbers):

Case 1: $R(i) \geq 0$, then the assumption was correct and $q_i = 1$.

Case 2: $R(i) < 0$ then, the assumption was wrong and $q_i = 0$, and restoration is necessary.

Let's illustrate the restoring division process for a binary division of $29/3$:

$$29 - 3 * 2^4 = -19 \qquad\qquad q_4 = 1$$
$$-19 + 3 * 2^4 = +29 \quad \text{restore} \quad \boxed{q_4 = 0}$$

$$29 - 3 * 2^3 = + 5 \qquad\qquad \boxed{q_3 = 1}$$

$$+ 5 - 3 * 2^2 = - 7 \qquad\qquad q_2 = 1$$
$$- 7 + 3 * 2^2 = + 5 \quad \text{restore} \quad \boxed{q_2 = 0}$$

$$+ 5 - 3 * 2^1 = - 1 \qquad\qquad q_1 = 1$$
$$- 1 + 3 * 2^1 = + 5 \quad \text{restore} \quad \boxed{q_1 = 0}$$

$$+ 5 - 3 * 2^0 = + 2 \qquad\qquad \boxed{q_0 = 1}$$

The left side of Figure 5–1 illustrates graphically the above division process. Using the following terminology:

$$Y = \text{Dividend},$$
$$Q = \text{Quotient (all quotient bits)},$$
$$R(0) = \text{Final Remainder},$$
$$D = \text{Divisor},$$

we have the following relationships:

$$Y = Q * D + R(0),$$
$$Q = q_4 * 2^4 + q_3 * 2^3 + q_2 * 2^2 + q_1 * 2^1 + q_0 * 2^0.$$

And in the above example

$$Y = 29 \quad \text{and } D = 3,$$
$$Q = 0 * 2^4 + 1 * 2^3 + 0 * 2^2 + 0 * 2^1 + 1 * 2^0 = 9,$$
$$29 = 9 * 3 + 2.$$

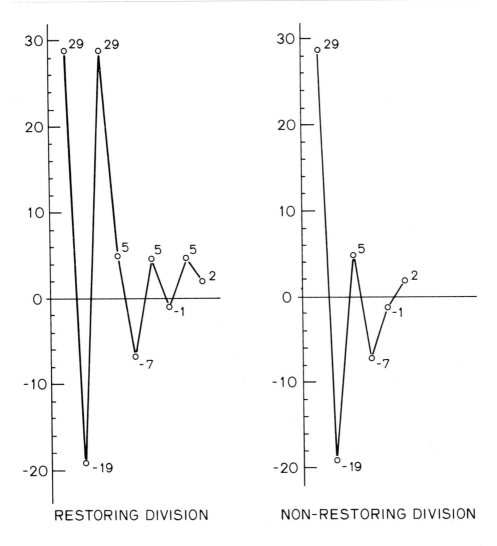

Figure 5–1. Graphical illustration of partial remainder computations in restoring and nonrestoring division.

It is obvious that for n bits we may need as many as $2n + 1$ cycles to select all the quotient digits, that is, there are $n + 1$ cycles for the trial subtractions, and there may be additional n cycles for the restoration. However, these restoration cycles can be eliminated by a more powerful class of division algorithm: nonrestoring division.

5.2 SUBTRACTIVE ALGORITHMS: NONRESTORING BINARY DIVISION

5.2.1 Introduction

For simplicity we start with an informal description using only positive numbers:

1. The first step (as in restoring division) subtracts the shifted divisor from the dividend.

2. The next step becomes an iteration whose action depends on the condition of the partial remainder (the dividend is the initial partial remainder).

   a. If the partial remainder is negative, then addition is performed.

   b. If the partial remainder is positive, then subtraction is performed.

3. The above iteration step is repeated until the partial remainder is smaller in magnitude than the divisor.

The quotient digit at each step is selected from the set $\{-1, +1\}$, where $q_i = +1$ is for subtraction, and $q_i = -1$ is for addition. Since a binary system can store only $\{0, 1\}$ we assign the following:

$$q_i = -1 \Rightarrow 0,$$

$$q_i = +1 \Rightarrow 1.$$

Let's illustrate the nonrestoring division for the previous example of $29/3$ (Figure 5–1 illustrates graphically this example and compares it with the restoring division).

	start with subtraction	$q_4 = 1$
$29 - 2^4 * 3 = -19$	negative result next operation is addition	$q_3 = 0$
$-19 + 2^3 * 3 = + 5$	positive result next operation is subtraction	$q_2 = 1$
$+ 5 - 2^2 * 3 = - 7$	negative result next operation is addition	$q_1 = 0$
$- 7 + 2^1 * 3 = - 1$	negative result next operation is addition	$q_0 = 0$
$- 1 + 2^0 * 3 = + 2$		

When all the above equations are combined the following relationship is obtained:

$$29 - 2^4 * 3 + 2^3 * 3 - 2^2 * 3 + 2^1 * 3 + 2^0 * 3 = 2,$$

$$29 - [2^4 - 2^3 + 2^2 - 2^1 - 2^0] * 3 = 2.$$

$$\underbrace{}$$

Q = Quotient

Therefore, $Q = q_4 * 2^4 + q_3 * 2^3 + q_2 * 2^2 + q_1 * 2^1 + q_0 * 2^0$ where $q_i = \{+1, -1\}$; that is, signed digit representation is as follows.

q_4	q_3	q_2	q_1	q_0
1	0	1	0	0
+16	-8	+4	-2	-1

5.2.2 Conversion of Signed Digit Representation to Binary Representation

The signed digit representation used in the last example is incompatible with a standard binary machine, since the bit pattern 10100 will be interpreted as 20 instead of 9. Fortunately, there is a fairly simple algorithm to convert from signed digit to standard binary; since $1 * 2^n - 1 * 2^{n-1} = 0 * 2^n + 1 * 2^{n-1}$. The algorithm is listed below.

   A.   Shift left 1-bit position.

   B.   Complement the MSB.

   C.   Shift in 1 into the LSB.

		16	8	4	2	1		$+1 \Rightarrow 1$
Signed Digit		q_4	q_3	q_2	q_1	q_0	$q_i = \{+1, -1\}$	$-1 \Rightarrow 0$
Q		1	0	1	0	0		
	0	0	1	0	0	1		
Std. Binary	k_5	k_4	k_3	k_2	k_1	k_0	$k_i = \{0, 1\}$	
K	-32	16	8	4	2	1		

Next, we prove that this conversion algorithm is valid for two's complement representation. We start with 5-bit numbers and then we generalize it for n bits.

Signed Digit $Q = q_4 * 16 + q_3 * 8 + q_2 * 4 + q_1 * 2 + q_0 * 1.$

After this value is shifted left and interpreted as conventional binary the relationship between the bits in each representation is:

$$q_i = 2k_{i+1} - 1.$$

The original mapping between $\{1, -1\}$ & $\{1, 0\}$ is apparent if:

$$\begin{array}{llll} \text{if} & q_i = 0 & k_{i+1} & q'_i = 2k_{i+1} - 1 = 2(0) - 1 = -1; \\ & q_i = 1 & k_{i+1} = 1 & q'_i = 2k_{i+1} - 1 = 2(1) - 1 = +1. \end{array}$$

Q shifted left appears as:

$$Q(A) = (2k_5 - 1)16 + (2k_4 - 1)8 + (2k_3 - 1)4 + (2k_2 - 1)2 + (2k_1 - 1)1.$$

After we complement the MSB we have the following:

$$Q(B) = (1 - 2k_5)16 + (2k_4 - 1)8 + (2k_3 - 1)4 + (2k_2 - 1)2 + (2k_1 - 1)1;$$

$$Q(B) = -32k_5 + 16k_4 + 8k_3 + 4k_2 + 2k_1 + 1.$$

Now in two's complement representation we should get the following (recall that in two's complement the MSB has a negative weight):

$$K = -32k_5 + 16k_4 + 8k_3 + 4k_2 + 2k_1 + 1k_0.$$

Therefore by making $k_0 = 1$, we get $Q(B) = K$. Now the above can be generalized for n-bit numbers:

$$\text{Signed Digit } Q = \sum_{i=0}^{n-1} q_i * 2^i; \qquad q_i = \{+1, -1\}.$$

$$q_i = 2k_{i+1} - 1; \qquad\qquad k_i = \{0, 1\}.$$

After Q is shifted left we get:

$$Q(A) = \sum_{i=0}^{n-1} (2k_{i+1} - 1) * 2^i.$$

After we complement the MSB, k_n, we have the following:

$$\underbrace{Q(B) = (1 - 2k_n) * 2^{n-1}}_{\text{MSB}} + \sum_{i=0}^{n-2}(2k_{i+1} - 1) * 2^i.$$

$$Q(B) = 2^{n-1} - 2^n * k_n + \sum_{i=0}^{n-2} 2k_{i+1} * 2^i - \sum_{i=0}^{n-2} 2^i.$$

Since

$$2^{n-1} - \sum_{i=0}^{n-2} 2^i = +1,$$

then

$$Q(B) = -2^n * k_n + \sum_{i=0}^{n-2} k_{i+1} * 2^{i+1} + 1;$$

or

$$Q(B) = -2^n * k_n + \sum_{i=1}^{n-1} k_i * 2^i + 1.$$

Now in two's complement representation we get the following:

$$K = -2^n * k_n + \sum_{i=0}^{n-1} k_i * 2^i.$$

Now let's separate the LSB from the summation.

$$K = -2^n * k_n + \sum_{i=1}^{n-1} k_i * 2^i + \underbrace{k_0 * 2^0}_{\text{LSB}};$$

therefore, by making $k_0 = 1$, we get $Q(B) = K$.

Now that we have the conversion algorithm from signed digit to standard binary representation, let us go back to the nonrestoring division and analyze negative numbers also. Recall from Chapter 1 the discussion of signed division. For this conventional type of division, the general principle is that we want each operation to bring the partial remainder closer to zero. Therefore, if we have the following:

$$\text{Dividend} = -29,$$
$$\text{Divisor} = +3,$$

then the first operation is addition

$$-29 + 3 * 2^4 = +19;$$

and if we treat the dividend as the initial partial remainder, then at each step we have one of the following four possibilities.

Sign of Partial Remainder	Sign of Divisor	Next Operation	q_i
+	+	Subtraction	1
+	−	Addition	0
−	+	Addition	0
−	−	Subtraction	1

Now, at each step the operation is a function of the previous quotient bit, where:

$$q_i = (\text{SIGN OF DIVISOR}) \oplus \overline{\text{SIGN OF REMAINDER (i)}},$$

and the algorithm for two's complement division is as follows:

First step:

1. Generate the MSB quotient bit q_{n-1},

$$q_{n-1} = (\text{SIGN OF DIVISOR}) \oplus \overline{(\text{SIGN OF DIVIDEND})};$$

Iterative steps (repeat Steps 2 and 3 for $i = n-1, n-2, \ldots, 0$; Step 3 not repeated for $i = 0$).

2. Generate the next partial remainder (Ri):

$$R(i) = R(i+1) \pm 2^i * D \begin{cases} +\text{if } q_i = 0 \\ -\text{if } q_i = 1 \end{cases}$$

3. Generate the next quotient bit,

$$q_{i-1} = (\text{SIGN OF DIVISOR}) \oplus \overline{(\text{SIGN OF R(i)})}.$$

This algorithm generates only the signed digit quotient bits, which will have to be converted to conventional binary representation, but at this point we have enough information to illustrate a hardware implementation.

5.2.3 Hardware Implementation

Figure 5–2 is a simplified block diagram of two's complement nonrestoring division. It is made up of three registers and an add/subtract unit. Assume that we start with a $2n$-bit dividend in the Z, W registers, and an n-bit divisor in the X register. The quotient bits are generated one at a time and are left shifted into the W register, while Z contains the partial remainder. Thus, after n cycles, the W register has the signed digit quotient, and Z has the remainder R(0). The hardware algorithm is as follows:

Step 1:

    a.   Shift Z left 1-bit position and load DVDS with Z(MSB).

    b.   Shift W left 1-bit position—note that the MSB of the W register is shifted into the LSB of the Z register.

    c.   Generate the next quotient bit: $q_{i-1} = X(MSB) \oplus C_{out}$. Note that C_{out} is valid in this step since the X and Z registers were assumed to be loaded before we started the iteration.

    d.   Shift in q_{i-1} into W_0.

Steps 2 through $n + 1$:

    a.   If $W_0 = 1$ then $S = Z - X$, otherwise $S = Z + X$.

    b.   Shift S left 1-bit position and load into Z.

    c.   Same as b in Step 1.

    d.   Generate the next quotient bit: $q_{i-1} = X(MSB) \oplus C_{out}$.

    e.   Same as d in Step 1.

Figure 5–3 shows the register contents before each step, and the way the quotient bits are generated in the division of 29/3.

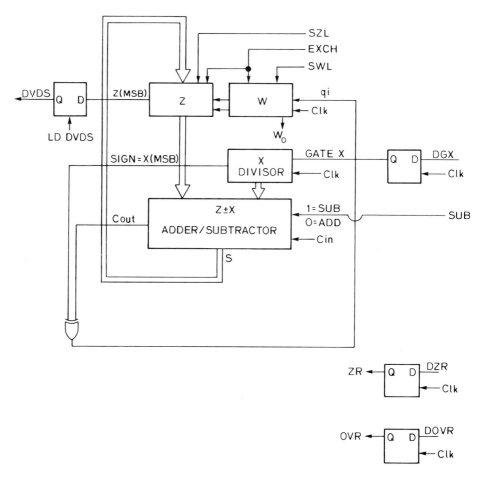

Figure 5–2.   Hardware implementation of two's complement nonrestoring division.

The following shorthand notation is used in the above figure to describe the various signals:

$$SZL = \text{Shift Z left}$$
$$EXCH = \text{Exchange the contents of Z and W registers}$$
$$SWL = \text{Shift W register left}$$
$$DVDS = \text{Dividend Sign}$$

Flags:

$$ZR = \text{Zero remainder}$$
$$OVR = \text{Overflow}$$
$$GATE\ X = \text{Gate X register to the adder/subtractor}$$
$$DZR,\ DOVR,\ DGX = \text{D input to the above flag (flags are stored in D flip-flop)}$$

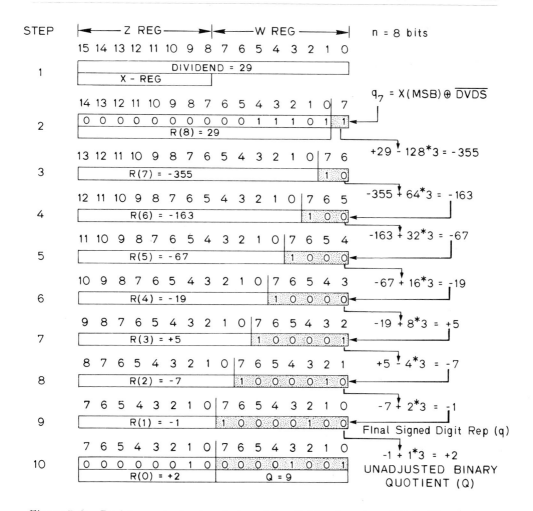

Figure 5–3.   Register contents at each step of the division iteration of 29/3. The numbers
above the unshaded side of the registers are the binary power of the partial
remainder. The numbers above the shaded side are the weights of the signed
digit representation of the quotient, except in the last step where the quotient
(Q) is represented by a conventional binary number.

5.2.3.1   Remainder Correction and Quotient Adjustment

The algorithm for converting signed digit to standard binary representation
always makes $q_0 = 1$, which means that all quotients are odd. But, this does not
seem right since many divisions yield even quotients. For example:

$$\frac{31}{3} = 10 + \frac{1}{3}; \qquad \text{i.e., } Q = 10.$$

Let us go through the nonrestoring algorithm to see if this case gives us the wrong result:

$$
\begin{aligned}
&\text{Start with subtraction} && q_4 = 1 \\
R(4) &= +31 - 16*3 = -17 && q_3 = 0 \\
R(3) &= -17 + 8*3 = +7 && q_2 = 1 \\
R(2) &= +7 - 4*3 = -5 && q_1 = 0 \\
R(1) &= -5 + 2*3 = +1 && q_0 = 1 \\
R(0) &= +1 - 1*3 = -2 &&
\end{aligned}
$$

Thus, $Q = 10101$ (signed digit representation) and after the left shift and making $q_0 = 1$ we get:

$$Q = 101011_2 = 11_{10}$$

$$\frac{31}{3} = 11 - \frac{2}{3}; \quad \text{or} \quad 31 = 3*11 - 2.$$

Therefore, the algorithm produces a valid result, but the remainder polarity is opposite to the convention. In signed division, the remainder sign should equal the dividend sign, so in the previous example we need to correct the remainder by adding it to the divisor:

$$R(\text{FINAL}) = R(0) + X.$$

Conversely, if we start with a negative dividend and we get a positive remainder, the correction is to subtract the divisor from $R(0)$:

$$R(\text{FINAL}) = R(0) - X\text{---(assuming positive divisor)}.$$

Similarly, we can analyze all eight permutations of the signs of the dividend, divisor, and remainder. But, before we do this, let us analyze the hardware shown in Figure 5–2. To convert the sign digit to standard binary we simply shift left the W register, and at the same time we shift in q_i:

$$\text{when } i = 0 \quad q_0 = q_i = X(\text{MSB}) \oplus C_{\text{out}},$$

rather than $q_0 = +1$. Therefore, in the case of 31/3 we will get $Q = 10$ (correct quotient) but the remainder still requires correction, since $R(0) = -2$. In Figure 5–4 we list all permutations, while taking into account the actual hardware used.

	Mathematical Interpretation					Hardware Implementation	
	Sign of			q_0 Ignoring Remainder Correction	Quotient Adjustment for Remainder Correction	Remainder Correction	Actual $q_0 = X(MSB) \oplus \overline{R(MSB)}$	Composite Quotient Correction
Case	Dividend DVDS	Divisor X(MSB)	Remainder R(0)					
0	0	0	0	1	NONE	NONE	1	NONE
1	0	0	1	1	Q←Q−1	R←R(0)+D	0	NONE
2	0	1	0	1	NONE	NONE	0	Q←Q+1
3	0	1	1	1	Q←Q+1	R←R(0)+D	1	Q←Q+1 Negative
4	1	0	0	1	Q←Q+1	R←R(0)+D	1	Q←Q+1 Quotients
5	1	0	1	1	NONE	NONE	0	Q←Q+1
6	1	1	0	1	Q←Q−1	R←R(0)+D	0	NONE
7	1	1	1	1	NONE	NONE	1	NONE

Figure 5–4.   Remainder correction and quotient adjustment.   Remainder is corrected if the sign of R(0) is different than the dividend sign.   Quotient has to be adjusted to compensate for a remainder correction and/or wrong value of q_0 due to the hardware implementation.

Note: R(MSB) = Sign bit of the remainder R(0) = $\overline{C_{out}}$

185

The following hardware bits are used in performing the remainder correction and the quotient adjustment:

$$\text{DVDS} = \text{Dividend sign,}$$
$$\text{X(MSB)} = \text{Divisor sign,}$$
$$\text{S(MSB)} = \text{Partial remainder sign,}$$
$$\text{DGX} = \text{D input to the ``gate X'' flag (D flip-flop).}$$

From the tabulation in Figure 5–4 we see that correction is necessary only if $\text{DVDS} \neq \text{S(MSB)}$, therefore:

$$\text{DGX} = \text{DVDS} \oplus \text{S(MSB)}.$$

(The signal "gate X" is used in the hardware implementation to gate the X register to the adder/subtractor. When the signal is not active zeros are gated instead.)

If correction is necessary, then it is a function of the divisor sign and the remainder sign;

$$\text{Subtract} = \text{X(MSB)} \oplus \overline{\text{Z(MSB)}} = \text{X(MSB)} \oplus C_{\text{out}}.$$

But that is exactly the value of q_0 shifted in the last iteration step; so, again, W_0 can be used as the SUBTRACT control like it was used in the rest of the iteration.

Next, the quotient has to be adjusted according to Figure 5–4. But since W does not have an access to the ALU, it is necessary to exchange W and Z, after which Z contains the unadjusted quotient. From Figure 5–4 the only correction necessary is incrementing Q when the DIVIDEND SIGN $\neq$ DIVISOR SIGN:

$$C_{\text{in}} = \text{DVDS} \oplus \text{X(MSB)}$$

$$\text{Gate X} = 0$$

At this point we can summarize all the steps necessary in microprogramming the nonrestoring division for n bits (dividend is actually $2n$ bits).

Step 1:	Generate q_{n-1},
Steps 2 through n:	Generate q_i and $R(i)$,
Step $n + 1$:	Convert signed digit to conventional binary,
Step $n + 2$:	Remainder correction,
Step $n + 3$:	Exchange Z and W,
Step $n + 4$:	Quotient adjustment and OVERFLOW detection.

Before we give the details of the microprogram it is necessary to consider a special case we overlooked so far—the case of a zero partial remainder.

5.2.3.2   Zero Remainder

At any point in the division iteration, if we encounter a case of a zero partial remainder, then the division process is complete and should be terminated. However, if the quotient is at the wrong position, and if the division process is continued, the result will be the wrong remainder, as illustrated by the following example.

Recall that the iteration is:

$$R(i) = R(i+1) \pm 2^i * D,$$

assume: $D = 3,$

also assume that at $i = 5$ we get R(5)=0;   (i.e., zero partial remainder) and

$$R(5) = 0,$$
$$R(4) = 0 - 3 * 2^4 = -48,$$
$$R(3) = -48 + 3 * 2^3 = -24,$$
$$R(2) = -24 + 3 * 2^2 = -12,$$
$$R(1) = -12 + 3 * 2^1 = -6,$$
$$R(0) = -6 + 3 * 2^0 = -3,$$

Therefore, $R(0) = -3$ and a correction is necessary to restore the zero remainder.

$$R = R(0) + D = -3 + 3 = 0.$$

Whenever a zero partial remainder is encountered, the remainder $R(0)$ is always negative and

$$|R(0)| = |D|.$$

The proof is as follows:

$$R(i) = R(i+1) \pm 2^i * D.$$

Assume $R(i+1) = 0$ and $D \geq 0.$

$$R(i) = 0 - 2^i * D,$$
$$R(i-1) = -2^i * D + 2^{i+1} * D = -D * 2^{i-1},$$
$$R(0) = -D * 2^0 = -D;$$

and for negative divisor similar reasoning leads to:

$$R(0) = +D.$$

Now that we have established that $R(0)$ is always negative we go back to the tabulation of Figure 5–4, to see how this affects the remainder correction and the quotient adjustment. From all eight permutations in the table we are interested only in the two cases of negative remainder and negative dividend (since positive dividend will invoke remainder correction anyhow due to opposite polarity with the remainder). We assume the existence of a flag called ZERO-REMAINDER and abbreviated as ZR (design details of zero detection will be given later on). $ZR = 1$ if any $R(i) = 0$.

					ZR = 0		ZR = 1	
Case	DVDS	X(MSB)	S(MSB)	Q$_0$	Remainder Correction	Quotient Correction	Remainder Correction	Quotient Correction
5	1	0	1	0	None	$Q = Q+1$	$R = R(0) \div D$	None
7	1	1	1	1	None	None	$R = R(0) - D$	$Q = Q+1$

Before the zero remainder was taken into account we had the control for the remainder correction as:

$$DGX = DVDS \oplus S(MSB).$$

But now it becomes:

$$DGX = [DVDS \oplus S(MSB)] + DVDS \cdot ZR.$$

Note that Q_0 still provides the proper add/subtract control. The quotient adjustment before ZR being considered was:

$$C_{in} = X(MSB) \oplus DVDS = X(MSB) \cdot \overline{DVDS} + \overline{X(MSB)} \cdot DVDS.$$

But from the table the new quotient adjustment is opposite to the previous one in the two cases listed above, therefore:

$$C_{in} = X(MSB) \cdot \overline{DVDS} + \overline{X(MSB)} \cdot DVDS \cdot \overline{ZR} + X(MSB) \cdot DVDS \cdot ZR.$$

But with all of the above we still have one more special case of a zero remainder, that is the case when $R(0) = 0$; i.e., zero remainder happens exactly at the end of the iteration; and therefore no remainder correction were required. Again the concern is just with negative dividend because for such a case a zero remainder with $S(MSB) = 0$ appears as if a correction is required due to opposite polarity. The signal $S = ZERO$, abbreviated as SZ, is used to prevent the otherwise necessary correction. Therefore, the final equation for the remainder correction is:

$$DGX = \overline{DVDS} \cdot S(MSB) + DVDS \cdot \overline{S(MSB)} \cdot \overline{SZ} + DVDS \cdot ZR \cdot \overline{SZ}.$$

To see if the equation for the quotient adjustment needs to be modified, let us tabulate the two cases of interest.

Case	DVDS	X(MSB)	S(MSB)	q_0	Quotient Adjustment
4	1	0	0	1	None, since $q_0 = 1$
6	1	1	0	0	Make $q_0 = 0$ by $Q = Q + 1$

From this table we can see the quotient adjustment does not need to be modified, and the previous equation for C_{in} is final.

Before we conclude the section on zero remainder let us go through the design details of the zero detector. The difficulty is in the varying number of bits in the partial remainder, as can be seen in Figure 5–3; and, therefore, a simple NOR gate (as for SZ above) is not adequate. Instead, a flag (flip-flop) is set whenever $SZ = 1$ and $W(MSB) = 0$, because these signals represent the new value to be loaded into Z. The flag will remain set as long as the new bits that are left shifted into the Z register are also zero. The following table summarizes the value of the D input (to the ZR flag) at each step of the division algorithm.

Step No.	DZR
1	$SZ \cdot \overline{W(MSB)}$
$2, \ldots, n$	$SZ \cdot \overline{W(MSB)} + ZR \cdot \overline{W(MSB)}$
$n + 1$	$ZR + SZ$
$n + 2, n + 3, n + 4$	ZR

5.2.3.3 Overflow Detection

For n-bit systems, the dividend is $2n$ bits, and the divisor is n bits. If the resultant quotient requires more than n bits, then an OVERFLOW flag should be set. At the beginning of the division the most significant portion of the dividend is in the Z register, the least significant portion is in the W register, and the divisor resides in the X register.

$$|Q| < 2^{n-1} \qquad \text{for positive quotients,}$$
$$|Q| \leq 2^{n-1} \qquad \text{for negative quotients,}$$
$$|Q| = \left| \frac{Z * 2^n + W}{X} \right| < 2^{n-1}.$$

Since W is the least significant portion of the dividend it is always positive and its largest value is less than W(MSB)$*2^n$.

$$W < W(MSB) * 2^n.$$

$$|Q| = \left| \frac{Z * 2^n + W}{X} \right| < \left| \frac{Z * 2^n + W(MSB) * 2^n}{X} \right|,$$

$$\left| \frac{[Z + W(MSB)] * 2^n}{XD} \right| < 2^{n-1},$$

$$|[Z + W(MSB)]2| < |X|;$$

$$|X| > |2Z + 2W(MSB)| \quad \text{for positive quotients}$$
$$\text{and } |X| \geq |2Z + 2W(MSB)| \quad \text{for negative quotients} \Big\} \quad \text{to avoid OVERFLOW.}$$

The last result explains why the first step in the division algorithm is simply a left shift of the Z register. After the Z register is shifted left (Z $\Leftarrow$ 2Z and Z(LSB) $\Leftarrow$ W(MSB)) the first operation(Z $\pm$ X) takes place. This operation is a subtraction if the signs of the dividend and divisor are the same, otherwise the operation is addition.

The following table lists the most significant quotient bit as a function of the dividend and the divisor signs and the relative magnitude of Z and X. The overflow conditions are marked in square brackets.

Case	DVDS	Divisor Sign X(MSB)	Operation	$q(MSB) = q_{n-1}$ $\|X\| > \|X\|$	$\|X\| < \|Z\|$	$\|X\| = \|Z\|$	$q_{n-1}, \ldots, q_0$ $\|X\| = \|Z\|$
1	+	+	Z−X	+	[−]	[−]	100...00
2	−	+	Z+X	−	[+]	−	100...00
3	+	−	Z+X	−	[+]	+	011...11
4	−	−	Z−X	+	[−]	[+]	011...11

If we ignore the cases of $|X| = |Z|$, then overflow detection occurs when $|Z| < |X|$, and inspection of the table gives:

$$\text{OVERFLOW} = \text{DVDS} \oplus \text{X(MSB)} \oplus \text{Q(MSB)},$$

(assuming a plus sign is a zero and a minus sign is one).

If the overflow flag is to be set at Step $n + 4$, then the quotient resides in the Z register and, therefore, the D input to the overflow register is:

$$\text{DOVR} = \text{DVDS} \oplus \text{X(MSB)} \oplus \text{Z(MSB)}.$$

Now let us analyze the cases of $|Z| = |X|$. Cases 1 and 4 should generate overflow, but not Cases 2 and 3 (since they result in the most negative number -2^{n-1}). Examining the equation above for DOVR and the table reveals that Cases 3 and 4 give the negation of the OVERFLOW. Note that the bit pattern for these two cases (ignoring the sign bit) is 111...111, so if we use the signal "ONES" to indicate the condition of all one's the final equation is:

$$\text{DOVR} = \text{DVDS} \oplus \overline{\text{X(MSB)}} \cdot \text{Z(MSB)} \oplus \text{X(MSB)} \cdot \overline{\text{Z(MSB)}} \cdot \overline{\text{ONES}}.$$

5.2.3.4   Microprogram of the Nonrestoring Division

The table below lists the microprogram to perform two's complement nonrestoring division using the hardware of Figure 5–2 where:

$$
\begin{aligned}
\text{X} &= \text{Don't care,} \\
\text{SZL} &= \text{Shift Z left 1-bit position,} \\
\text{SWL} &= \text{Shift W left 1-bit position,} \\
\text{EXCH} &= \text{Exchange Z} \leftrightarrow \text{W,} \\
\text{DVDS} &= \text{Dividend sign,} \\
\text{SUB} &= \text{If SUB} = 1, \text{ then S} = \text{Z} - \text{X; otherwise S} = \text{Z} + \text{X,} \\
\text{DGX} &= \text{D input to GATE X flip-flop,} \\
\text{DZR} &= \text{D input to ZERO REMAINDER flag,} \\
\text{DOVR} &= \text{D input to the OVERFLOW flag.}
\end{aligned}
$$

| | | Micro Instruction | | | | Data Dependent Controls | | | | |
| | | | | | Load | | | | | |
Step	Description	SZL	SWL	EXCH	DVDS	SUB	C_{in}	DGX	DZR	DOVR
1	Generate q_{n-1}	1	1	0	1	[1]	0	1	[4]	X
$2 \rightarrow n$	Iteration, q_i, R(i)	1	1	0	0	W_0	0	1	[5]	X
$n + 1$	Convert q to Q	0	1	0	0	W_0	0	[3]	[6]	X
$n + 2$	Remainder Correction	0	0	0	0	W_0	0	X	ZR	X
$n + 3$	Exchange	0	0	1	0	X	0	0	ZR	[7]
$n + 4$	Quotient Adjustment	0	0	0	0	0	[2]	0	ZR	OVR

Data Dependent Logic Equations: the numbers in brackets refer to the equations summarized below.

1. $\text{SUB} = \text{X(MSB)} \oplus \overline{\text{Z(MSB)}}$
2. $C_{\text{in}} = \text{X(MSB)} \cdot \overline{\text{DVDS}} + \overline{\text{X(MSB)}} \cdot \text{DVDS} \cdot \overline{\text{ZR}} + \text{X(MSB)} \cdot \text{DVDS} \cdot \text{ZR}$
3. $\text{DGX} = \overline{\text{DVDS}} \cdot \text{S(MSB)} + \text{DVDS} \cdot \overline{\text{S(MSB)}} \cdot \overline{\text{SZ}} + \text{DVDS} \cdot \text{ZR} \cdot \overline{\text{SZ}}$
4. $\text{DZR} = \text{SZ} \cdot \overline{\text{W(MSB)}}$
5. $\text{DZR} = \text{SZ} \cdot \overline{\text{W(MSB)}} + \text{ZR} \cdot \overline{\text{W(MSB)}}$
6. $\text{DZR} = \text{ZR} + \text{SZ}$
7. $\text{DOVR} = \text{DVDS} \oplus \overline{\text{X(MSB)}} \cdot \text{Z(MSB)} \oplus \text{X(MSB)} \cdot \overline{\text{Z(MSB)}} \cdot \overline{\text{ONES}}$

5.2.4 Higher-Radix Subtractive Division

Even with nonrestoring division, the speed of quotient formation is seriously limited by the requirement of an inspection and conditional operation in order to form each new bit of the quotient. An n-bit quotient requires n-serial addition/subtraction operations—significantly slower than multiplication.

A good deal of the early literature on division concerned methods of improving division speed by developing two or more quotient bits per serial addition/subtraction time. These algorithms use multiple simultaneous subtractions or comparisons to situate the new quotient bits.

The basis for these algorithms is that multiple trial divisors can be simultaneously compared with the present partial remainder to determine both the new quotient bits as well as the next trial divisor action. In order to form n bits of quotient in an iteration $2^n - 1$ equally spaced divisor partitions must be derived. These partitions together with the two extreme trial divisors, 0 and D, define 2^n possible outcomes. Thus, $2^n - 1$ comparisons are simultaneously made with the present partial remainder. The smallest partition that has a positive comparison determines the next n quotient bit configuration.

E.g., for two bits per iteration, we partition the trial divisors by $\frac{D}{4}$, $\frac{D}{2}$, and $\frac{3}{4}D$. Note that the formation of $\frac{3D}{4}$ requires an initial addition of D and 2D forming 3D—the division by 2 or 4 is trivially accomplished by shifting one or two places. Now on each iteration the three scaled (shifted) trial divisor partitions are compared against the partial remainder, R. If the scaled divisor is designed D′, then

$$\text{if } R - \frac{D'}{4} < 0, \text{ then } 0 \leq R < \frac{D'}{4} \rightarrow Q = 00;$$

$$\text{if } 0 \leq R - \frac{D'}{4} < \frac{D'}{2}, \text{ then } \frac{D'}{4} \leq R < \frac{D'}{2} \rightarrow Q = 01;$$

$$\text{if } 0 \leq R - \frac{D'}{2} < \frac{3D'}{4}, \text{ then } \frac{D'}{2} \leq R < \frac{3D'}{4} \rightarrow Q = 10;$$

$$\text{if } 0 \leq R - \frac{3D'}{4} < D', \text{ then } \frac{3D'}{4} \leq R < D' \rightarrow Q = 11.$$

In order to form n quotient bits per iteration, algorithms of this type require $2^n - 1$ comparisons and a selection per iteration. With the advent of fast multipliers such algorithms are not currently competitive (cost-performance) with multiplicative based division—their disadvantage is significant for $n > 2$.

5.3 MULTIPLICATIVE ALGORITHMS

Algorithms of this second class obtain a reciprocal of the divisor, and then multiply the result by the dividend. Thus, the main difficulty is the evaluation of a reciprocal. Flynn [FLY 70] points out that there are two main ways of iteration to find the reciprocal. One is the series expansion, and the other is the Newton-Raphson iteration.

5.3.1 Division by Series Expansion

The series expansion is based on the Maclaurin series (a special case of the familiar Taylor series). Let b, the divisor, equal $1 + x$.

$$g(X) = \frac{1}{b} = \frac{1}{1 + X} = 1 - X + X^2 - X^3 + X^4 - \ldots$$

Since $X = b - 1$, then the above can be factored $(0.5 \le b < 1.0)$:

$$\frac{1}{b} = (1 - X)(1 + X^2)(1 + X^4)(1 + X^8)(1 + X^{16})\ldots$$

The two's complement of $1 + X^n$ is $1 - X^n$ since:

$$2 - (1 + X^n) = 1 - X^n.$$

Conversely, the two's complement of $1 - X^n$ is $1 + X^n$.

This algorithm was implemented in the IBM 360/91 [AND 67], where division to 32-bit precision was evaluated as shown below.

1. $(1 - X)(1 + X^2)(1 + X^4)$ is found from a ROM look-up table.

2. $1 - X^8 = [(1 - X)(1 + X^2)(1 + X^4)](1 + X)$.

3. $1 + X^8$ is the two's complement of $1 - X^8$.

4. $1 - X^{16}$ is computed by multiplication $(1 + X^8)(1 - X^8)$.

5. $1 + X^{16}$ is the two's complement of $1 - X^{16}$.

6. $1 - X^{32}$ is the product of $(1 + X^{16})(1 - X^{16})$.

7. $1 + X^{32}$ is the two's complement of $(1 - X^{32})$.

In the ROM table look-up the first i bits of the b are used as an address of the approximate quotient. Since b is bit-normalized $(0.5 \le b < 1)$, then $|X| \le 0.5$ and $|X^{32}| \le 2^{-32}$; i.e., 32-bit precision is obtained in Step 7.

The careful reader of the above steps will be puzzled by a seeming sleight of hand. Since all divisors of the form $b_0 \ldots b_i xxx \ldots$ have same leading digits they will map into the same table entry *regardless* of the value of $0.00 \ldots 0xxxx \ldots$. Then how will the algorithm use the different trailing digits to form the proper quotient?

If we wish the quotient of $1/b$,

$$\frac{1}{b} = \frac{1}{1+X} = \underbrace{(1-X)(1+X^2)(1+X^4)}\ldots$$

table entry—approximate quotient.

Suppose we look up the product of the indicated three terms. Since our look-up cannot be exact, we have actually found

$$(1-X)(1+X^2)(1+X^4) + \epsilon_0.$$

Let us make the table sufficiently large so that

$$|\epsilon_0| \leq 2^{-9}.$$

Now in order to find $1 + X^8$ multiply the above by b, i.e., the entire number $.b_0 \ldots b_8 xxxx \ldots$, then since $b = 1 + X$,

$$\overbrace{(1+X)}^{b}\overbrace{(1-X)(1+X^2)(1+X^4)}^{\text{table entry}} = 1 - X^8$$

$$\underbrace{(1-X^2)}$$

$$\underbrace{(1-X^4)}$$

$$(1-X^8)$$

Thus by multiplying the table entry by b we have actually found

$$(1-X^8) + b\epsilon_0.$$

Upon complementation we get

$$1 + X^8 - b\epsilon_0;$$

and multiplying we get:

$$1 - X^{16} + 2X^8\epsilon_0 b - (b\epsilon_0)^2.$$

Since $X = b - 1$ the new error is actually

$$\epsilon_1 = 2b(b-1)^8 \epsilon_0 - (b\epsilon_0)^2,$$

whose max value over the range

$$\frac{1}{2} \le b < 1$$

occurs at

$$b = \frac{1}{2};$$

thus

$$\epsilon_1 < 2^{-8}\epsilon_0 - 2^{-2}\epsilon_0^2 = \epsilon_0(2^{-8} - 2^{-2}\epsilon_0).$$

If in the original table ϵ_0 was selected such that

$$|\epsilon_0| \le 2^{-9},$$

then

$$|\epsilon_1| < 2^{-17}.$$

Thus the error is decreasing at a rate equal to the increasing accuracy of the quotient.

The ROM table for quotient approximations warrants some further discussion as the table structure is somewhat deceptive. One might think, for example, that a table accurate to 2^9 would be a simple structure $2^8 \times 8$, but division is not a linear function with the same range and domain. Thus the width of an output is determined by the value of the quotient; when $1/2 \le b < 1$ the quotient is $2 \ge q > 1$. The table entry should be 10 bits: $xx.xxxxxxxx$ in the example. Actually, by recognizing the case $b = 1/2$ and avoiding the table for this case q will always start $1.xx \ldots x$ and the "1" can be omitted and we again have 8 bits per entry.

The size of the table is determined by the required accuracy. Suppose we can tolerate error no greater than ϵ_0. Then

$$\left| \frac{1}{b} - \frac{1}{b - 2^{-n}} \right| \le \epsilon_0.$$

That is, when truncating b at the nth bit the quotient approximation must not differ from the true quotient by more than ϵ_0.

$$\left| \frac{b - 2^{-n} - b}{b^2 - b2^{-n}} \right| \le \epsilon_0;$$

$$2^{-n} \leq b^2 \epsilon_0 - b2^{-n}\epsilon_0.$$

Since $b^2 \epsilon_0 \gg b2^{-n}\epsilon_0$ $(1/2 \leq b < 1)$, we rewrite as

$$2^{-n} \leq b^2 \epsilon_0.$$

Thus if $|\epsilon_0|$ were to be 2^{-9},

$$2^{-n} \leq 2^{-9} \cdot 2^{-2},$$

$$n = 11 \text{ bits.}$$

Now again by recognizing the case $b = 1/2$ and that the leading bit of $b = 0.1x$ we can reduce the table size; i.e., $n = 9$ bits.

5.3.2 The Newton-Raphson Division

The Newton-Raphson iteration is based on the following procedure to solve the equation $f(X) = 0$ [THO 62]:
- make a rough graph $y = f(X)$
- estimate the root where the $f(X)$ crosses the X axis
- this estimate is the first approximation; call it X_1
- the next approximation, X_2, is the place where the tangent to $f(X)$ at $(X_1, f(X_1))$ crosses the X axis
- from Figure 5–5 the equation of this tangent line is:

$$y - f(X_1) = f'(X_1)(X - X_1).$$

- the tangent line crosses the X axis at $X = X_2$ and $y = 0$

$$0 - f(X_1) = f'(X_1)(X_2 - X_1)$$

$$X_2 = X_1 - \frac{f(X_1)}{f'(X_1)}$$

- more generally

$$X_{i+1} = X_i - \frac{f(X_i)}{f'(X_i)}$$

- NOTE: the resulting subscripted values, X_i, are successive approximations to the quotient; they should not be confused with the unsubscripted X used in the preceding section on binomial expansion where X is always equal to $b - 1$.

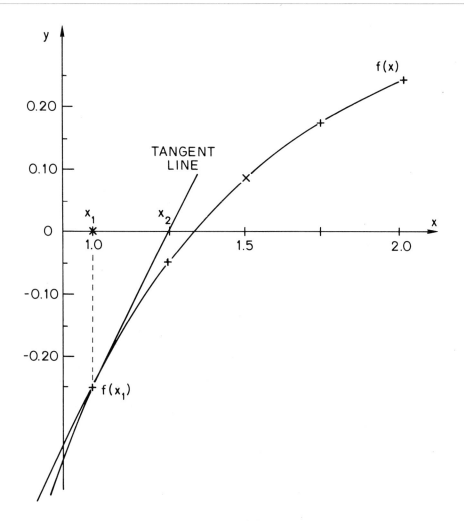

Figure 5–5. Plot of the curve $f(\mathrm{X}) = 0.75 - \frac{1}{\mathrm{X}}$ and its tangent at $f(\mathrm{X}_1)$, where $\mathrm{X}_1 = 1$ (first guess).

The above formula is a recursive iteration that can be used to solve many equations. In our specific case we are interested in computing the reciprocal of b. Thus, the equation $f(\mathrm{X}) = \frac{1}{\mathrm{X}} - b = 0$ can be solved using the above recursion. Note that if

$$f(\mathrm{X}) = \frac{1}{\mathrm{X}} - b,$$

then

$$f'(\mathrm{X}) = -\left(\frac{1}{\mathrm{X}}\right)^2;$$

and at $\mathrm{X} = \mathrm{X}_i$,

$$f'(X_i) = -\left(\frac{1}{X_i}\right)^2.$$

After substitution, the following recursive solution for reciprocal is obtained:

$$X_{i+1} = X_i(2 - bX_i),$$

where $X_0 = 1$.

The following decimal example illustrates the simplicity and the quadratic convergence of this scheme.

Example:
Find $\frac{1}{b}$ where $b = 0.75$ (error $= \epsilon$).

$$
\begin{array}{llll}
X_0 = & = 1 & \epsilon_1 = 0.333334 \\
X_1 = 1(2 - 0.75) & = 1.25 & \epsilon_2 = 0.083334 \\
X_2 = 1.25(2 - (1.25 \times 0.75)) & = 1.328125 & \epsilon_3 = 0.005208 \\
X_3 = X_2(2 - (1.328125 \times 0.75)) & == 1.333313 & \epsilon_4 = 0.000021
\end{array}
$$

The quadratic convergence of this scheme is proved below. That is, $\epsilon_{i+1} \leq (\epsilon_i)^2$:

$$X_{i+1} = X_i(2 - bX_i),$$
$$\epsilon_i = \frac{1}{b} - X_i$$

and

$$X_i = \frac{1}{b} - \epsilon_i$$

or

$$= \frac{1 - b\epsilon_i}{b},$$
$$\epsilon_{i+1} = \frac{1}{b} - X_{i+1},$$
$$\epsilon_{i+1} = \frac{1}{b} - [X_i(2 - bX_i)] = \frac{1 - 2bX_i + (bX_i)^2}{b},$$

substituting for X_i,

$$\epsilon_{i+1} = \frac{1 - 2b\left(\frac{1-b\epsilon_i}{b}\right) + (1 - b\epsilon_i)^2}{b}$$
$$\epsilon_{i+1} = 1 - 2 + 2b\epsilon_i + 1 - 2b\epsilon_i + b\epsilon_i^2,$$
$$\epsilon_{i+1} = b\epsilon_i^2;$$

(recall that $1 < b$)

The division execution time, using the Newton-Raphson approximation, can be reduced by using a ROM look-up table. For example, computing the reciprocal of a 32-bit number can start by using 1024×8 ROM to provide the 8 most significant bits, the next iteration will provide 16 bits, and the third iteration produces a 32-bit quotient. The Newton-Raphson seems similar in many ways to the previously discussed binomial approximation. In fact for the Newton-Raphson iteration:

$$X_{i+1} = X_i(2 - bX_i);$$

if

$$X_0 = 1,$$

then

$$X_1 = (2 - b)$$
$$X_2 = (2 - b)(2 - 2b + b^2)$$
$$= (2 - b)(1 + (b - 1)^2)$$

.

.

.

$$X_i = (2 - b)(1 + (b - 1)^2)(1 + (b - 1)^4)\ldots(1 + (b - 1)^{2i}),$$

which is exactly the binomial series when $X = b - 1$.

Thus the Newton-Raphson iteration on $f(X) = \frac{1}{X} - b$ and the binomial expansion of $\frac{1}{b} = \frac{1}{1+X}$ are different ways of viewing the same algorithm [FLY 70].

5.3.3 Higher-Radix Multiplicative Division (Byte Division)

This is more commonly called Byte Division since a number of implementations (such as Amdahl and Honeywell processors) use a byte at a time multiplication to form a byte of quotient per iteration. The basic iteration is the previously discussed binomial expansion or Newton-Raphson iteration—remember they are identical for similar starting approximations. Rather than take advantage of the quadratic convergence, these approaches provide lower cost implementations which restrict the size of the multiplier and provide a uniform convergence to the quotient. The technique is best understood by considering the Newton-Raphson iteration.

$$X_{i+1} = X_i(2 - bX_i).$$

Now we wish to "partition" the ith quotient approximation X_i into i 8-bit digits, labeled $q_0, q_1, q_2 \ldots q_{i-1}$. Byte division finds a new byte of quotient on each iteration; thus, the ith iteration finds q_i. While the digits formed are largely disjoint, the reader should recognize that there maybe partial digit overlap so that,

$$X_i = \sum_{j=0}^{i-1} q_j.$$

Suppose the division starts with a table look-up of an 8-bit quotient (reciprocal), $X_0 = q_0$. Then,

$$X_1 = X_0(2 - bX_0),$$

or

$$X_1 - X_0 = X_0(1 - bX_0).$$

Since $X_1 = q_1 + q_0$ and $X_0 = q_0$,

$$q_1 = X_0(1 - bX_0).$$

A byte multiplier ($8 \times$ precision of b) can easily be used to form $bX_0 = b \cdot q_0$ and then q_1. Extending this, let

$$d_0 = 1 - b \cdot q_0$$

and

$$d_i = 1 - b \cdot q_0 - b \cdot q_1 - \cdots - b \cdot q_i$$

or

$$d_i = d_{i-1} - b \cdot q_i$$

Now we have the desired byte iteration:

$$q_{i+1} = X_i(d_{i-1} - b \cdot q_i)$$
$$= X_i(d_i)$$

The term $b \cdot q_i$ is a multiplication operation followed by a subtraction forming d_i. The leading digit of d_i is used as the multiplier forming q_{i+1}. This latter multiplication is actually an 8×8 operation. The formation of X_{i+1} may require an addition (actually an increment) to X_i if q_{i+1} overlaps the previously formed bits of X_i.

The advantage of byte division lies not only in reduced hardware. While six iterations, following the table look-up, are required to form a 56-bit quotient instead of three, the required multipliers themselves are faster. Depending on implementation the 8×56 or 8×8 may be $2 - 4$ times faster than 56×56 thus, gaining back much of the time lost in the additional iterations.

Since a four input adder suffices (with modified Booth multiplier encoding) to serve as the byte multiplier, one can understand the increasing popularity of multiplicative algorithms. With higher-radix subtractive division, the formation of 8 bits of quotient might require 255 comparisons!

5.3.4 Quotient Representation

Several important issues remain related to the kind of quotient representation developed by these algorithms.

Will the quotient be the same as with subtractive algorithms? The answer is that it can be made the same or it can be different and more precise. The subtractive algorithm always provides a quotient *and* a positive remainder (division and dividend are always assumed positive in our discussion); that is, it is a truncated representation of the true quotient.

Now in the multiplicative division, the algorithm on each iteration will also provide a negative error bias; that is, the sequence of quotient estimates will approach $1/b$ from below.

If ϵ is a positive number and at any iteration our quotient estimate is $\frac{1}{b} - \epsilon = X_i$ or $\epsilon = \frac{1}{b} - X_i$ (X_i approaching $1/b$ from below), then:

$$
\begin{aligned}
X_{i+1} &= X_i(2 - bX_i), \\
&= (1/b - \epsilon)(2 - b(1/b - \epsilon)), \\
&= (1/b - \epsilon)(1 + b\epsilon), \\
&= 1/b - \epsilon + \epsilon - b\epsilon^2, \\
&= 1/b - b\epsilon^2.
\end{aligned}
$$

Note that even if ϵ were negative (after an initial table look-up), all subsequent iterations would approach $1/b$ from below.

While seemingly solving the problem this strict approach from below actually is the cause of inconsistent quotient representations between the two approaches. Suppose for $q/b \cdot q + r = 1$, where $r = 0$; i.e., q is an a factor. Strictly speaking there are two representations for an integer in the real number system:

$$XXX.0000\ldots 0,$$

and

$$XXX.999999\ldots - 1.0.$$

Now when q is a (scaled) integer our algorithm will find the diminished representation. The following example illustrates the problem.

Example:
Find $1/b$ where $b = .8$ ($Q = 1.250$).
    Use the iterative formula:

$$X_{i+1} = X_i(2 - b \cdot X_i).$$

Start with $X_1 = 1$, then

$$X_2 = X_1(2 - bX_i) = 1(2 - 0.8 \times 1) = 1.2.$$

Similarly, we get the following results which approach the precise quotient of 1.25.

$$X_1 = 1,$$
$$X_2 = 1.2,$$
$$X_3 = 1.248,$$
$$X_4 = 1.2499968,$$
$$X_5 = 1.24999999976.$$

Thus, we have a problem preserving the integrity of (scaled) integers. If we wish the exact answer of the subtractive algorithm, we must ensure that the remainder is zero; i.e., in (b is positive)

$$bQ + r = 1,$$

where
$$r = 0.$$

Now if b and q are normalized n-bit numbers, their product is $2n$ bits. In order to find $r = 0$, the low-order n bits of bQ must be examined (see Figure 5–6). If this resulting Q differs from the desired quotient representation Q' by 2^{-n-1}, then

$$Q = Q' - 2^{-n-1} \text{ and}$$
$$bQ = bQ' - b2^{-n-1}$$

but
$$bQ' = 1$$

thus
$$bQ = 1 - b2^{-n-1}$$

For complete compatibility of the approaches this is the only case which should be modified.

Figure 5–6 shows the bQ partial products and the product. If the leading n bits of bQ are all 1's, the correction of Q should be performed; i.e., a low-order 1 should be added to Q to find Q'.

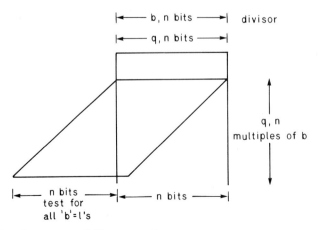

Figure 5–6.   Quotient compatibility correction.

It is also possible to force a positive bias into the last iteration to have integer convergence. The corrections must be small enough to ensure that the overall rate of convergence is not materially affected.

In systems such as System 360 Model 91 a compromise was used where the quotient was computed to 12 bits greater accuracy than necessary and then rounded. This provides a "better" (i.e., more accurate) representation of the quotient and better preserves integer integrity but does not always provide a truncated quotient in the case of nonzero remainders. In the example above rounding X_5 at the 10th digit following the decimal point provides the correct (scaled) integer result, 1.2.5.

As can be seen, for all of this discussion the remainder is not required to extend the precision of a quotient. The iteration will double the precision. In cases where the remainder is to be provided, it is found from:

$$r = a - bQ,$$

where only the low-order bits of bQ need be formed.

5.3.5 Hardware Implementation of Multiplicative Division

We conclude this section by illustrating the implementation of a 56-bit division (56 bits is a typical mantissa size in many floating point formats).

$$Q = \frac{a}{b} = a \cdot \frac{1}{b}.$$

Based on $X_{i+1} = X_i(2 - bX_i)$:

$$a = 56 \text{ bits dividend,}$$
$$b = 56 \text{ bits divisor,}$$
$$\text{Temp (A)} = \text{ Temporary register for the A port,}$$
$$\text{Temp (B)} = \text{ Temporary register for the B port,}$$
$$X_1 = 8 \text{ MSBs of the reciprocal,}$$
$$X_2 = 16 \text{ MSBs of the reciprocal,}$$
$$X_3 = 32 \text{ MSBs of the reciprocal,}$$
$$X_4 = 56 \text{ bits of the reciprocal.}$$

X_1 is obtained from the reciprocal ROM look-up table, while X_2, X_3, and X_4 are computed by the following equations:

$$X_2 = X_1(2 - bX_1),$$
$$X_3 = X_2(2 - bX_2),$$
$$X_4 = X_3(2 - bX_3).$$

However, since we are dealing with normalized operands, some simple scaling is necessary during the execution of the above equations. To start with, the value of X_1 requires scaling because $1 < X_1 \leq 2(X_1 \simeq 1/b$ and $.5 \leq b < 1)$. X_1 is scaled (normalized) by shifting right 1-bit position. The normalized value, X_1^n, obviously relates to X_1 by:

$$X_1 = 2X_1^n.$$

X_2 is computed by:

$$X_2 = X_1(2 - bX_1).$$

Since we are using the normalized value X_1^n then:

$$X_2 = 2X_1^n(2 - 2bX_1^n),$$
$$X_2 = 4X_1^n(1 - bX_1^n).$$

But
$$X_2 = 2X_2^n,$$

therefore
$$X_2^n = 2X_1^n(1 - bX_1^n).$$

Let's investigate the scaling required in the last equation:

$$bX_1 \simeq 0.99 \quad \text{since} \quad (X_1 + \Delta X) = 1/b \text{ and } \Delta X \leq 2^{-8}$$
$$bX_1^n \simeq 0.49 \quad \text{since} \quad X_1^n = \tfrac{1}{2}X_1$$
$$1 - bX_1^n \simeq 0.51$$

thus $(1 - bX_1^n)$ is normalized and no scaling is needed.
    Next we multiply X_1^n by $(1 - bX_1^n)$,

$$0.5 \leq X_1^n < 1.$$

$$(1 - bX_1^n) \simeq 0.51.$$

A detailed analysis produces the following:

$$0.25 < X_1^n(1 - bX_1^n) < 0.5.$$

The last result has one leading zero, therefore, one left shift is required to normalize the result. This explains the 2 in the following equation:

$$X_2^n = 2X_1^n(1 - bX_1^n).$$

The 1-bit left shifting is accomplished by the left shifter shown in Figure 5–7a, which illustrates the hardware realization of the division. The recursive divide algorithm is implemented by the microprogram of Figure 5–7b.

Example:

Step 1:

Load the contents of ROM into the Temp (A) register.

Step 2:

• Gate Temp (A) register to the A port of the multiplier;

• Simultaneously gate the B register to the B port of the multiplier;

• At the same time select the input to the B register to perform two's complement of the multiplier result;

Thus in Step 2 the operation performed is $1 - bX_1^n$ and the result is loaded into the Temp (B) register.

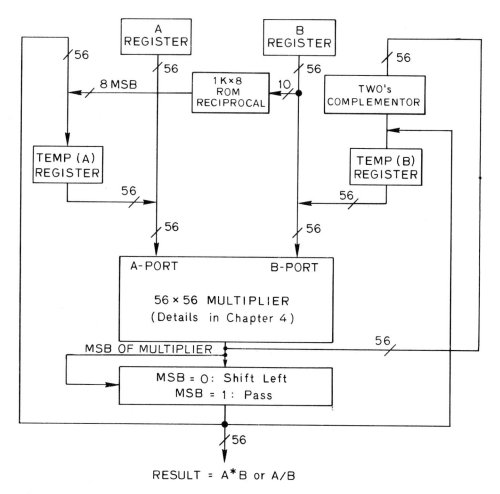

Figure 5–7a.   Hardware realization of a 56 $\times$ 56 multiplier/divider.

Step	A Port	B Port	What was computed? Where did it go?
1			ROM $\to$ Temp (A)
2	$X_1^n = $ Temp (A)	B	$1 - bX_1^n \to$ Temp (B)
3	$X_1^n = $ Temp (A)	Temp (B)	$X_2^n = 2X_1^n(1 - bX_1^n) \to$ Temp (A)
4	$X_2^n = $ Temp (A)	B	$1 - bX_2^n \to$ Temp (B)
5	$X_2^n = $ Temp (A)	Temp (B)	$X_3^n = 2X_2^n(1 - bX_2^n) \to$ Temp(A)
6	$X_3^n = $ Temp (A)	B	$1 - bX_3^n \to$ Temp (B)
7	$X_3^n = $ Temp (A)	Temp (B)	$X_4^n = 2X_3^n(1 - bX_3^n) \to$ Temp (B)
8	A	$X_4^n = $ Temp (B)	$a/b = aX_4^n \to$ Result

Figure 5–7b. Microprogram for computing 56-bit division, using the block diagram of Figure 5–7a.

5.4 FLOATING POINT MULTIPLICATION AND DIVISION

In this section we use the same floating point format that we used in Section 3.2.1 to describe floating point addition/subtraction. We assume that there are two operands; A and B. Multiplication is $A * B$ and division is A/B. The mantissa, the characteristic, and the sign of the A operand are designated MA, CA, and SA respectively, while MB, CB, and SB are similar parts of the B operand. The result of multiplication or division is designated by R; and MR, CR, and SR are the mantissa, the characteristics, and the sign of the R result.

5.4.1 Algorithm

1. IF ANY OPERAND IS ZERO, then use the following table and then exit the algorithm (X is a don't care case) otherwise, go to Step 2.

Instruction	A	B	Action
Multiply	0	X	Set final result to
	X	0	a normalized zero
Divide	0	$B \neq 0$	
	X	0	Set overflow flag

2. ADD (or SUBTRACT) the two characteristics, and correct for the bias:

$$CA + (CB - 128) \text{ or } CA - (CB - 128).$$

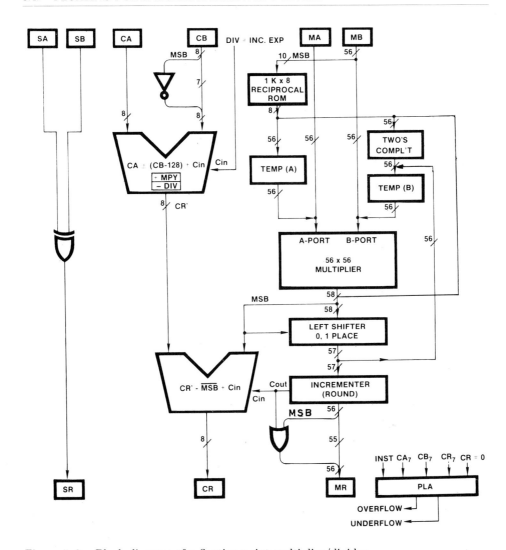

Figure 5–8.   Block diagram of a floating point multiplier/divider.

3. Perform fixed point MULTIPLICATION (or DIVISION) of the mantissas of the two operands:

$$MA * MB \text{ (or } MA/MB).$$

∗ In case of division this step is made of several microcycles as outlined in Figure 5–7b.

4. NORMALIZE the result of the mantissa multiplier/divider. This may require one left shift (and decrement the characteristic if the MSB is zero).

5. ROUND the result of Step 4 by adding 1 to the first guard bit. If the mantissa overflows as a result of the rounding, then shift right one place and increment the characteristic.

6. Check for OVERFLOW or UNDERFLOW.

5.4.2 Hardware Implementation

Figure 5–8 illustrates the hardware realization of the floating point multiplication/division. The block diagram is made of two distinct sections. On the right side the mantissas are handled as fixed point operands, while the left side computes the exponent and the sign. The fixed point multiplier/divider was described in Section 5.2.3, and the rounding mechanism is the same as for the floating point addition/subtraction. Therefore, we just need to describe the exponent section.

5.4.3 Exponent Computation

In floating point multiplication

$$R = A * B.$$

The exponents of the two operands are added together to generate the exponent of the result.

Because the exponents are represented by biased code (characteristic) a correction is necessary.

The characteristic of A is:	$CA = EA + 128.$
The characteristic of B is:	$CB = EB + 128.$
Adding the two characteristics gives:	$CA + CB = (EA + EB) + 256.$
The characteristic of the result should be:	$C(A + B) = (EA + EB) + 128.$
Thus, we correct by subtracting the bias:	$C(A + B) = CA + CB - 128.$

Let's call the corrected characteristics of the result CR'; then for multiplication:

$$CR' = CA + (CB - 128).$$

(By the way, we use CR' rather than CR since the final characteristics of the result may require adjustment for mantissa overflow, as we will see later.)

Now let's compute the exponent in the case of division where: $R = A/B$. The exponent of the divisor is subtracted from the exponent of the dividend,

$$ER = EA - EB,$$

where $ER = $ exponent of the result.

If we simply subtract the corresponding characteristics then:

$$CA - CB = EA - EB,$$

and we need to correct by adding the bias to the above difference.

$$CR' = (CA - CB) + 128 = (EA - EB) + 128,$$

and to make this compatible with multiplication rewrite as:

$$CR' = CA - (CB - 128).$$

Now we can generalize for both cases:

$$CR' = CA \pm (CB - 128),$$

use $+$ for multiply, use $-$ for divide. Thus, in both cases the input to the two's complement characteristic adder is $CB - 128$. This is accomplished by simply inverting the MSB of CB.

Example:

$$CB = 00000001 = 1.$$
$$CB - 128 = 10000001 = -127.$$

The characteristic CR' is the proper characteristic for the unnormalized mantissa. Next, we investigate the necessary updating of the exponent after normalization.

In multiplication each mantissa is between 0.5 and 0.999... thus, their product is between 0.25 and 0.999...

$$0.5 \leq MA < 1.$$

$$0.5 \leq MB < 1.$$

Therefore $0.25 \leq MR < 1$ where $MR = MA * MB$.

This product can be expressed as two cases:

Case 1: $0.25 \leq MR < 0.5$ (Requires one left shift);

Case 2: $0.5 \leq MR < 1$ (Requires no shift).

In the first case there is one leading zero, therefore, 1-bit left shift is required to normalize the product. In the second case the product is already normalized and no shifting is required. To update the characteristic we simply subtract the complement of the mantissa's MSB from the characteristics (CR′) generated in Step 2 of the algorithm (CR′ in Figure 5–8).

Finally, in the case of a rounding overflow we need to increment the characteristic to compensate for the right shift of the overflowing mantissa. This is accomplished, just as in the floating point adder/subtractor, by connecting the incrementer carry-out into the carry-in of the characteristic update, and the final characteristic is:

$$CR = CR' - \overline{MSB} \text{ mantissa } + C_{in}.$$

The exponent computation for division is almost identical to multiplication, since the division is implemented by multiplying the operand A by the reciprocal of B. The only difference is due to the reciprocal:

$$0.5 \leq MB < 1;$$

$$1 < (1/MB) \leq 2.$$

But (1/MB) was normalized by shifting it right 1-bit position. This scaling needs to be compensated by incrementing the characteristic. This is shown on the upper left side of Figure 5–8. During the divide instruction $C_{in} = 1$ and during the multiplication $C_{in} = 0$.

5.4.4 Overflows and Underflows

OVERFLOW may occur if two large operands are multiplied together or if a large operand is divided by a small operand. In both cases the characteristic of the result (CR) will be larger than the maximum allowed value of 255. This will cause the MSB of CR to be zero. An OVERFLOW in the case of a zero divisor is handled separately as was pointed out in Step 1 of the algorithm.

UNDERFLOW may occur if two small operands are multiplied together, or if a small operand is divided by a large operand. In either case, the characteristic of the result will be less then the minimum allowed value of 1. This will cause the MSB of CR to be one, or else the bits of CR will be zero (CR = 0), which is a reserved representation for normalized zero.

The table below illustrates all the cases of OVERFLOW and UNDERFLOW as a function of the characteristic range and the instruction.

	$1 \leq CB < 128$	$128 \leq CB < 255$	
$1 \leq CA < 128$	UNDERFLOW if: $CA + (CB - 128) < 1$	Result in range	Multiply
$128 \leq CA \leq 255$	Result in range	OVERFLOW if $255 < CA + (CB - 128)$	$CR' = CA + (CB - 128)$
$1 \leq CA < 128$	Result in range	UNDERFLOW if: $CA - (CB - 128) < 1$	Divide
$128 \leq CA \leq 255$	OVERFLOW if: $255 < CA - (CB - 128)$	Result in range	$CR' = CA - (CB - 128)$

From the above matrix it is very easy to construct the truth table below to decode the OVERFLOW and UNDERFLOW conditions. This truth table is implemented by a simple PLA shown in the lower section of Figure 5–8.

	MSB of			
Inst	CA	CB	CR	
MPY	1	1	0	Overflow
DIV	1	0	0	Overflow
MPY	0	0	1	Underflow
DIV	0	1	1	Underflow
	CR = 0			Underflow

5.5 ADDITIONAL READINGS

Session 14 of the 1980 WESCON included several good papers on the theme of "Hardware Alternative for Floating Point Processing."

Undheim [UND 80] describes the floating point processor of the NORD-500 computer, which is made by NORSK-DATA in Norway. The design techniques are very similar to the ones described in this book, where a combinatorial approach is used to obtain maximum performance. The entire floating point processor is made of 579 ICs and it performs floating point multiplication (64 bits) in 480 ns.

Birkner [BIR 80] describes the architecture of a high-speed matrix processor which uses a subset of the proposed IEEE (short) floating point format for data representation. The paper describes some of the trade-off used in selecting the above format, and it also discuss the detailed implementation of the processor using LSI devices.

Cheng [CHE 80] and McMinn [McM 80] describe single chip implementation of the proposed IEEE floating point format. Cheng describes the AMD 9512 and McMinn the Intel 8087.

Much early literature was concerned with higher-radix subtractive division. Robertson, [ROB 58] was a leader in the development of such algorithms. Both Hwang [HWA 77] and [SPA 81] contain reviews of this literature.

Flynn, [FLY 70], provides a review of multiplicative division algorithms.

5.6 SUMMARY

For low-cost division implementations one one quotient bit per iteration can be formed by restoring or nonrestoring division. The latter algorithm has the significant advantage of requiring only a single addition or subtraction per iteration while the former algorithm may require both an addition and a subtraction.

For higher-speed division, subtractive algorithms become quite complex, probably being practically limited to two quotient bits per iteration. For speed requirements beyond this, multiplication is the practical basis for the iteration. With the advent of low-cost ROM chips, table look-up for the reciprocal function is possible for arguments in the 8-bit to 16-bit range. Quotients are found by multiplying by the numerator. To extend the precision of the reciprocal a simple multiplier provides 8 bits of quotient per iteration. For faster convergence full-length multipliers double the precision of the result on each iteration.

5.7 EXERCISES

1. Using restoring two's complement division perform $\frac{a}{b}$, where

$$a = 0.110011001100,$$
$$b = 0.100111.$$

Show each iteration.

2. Repeat the above using nonrestoring two's complement division.

3. Using the Newton-Raphson iteration, compute $1/b$ where

$$b = .9$$
$$b = .6$$
$$b = .52$$

4. Construct a look-up table for two decimal digits (20 entries only; i.e., divisors from .60 to .79). Use this table to find $b = 0.666$.

5. Using Newton-Raphson, find the reciprocal (accurate to seven digits) of 0.825730 with a hand calculator. Show each iteration.

6. Repeat Problem 5 using "byte" division modified to form a decimal digit per iterations.

7. An alternate Newton-Raphson iteration uses $f(x) = \frac{X-1+1/b}{X-1}$ (converges quadratically toward the complement of the reciprocal) which has a root at the complement of the quotient.

    a.   Find the iteration

    b.   Compute the error term

    c.   Use this find $1/b$ when:

$$b = .9$$
$$b = .6$$

    d.   Comment on this algorithm as compared to that described in the text.

8. Another suggested approach uses:

$$f(x) = \exp\left[\frac{-1}{b(1-bx)}\right]$$

(This recursion is unstable and converges very slowly). Repeat Problem 3 for this function.

9. Draw a block diagram for:

    a.   A 2-bit per iteration quotient formation using subtraction as the basis.

    b.   Repeat for 3 bits at a time.

5.8 DESIGN EXERCISES

1. Design a simple *restoring* two's complement divider for 24-bit integers.

2. Extend the design of Problem 2 in Section 4.9 to include *restoring* two's complement division.

3. Show a detailed layout for a *byte* multiplier based division (56 $\times$ 8). Use the 56-bit example as a guide. Show the microprogram.

Chapter 6

PIPELINING OF ARITHMETIC
OPERATIONS

The previous chapters presented algorithms and hardware implementation for minimum latency (delay). In this section we address techniques for increasing bandwidth. Bandwidth is defined as the number of tasks that can be performed in a unit time interval. For a system that operates on only one task at a time, latency is the inverse of the bandwidth. However, for a given latency the bandwidth can be increased by pipelining, that is, allowing simultaneous execution of many tasks. Figure 6–1a illustrates the pipelining concept by showing that a system with latency of n gate delays can operate at bandwidth of $1/n$, $2/n$, $3/n$, etc. The increased bandwidth is accomplished by dividing the combinatorial logic into stages separated by latches. However, increasing the bandwidth (by pipelining) results in higher gate count due to the additional latches. Thus, it is necessary to analyze the cost of bandwidth using pipelining. (An alternate way to increase bandwidth is to simply operate several units in parallel.) As the title of this chapter indicates, we are primarily concerned about pipelining *within* arithmetic functional units and *not* about the more general issues of coordination and design of pipelined processors which use such functional units. Koege, [KOE 80], and Chen (see Chapter 11 in [STO 75]) provide very useful information on the more general problem of pipeline processor design.

This chapter is divided into four parts. The first part explains how to achieve maximum bandwidth while the cost of bandwidth (on a gate level) is analyzed in the second part. The third part illustrates the increased performance of floating point operations (on an IC level) and the fourth part is a case study of a commercially available system with pipelined arithmetic.

6.1 ACHIEVING MAXIMUM BANDWIDTH

Assume that a logical function is decomposed into a sequence of combinatorial pieces, each latched by a corresponding storage element. In this model (Figure 6–1a) results are stored in distinct elements called latches which are "clocked" and we do not rely on inherent delay in the logic itself for storage.

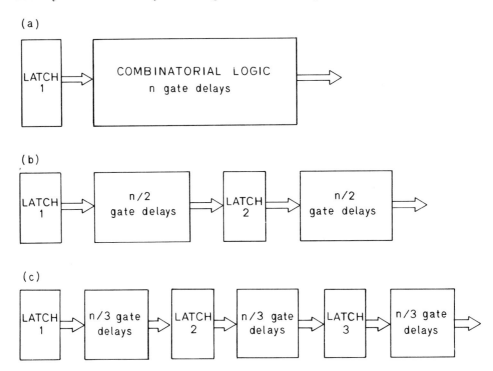

Figure 6–1a.   Increasing bandwidth by pipelining.
      a.   nonpipelined system bandwidth $= 1/n$.
      b.   2-stage pipelined system bandwidth $= 2/n$.
      c.   3-stage pipelined system bandwidth $= 3/n$.

What is the maximum rate at which this pipeline can produce results? In order to analyze this consider one stage of the pipeline (Figure 6–1b) and use the following definitions:

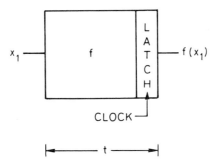

Figure 6–1b.   Pipeline stage.

$t_{\max}$ = maximum propagation time through combinatorial logic (f) for this stage of the pipeline.

$t_{\min}$ = minimum propagation time through the combinatorial logic (f) for this stage of the pipeline.

t_g = gate width or setup time; i.e., the total amount of time data has to be valid at the latch for proper storage into the latch.

Suppose an input x_1 is applied at time t_1, then $f(x_1)$ is guaranteed to be valid at the output after $t_1 + t_{\max}$. Then in order for proper latching of $f(x_1)$ to take place it must continue to remain valid until $t_1 + t_{\max} + t_g$. How soon can we apply new data x_2 at the input, and still meet the constraints on $f(x_1)$? If new data x_2 is applied at time t_2, it takes at least $t_2 + t_{\min}$ for its effect to be felt at the output:

$$t_2 + t_{\min} > t_1 + t_{\max} + t_g,$$
$$(t_2 - t_1) > t_{\max} - t_{\min} + t_g.$$

Let

$$\Delta t = t_2 - t_1.$$

Now Δt is the minimum clock period $(t_2 - t_1)$ and

$$\boxed{\Delta t > t_{\max} - t_{\min} + t_g.}$$

This difference between t_2 and t_1 defines the maximum rate $(1/\Delta t)$ at which the pipeline operates. This significant observation is discussed in detail in Section 6.2.2.

If the various pieces of the pipeline f_i have different pipeline rates, then the slowest element determines the maximum rate:

$$\text{max rate} = \max_i (1/\Delta t_i).$$

Thus far we have ignored the effect of the delay within the latch itself. Latches can be designed or integrated into the combinatorial logic. One such example of this is called the Earle latch.

6.2 THE COST OF BANDWIDTH: GATE LEVEL ANALYSIS

6.2.1 The Earle Latch

In Figure 6–1a the latches between the various stages did not add any additional delays. This type of a latch is called Earle latch, after its inventor J. G. Earle [EAR 65]. Figure 6–2 shows the logic diagram of the latch. The output data (Z) follows the input data (D) whenever the clock (C) is a logical one. The clock transition from one to zero latches the input data onto Z. The latch is then insensitive to further changes in the input data as long as the clock is at zero.

Earle has designed this latch specifically for latching carry-save adders, and its first use was in the IBM System 360/91. This latch is a very attractive element in a pipelined system, since it can incorporate two level AND-OR logic functions without introducing additional delay over the time required to perform an AND-OR function.

For example, suppose it is desired to latch the function

$$D = AB + EF.$$

From Figure 6–2 the logic equations for the Earle latch are:

$$G1 = CD,$$
$$G2 = ZD,$$
$$G3 = \overline{C}Z.$$

Now substitute the desired function instead of the data input (D).

$$G1 = CD = C(AB + EF) = CAB + CEF.$$
$$G2 = ZD = Z(AB + EF) = ZAB + ZEF.$$
$$G4 = G1 + G2 + G3.$$
$$G4 = CAB + CEF + ZAB + ZEF + \overline{C}Z.$$

Thus, latching a 2-level logic function is accomplished in only two gate delays, however, the gate count is increased (see Figure 6–3).

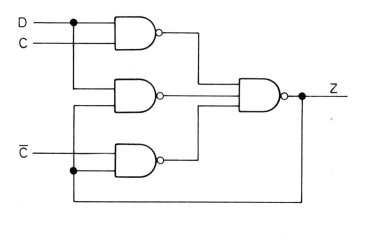

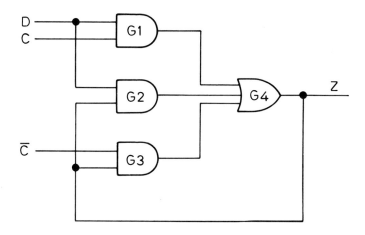

Figure 6–2.   The Earle latch (the two logic representations are equivalent).
The output data (Z) follows the input data (D) whenever the clock (C) is
logical one.   The clock transition from one to zero latches the input data
onto Z. The latch is insensitive to further changes of the input data as long
as the clock is at zero.

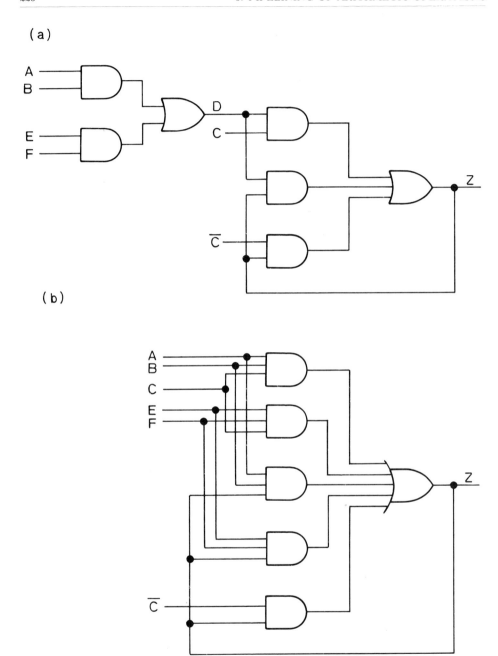

Figure 6–3.   Latching the AND-OR function.
              a. External latching results in additional 2-gate delays.
              b. By incorporating the AND-OR function into the
                 Earle latch, no additional delay is required.

6.2.2 Timing Constraints of the Earle Latch

Hallin and Flynn [HAL 72] developed timing constraints using the Earle latch to maximize pipelining without introducing a discussion of skew and logic hazards. In their study they determined minimum and maximum widths of the clock pulse, and also established a minimum path delay between latches. Their study was expanded later on in a master's thesis by Fawcett [FAW 75] who took into account various clock skews. We present here only a summary of Fawcett's very detailed study. But first we have to introduce his terminology.

t_{max}—maximum propagation delay time for a logic gate (in this case, a NAND gate in the Earle latch).

t_{min}—minimum propagation delay time for a logic gate.

C_{high}—the duration of $C = 1$ (clock high).

C_{low}—the duration of $C = 0$ (clock low).

P_{max}—maximum delay on the maximum data path of logic between storage registers (one segment) in the pipeline—not including delay in the register itself.

P_{min}—minimum delay on the minimum data path between registers in the pipeline.

Skew is defined as the difference in the time of the arrival of the two edges involved. $S(X,Y)$ is positive only if the first edge listed, X, precedes the second, Y; otherwise, it is defined to be zero. The algebraic skew, $AS(X,Y)$, is negative if Y occurs before X; if X occurs before Y, it is, of course, positive.

The first timing constraint is on the minimum width of the clock pulse C_{high}. The pulse has to be wide enough: (a) to ensure that valid data is stored in the latch, and (b) to avoid logic hazard if C leads $\overline{C}$.

$$\boxed{C_{high} \geq 3t_{max} - t_{min} + S(C \uparrow, \overline{C} \downarrow).}$$

where

$$t_{max} = \text{maximum propagation delay for a logic gate;}$$
$$t_{min} = \text{minimum propagation delay time for a logic gate;}$$
$$S(C \uparrow, \overline{C} \downarrow) = \text{skew between C going high and } \overline{C} \text{ going low at the}$$
$$\text{input to the latch.}$$

The second timing constraint is on the maximum width of the clock pulse C_{high}. If we ignore skews, then obviously the clock width should be shorter than the fastest time that a new data can propagate through one segment of the pipeline; i.e.,

$$C_{high} \leq P_{min} + 2t_{min},$$

where P_{min} = minimum delay on the minimum data path between storage registers (one segment) in the pipeline—not including delay in the register itself.

However, a more precise constraint includes the skew between segments of the pipeline, a $t_{max} - t_{min}$ term to avoid logic hazards, and two clock skews.

$$C_{high} + AS(C_{i-1} \uparrow, C_i \uparrow) \leq 2t_{min} + P_{min} - S(\overline{C} \downarrow, C \uparrow)$$
$$- \max\{0, t_{max} - t_{min} + AS(C \uparrow, \overline{C} \downarrow)\}$$

where

$AS(C_{i-1} \uparrow, C_i \uparrow)$ is the algebraic skew between C going high at a given segment in the pipeline and C going high at the segment succeeding it.

$AS(C \uparrow, \overline{C} \downarrow)$ is the algebraic skew between C going high and $\overline{C}$ going low.

The third timing constraint is a minimum clock period of:

$$C_{high} + C_{low} = P_{max} - P_{min} + 5t_{max} - 3t_{min} + 2S(C \uparrow, \overline{C} \downarrow)$$
$$+ S(\overline{C} \downarrow, C \uparrow) + \max\{0, t_{max} - t_{min} + AS(C \downarrow, \overline{C} \uparrow)\}$$

This equation leads Fawcett to the important observation that the minimum clock period, which determines the maximum possible throughput, is dependent on the difference $P_{max} - P_{min}$ as has been pointed out. A decade earlier the designers of the IBM 360/91 made a similar observation [AND 67]:

Clock period > (maximum delay—minimum delay) + gate width;

and they even "padded" the short paths with additional delay to minimize the difference between the maximum and the minimum delay.

Note: Gate width is the setup time the data has to be valid before the clock goes to zero, plus the hold time on the data needed after the clock went to zero.

6.2.3 Efficiency—The Figure of Merit for the Cost of Bandwidth

Hallin and Flynn developed the concept of efficiency in order to measure the cost of bandwidth. The cost is assumed to be directly proportional to the total gate count. Thus, for a given operand length and a given bandwidth, the fewer gates necessary to realize a function the more efficient the unit is. Similarly, if two circuits, having the same number of gates, perform the same function, the circuit with the **higher bandwidth** is more efficient. This leads to the following definition of efficiency:

$$\boxed{\text{EFFICIENCY} = \frac{N}{D \cdot G}}$$

where

N = number of bits in the operands;

D = the delay of each pipeline stage in units of gate delays;

G = total number of gates (including those used for latching).

This measure is really a figure of merit rather than an "efficiency" measure in the familiar sense. It is not normalized with respect to an ideal, but simply provides a comparative measure for algorithms of slightly varying word sizes. The resulting measure includes no notion of computational complexity, thus its validity is strictly limited to comparisons of several implementations of the *same* arithmetic operation. That is, there is no comparability between an addition efficiency measure and a multiplication measure.

6.2.4 Efficiency of Pipelined Adders and Multipliers

Using the previously developed definition of efficiency Hallin and Flynn tabulate the pipelining efficiency of two addition schemes (on 48-bit operands) using various numbers of pipelining stages (see Figure 6–4). For example, in the carry-look-ahead addition scheme the delay is reduced from 14 gates per addition in a nonpipelined system (a factor of 3.5). The total gate count increases from 700 to 2000 (a factor of 2.8). Thus, the efficiency of pipelining carry-look-ahead addition is about 25% higher than the equivalent nonpipelining addition ($3.5/2.8 = 1.25$).

Addition Scheme	Stages	Stage Delay	Latches	Total Gates	Efficiency $\times 10^{-5}$
Carry-	1	14	49	700	490
look-	2	8	161	1152	520
ahead	3	6	282	1607	495
	4	4	376	2007	600
Conditional	1	12	49	934	428
sum	2	6	181	1426	561
	3	4	322	1904	630

Figure 6–4.   Pipelining efficiency of two addition schemes, with various numbers of stages. Operands are 48 bits long, and fan-in is 5. [HAL 72].

In Figure 6–5 the pipelining efficiency of various multiplication schemes is tabulated. This table is a combination of the results reported by Hallin and Flynn [HAL 72] and the more recent study done by Deverell [DEV 75]. From Figure 6–5 it is clear that the most efficient multiplication is obtained by pipelining a multiplier using the Booth's encoder to reduce the number of partial products, and a Wallace tree to sum the remaining partial products.

Multiplication Scheme	Stages	Stage delay	Latches	Total Gates	Efficiency $\times 10^{-5}$
Booth's encoder	1	32	97	22415	6.70
with	2	16	386	23667	12.60
Wallace tree	4	8	1299	27542	21.80
	8	4	3376	34499	34.80
4-pass Tree	1	42	925	10810	10.60
(IBM 360/91)	2	16	1166	11582	25.90
Guild	1	190	96	25728	0.98
Iterative	5	38	674	28337	4.45
Array	19	10	2697	37355	12.80
	48	4	5736	51675	23.00
Carry-save array	1	110	96	26044	1.67
With CLA (Figure 6–6)	48	4	8088	66718	18.00
Iterative array	1	196	96	33302	0.73
as a multiplier	48	100	5736	61692	0.77
Iterative array	1	4612	96	33302	0.03
as a divider	48	100	5736	61692	0.77

Figure 6–5.   Pipelining efficiency of various multiplication schemes of 48-bit operands. The first three schemes are based on Hallin and Flynn [HAL 72], and the rest are adapted from Deverell [DEV 75].

Multiplication arrays are not as efficient, but they have the important feature of being iterative, and therefore only one type of circuit is needed. Let's analyze some of the iterative multiplication arrays. For example, the Guild array (see also Figure 4–15) is made of the following carry-save adder cells:

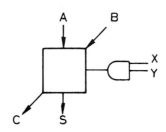

The logic equations for the cells are as follows (using the terminology of Chapter 4):

$$\text{SUM} = S = A \oplus B \oplus (XY);$$
$$S = (\overline{A}\,\overline{B})(X\,Y) + (A\,B)(X\,Y) + (\overline{A}\,B)(\overline{X}\,\overline{Y}) + (A\,\overline{B})(\overline{X}\,\overline{Y});$$
$$S = (\overline{A}\,\overline{B})(X\,Y) + (A\,B)(X\,Y) + (\overline{A}\,B)\overline{X} + (\overline{A}\,B)\overline{Y} + (A\,\overline{B})\overline{X} + (A\,\overline{B})\,\overline{Y};$$
$$\text{CARRY} = C = A(X\,Y) + B(X\,Y) + (A\,B).$$

Assuming fan-in of 6 and ignoring the necessity for inverters, each cell is implemented by 11 gates, and its delay is two gate delays. An unlatched Guild array has $11N^2$ gates in the bulk of the array with an additional 8N gates for one row of Earle latches. For the 48-bit case $N = 48$

$$\begin{aligned}
\text{Array gates} &= 11N^2 = 11 \times 48 \times 48 = 25{,}344\\
\text{Latch gates} &= 8N = 8 \times 48 = \phantom{25{,}}384\\
\hline
\text{Total gates} & 25{,}728
\end{aligned}$$

The worst-case path delay is along the diagonal on the right side (N) and across the bottom row (Figure 4–15) of $N - 1$ cells. Thus, the total delay is $2N - 1$ cells or $4N - 2$ gates, and for a 48-bit array and one row of latches the longest path is 190 gate delays.

If the Guild array is maximally pipelined, a delay of four gates per stage is obtained. But now we need two latches per cell, and in addition $(N/2)(N - 1)$ dummy latches to keep the timing correct. Thus, a total of $2N^2 + (N/2)(N - 1)$ latches is required. The total gate count for a maximally latched array is computed as follows:

$$\begin{aligned}
\text{Array gates} &= 11N^2 = 11 \times 48 \times 48 & &= 25{,}344\\
\text{Latch gates} &= (2N^2 + (N/2)(N - 1))4 = 4 \times 5736 & &= 22{,}944\\
\hline
\text{Total gates} & & &48{,}288
\end{aligned}$$

(This result is slightly different from the 51,675 gates reported by [HAL 72] and duplicated in Figure 6–5.)

Deverell points out that the Guild array is completely iterative when it is not latched, however, it loses its iterative nature when latches are added to it. Deverell suggests the latched carry-save adder array (Figure 6–6) as a structure that preserves its iterative nature in spite of latching, and yet maintains a relatively high efficiency (18×10^{-5}). For such a maximally latched carry-save adder array, three latches per cell are required. Thus, $3N^2$ latches for all the cells, plus $(N/2)(N + 1)$ latches to keep the timing correct, are required. This results in 8088 latches and a total gate count of 66,718 gates.

Finally, Deverell suggests the use of iterative dividing arrays, because they use row by row methods of division and are, therefore, ideal for latching. A latched $(N \times N)$ divider has an efficiency $(N/2)$ times greater than its unlatched equivalent. Of course, the efficiency of such a general array as a multiplier is not very high, but this is the price paid for the generality of the array as a multipurpose arithmetic unit.

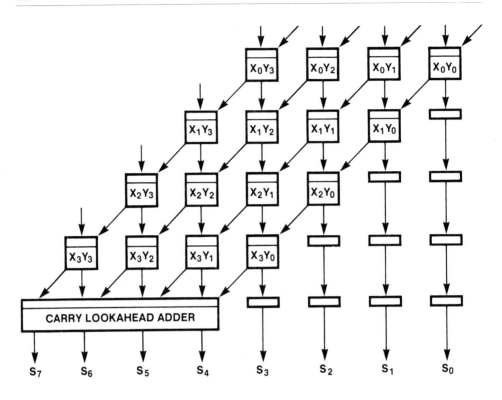

Figure 6–6.   Pipelined carry-save multiplication array. The square boxes are carry-save adders with three latches. Each square box has three inputs; a sum and a carry from previous carry-save adders, and the third is the partial product $X_i \cdot Y_i$. The ten unmarked rectangles on the right are 1-bit latches to keep correct timing.

6.3 PIPELINING OF A FLOATING POINT MULTIPLIER

In the previous section we analyzed the pipelining of arithmetic operations on a gate level. In other words, the minimum delay per stage was determined by the desired minimum number of gate delays. Now we turn our attention to the integrated circuit (IC) level, where the minimum delay per pipelined stage is determined by the propagation delay of the slowest IC. For example, in designing with 125 ns multipliers, the minimum delay per pipeline stage is 125 ns + register overhead.

Since the IC is the smallest integral unit used, it is necessary to redefine efficiency in these terms [MAJ 76]:

$$\mathrm{EFFICIENCY} = \frac{\mathrm{N}}{\mathrm{D \cdot I}}$$

where:

N = number of bits in the operands;

D = the longest delay of a pipeline stage in ns;

I = total number of IC modules used in the design.

The concepts of pipelining using ICs can best be illustrated by an example. It will show how to pipeline the floating point multiplier/divider of Figure 5–4. For simplicity we do not discuss the divider, but only the multiplier. The time to execute a single nonpipelined floating point multiplication is made up of the following delays:

• partial products generation (8×8 multipliers)	125 ns
• column compression (three ROM delays)	150 ns
• 64-bit addition of compressed columns	55 ns
• normalization (left shift)	20 ns
• rounding (incrementing)	50 ns
Total	400 ns

From Chapter 4 we can compute the total ICs necessary for the floating point multiplier:

• 56 $\times$56 single length multiplier	127
• left shifter	2
• incrementer	15
• exponent section	4
• 8-bit input registers	17
• 8-bit output registers	9
Total number of ICs	174

Figure 6–7 shows the pipelining of the floating point multiplier. Assuming we do not want to insert registers between the ROMs, then the column compression at 150 ns is the longest path and as such it determines the minimum clock period of the pipelined system. If we assume the use of 8-bit edge-triggered registers such as 74S374 [MMI 82], then the exact clock period is determined as follows:

• clock to register output delay	17 ns
• longest path delay	150 ns
• setup time	5 ns
Minimum clock period	172 ns

From Figure 6–7 it is obvious that pipelining requires an additional 82 register ICs, in addition to the 174 ICs. Thus, a total of 256 ICs are used in the pipelined floating point multiplier. From the table below it can be seen that pipelining more than doubles the bandwidth with only a 50% increase in the hardware, thus resulting in a more efficient system.

Stages	Stage Delay (ns)	Bandwidth (MOPS)	Total ICs	Efficiency $\times 10^{-5}$
1	400	2.5	174	94
3	172	5.8	256	145

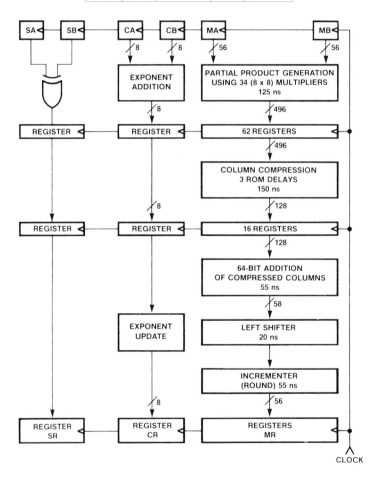

Figure 6–7. Pipelined floating point multiplier.

6.4 PIPELINED ARRAY PROCESSORS

An array processor is an add on high speed arithmetic processor that can be combined with a host computer to increase the system throughput at a relatively low cost. As used here, an array processor refers to a processor optimized for handling large arrays of data, not to the array of separate processors used in a machine like the ILLIAC IV. The table below illustrates the cost effectiveness of an array processor (AP-120B) as compared with large, fast mainframes. The benchmark program used for comparison is a phase demodulation algorithm [WIT 78]. (Megaflop = million floating point operations per second.)

Machine	CPU Cost (Million $)	Performance (Megaflops) Max	Actual	Performance/Cost (Megaflop/$M)
CRAY-1	4.5	80	20.00	4.4
STAR-100	8.0	50	16.60	2.1
CDC-760	3.0	8	3.30	1.1
CDC-6600	1.5	2	0.63	0.4
AP-120B	0.1	12	7.90	79.0

6.4.1 A Pipelined Array Processor

This section describes the AP-120B from Floating Point Systems, Inc. [FPS 78].

The AP-120B is an array processor that can be interfaced with various computers such as PDP-11, IBM/370, and several others. Array data is transferred from the host memory to internal data memory via a DMA channel. The data is converted from host floating point format to internal AP-120B floating point format "on the fly." The internal floating point format is as follows:

10 bits binary EXPONENT biased by 512	28 bits two's complement MANTISSA	3 GUARD bits

| ←——————————— 38 bits ——————————→ |

The dynamic range of this format is from 3.7×10^{-155} to 6.7×10^{153}, and the precision is about 8 decimal digits. The machine also rounds by adding 1 to the most significant guard bit.

Figure 6–8 is a block diagram of the AP-120B arithmetic paths. Data transfers occur under control of either the host computer or the AP-120B; therefore, the array processor is interfaced to both the programmed I/O and DMA channels. The system elements are interconnected with multiple parallel paths so that data transfer can occur in parallel. All internal data paths are 38 bits wide, to accommodate the above floating point format.

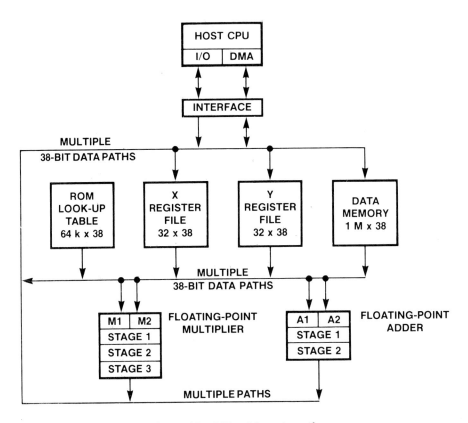

Figure 6–8.   Block diagram of the AP-120B arithmetic paths.

The data memory is organized in 8K-word modules, expandable up to 1 megawords. The effective memory cycle time (interleaved) is 333 ns.

The ROM look-up table is used for storage of frequently used constants in signal processing (complex roots of unity and transcendental values). Such a separate memory organization increases the throughput of the machine by allowing simultaneous fetching of data values and table values, (constants, coefficients, etc.).

The register files (X and Y) are effectively 32 floating point accumulators each. Each file is made of dual-port registers allowing one register to be read while another is written, all in the same microcycle (167 ns).

The floating point adder operates on the contents of the input registers A1 and A2. This structure is a 2-stage pipeline. In the first stage, alignment and addition (or subtraction) of the mantissas take place. In the second stage, normalization and rounding are performed. Thus, the bandwidth of addition is the inverse of 167 ns, while the latency is 333 ns. The floating point adder performs the conversion from fixed to floating point, and vice versa.

The floating point multiplier is a 3-stage pipeline structure. In the first stage, the 56-bit product (of the two 28-bit mantissas) is partially completed. The second stage completes the product of the mantissas. In the third stage, the exponents are added and the mantissa product is rounded. The bandwidth of multiplication is the same as of addition; i.e., every 167 ns a new multiplication can be started (it is interesting to note the similarity between the AP-120B multiplier and the one described in Section 6.3. Both are made of three pipelining sections, and their bandwidth is almost identical; 167 ns verses 172 ns). Finally, the latency of the AP-120B multiplier is the time to travel through the three pipelining stages; i.e., 500 ns.

The following table summarizes the latency and the bandwidth for various arithmetic operations of the AP-120B:

Operation	Latency	Pipeline Interval	Bandwidth (mf = megaflops)
Add/Subtract	333 ns	167 ns	6 mf
Multiply	500 ns	167 ns	6 mf
Multiply/Add	833 ns	167 ns	6 mf
Complex Add/Subtract	500 ns	333 ns	3 mf
Complex Multiply	1333 ns	667 ns	1.5 mf
Complex Multiply/Add	1667 ns	667 ns	1.5 mf

The control of the arithmetic paths in Figure 6–8 is provided by a microprogram stored in a 4K × 64 memory. The microprogram memory is loaded from the host CPU via the same DMA as the data. The 64 bits of the microinstruction word are divided into six fields as shown in Figure 6–9. This wide microinstruction allows parallelism for further throughput. For example, while the multiplier is operating at the rate of 167 ns on one set of data, the adder simultaneously operates on another set of data (also at 167 ns). Thus, the maximum arithmetic bandwidth of the system is twice the inverse of 167 ns; i.e., 12 megaflops.

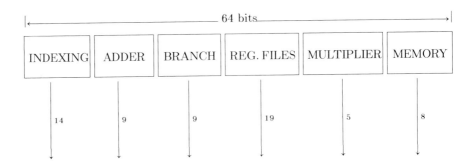

Figure 6–9.   The 64-bit microinstruction of the AP-120B is made up of six fields, enabling
highly parallel operations.

6.5 ADDITIONAL READINGS

Session 18 of the 1979 WESCON conference was dedicated to array processors. The session, entitled "High Speed, Low Cost Number Crunchers," described the implementation of array processors from Floating Point Systems, Inc. [WIN 79] and from Computer Design and Applications [BIR 79]. The latter describes a unique approach to increasing bandwidth while maintaining low cost by the use of pipelining serial techniques.

The September 1981 issue of *Computer* magazine,(published by IEEE) contains several excellent articles on array processors. The issue opens with a good introduction to array processor architecture by Theis [THE 81].

Karplus and Cohen [KAR 81] give an overview of array processors. They describe the evolution of these machines and evaluate them relative to other commercially available general purpose host computers on a cost/performance basis. Their article also includes a comparison of 13 commercially available array processors with key attributes such as instruction time, word size, and execution time for 1024-point complex FFT.

Cohen and Storer [COH 81] describe the architecture of another array processor. In their implementation bandwidth is increased by using asynchronous functional parallelism instead of the conventional pipelined architecture.

Maron and Brengle [MAR 81] discuss the integration of an array processor with a general purpose host computer. They show that during the integration process the high performance of the array processor is always compromised, preventing it from achieving the highest possible overall system performance.

Louie [LOU 81] gives a selected bibliography that includes 116 published papers and articles on various aspects of array processors.

6.6 SUMMARY

Arithmetic operational units may be pipelined to improve bandwidth: the supply of results per unit time. This is contrasted with the more conventional design emphasis of simply minimizing the operational execution time. Pipelined designs consist of partitioning the algorithmic logic into latched stages to store intermediate results. Each stage should have approximately the same delay since the bandwidth is determined by the slowest stage. The Earle latch is frequently used as a pipeline stage latch since it can be integrated into existing logic without causing additional stage delay.

Pipeline efficiency is a figure of merit for arithmetic algorithms which serves as an indicator of the value of a particular algorithm for pipeline implementations.

Conditional sum for addition and Booth's encoder with a Wallace tree for multiplication have among the highest respective pipeline efficiency factors.

6.7 EXERCISES

1. The Earle latch has a logic hazard.

   a. Show this on a Karnaugh map.

   b. Exactly under what conditions will the latch fail?

   c. During the C_{high} timing constraints, (see Section 6.2.2) at the latch, which needs be imposed to insure reliable operations?

2. The Earle latch;

   a. Propose a modified Earle latch without a hazard.

   b. Discuss the practical feasibility of your proposal.

3. Show that for the Earle latch, Fawcett's third timing constraint is derived from the Model 91 bound on minimum clock period.

4. A clock period at $4t_{max}$ was mentioned in Chapter 4, in the use of the Earle latch for iterating multiplication. What idealizations does this represent?

5. Show a realization of a 4-stage pipelined CLA for 48-bit operands, fan-in = 5. Compare your results to Figure 6–4.

6. Discuss the suitability of pipelining the canonic adder of Chapter 3. Use fan-in = 5 and 20-bit operands.

6.8 DESIGN EXERCISES

1. Design a 48-bit pipelined floating point adder. Use CLA, fan-in = 5, and binary floating point format (12-bit characteristic, 36-bit fraction including sign).

   a. What is the best latching point for a 2-stage pipeline?

   b. Repeat (a) for a 4-stage pipeline.

   c. Provide a rough estimate of the efficiency in (a) and (b).

DESIGN APPENDIX

TABLE OF CONTENTS

INTRODUCTION

We include here (courtesy of Monolithic Memories, Inc.) the data sheets for enough MSI/LSI as to be useful in the design assignments in the end of each chapter. Only four families of ICs are included in the appendix.

- Arithmetic ICs (ALU, look-ahead carry generator and combinatorial multipliers);

- PROMs (various sizes for look-up tables);

- Octal Registers, Latches, Buffers and Transceivers;

- PAL (combinatorial PLA and Registered PLA with internal feedback);

The inclusion of the PAL family eliminates the need for many SSI/MSI functions since the PAL can be programmed to implement the various Boolean logic transfer functions of SSI plus it can implement most MSI functions such as multiplexers, counters, shift registers, etc.

DESIGN IMPLEMENTATIONS IN THE LAB

For the instructor that wants to implement the design exercises in the lab, we have selected MSI/LSI in this design appendix with two criterias in mind:

a. Widely available (most parts are available from Advanced Micro Devices, Monolithic Memories, National Semiconductor, and Texas Instruments).

b. Fuse programmability. By using PROMs instead of ROMs, we avoid the high cost and the high volume associated with custom made ROMs. Lab facilities that include any computer microprocessor development system will find it very easy to interface to low-cost PROM/PAL programmers that are available from various commercial vendors (see list in the PAL data sheet). For the PAL there is a software program called PALASM that translates the Boolean transfer function to a fuse map. A copy of this software is available from the PAL applications department at Monolithic Memories.

SELECTION GUIDE

ARITHMETIC IC's

Device	Description
74S382	4-bit ALU
74S182	Look-ahead carry generator
74S558	8×8 Multiplier (Propagation delay = 60 ns)
29516	16×16 Multiply (Pipeline rate = 65 ns); see [AMD 82]

PROM

Device	Description		Access Time	
6381-2	$1K \times 8$	PROM	55 ns	
63S441A	$1K \times 4$	PROM	35 ns	
63S081	32×8	PROM	25 ns	
			Set-up time	Clock to Out
63RA441	Registered $1K \times 4$ PROM		50 ns	30 ns

REGISTERS AND BUFFERS

Device	Description
74S240/244	Octal Buffers (inverting/noninverting)
74LS245	Octal Transceiver
74S374	Octal Register
74S373	Octal Latch

PROGRAMMABLE LSI:PAL

Device	Description		
PAL16L8	Combinatorial PLA (Propagation delay = 25 ns)		
		Set-up time	Clock to Out
PAL16R8	PLA with output registers	25 ns	15 ns

Arithmetic Logic Unit/ Function Generator
SN54S381 SN74S381

Features/Benefits

- A Fully Parallel 4-Bit ALU in 20-Pin Package for 0.300-inch Row Spacing

- Ideally Suited for High-Density Economical Processors

- Parallel Inputs and Outputs and Full Look-Ahead Provide System Flexibility

- Arithmetic and Logic Operations Selected Specifically to Simplify System Implementation:

    A Minus B
    B Minus A
    A Plus B
    and Five Other Functions

Description

The 'S381 is a Schottky TTL arithmetic logic unit (ALU)/function generator that performs eight binary arithmetic/logic operations on two 4-bit words as shown in the function table. These operations are selected by the three function-select lines (S0, S1, S2). A fully carry look-ahead circuit is provided for fast, simultaneous carry generation by means of two cascade outputs ($\overline{P}$ and $\overline{G}$) for the four bits in the package.

Logic Symbol

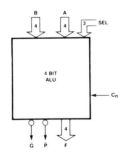

Ordering Information

PART NUMBER	PACKAGE	TEMPERATURE
SN54S381	J20,F20	Military
SN74S381	J20	Commercial

Pin Configuration

SN54S381, SN74S381

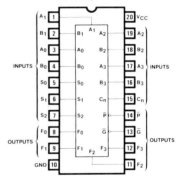

Function Table

SELECTION			ARITHMETIC/LOGIC OPERATION
S2	S1	S0	
L	L	L	Clear †
L	L	H	B minus A
L	H	L	A minus B
L	H	H	A plus B
H	L	L	A $\oplus$ B
H	L	H	A + B
H	H	L	AB
H	H	H	Preset ††

† Force all F outputs to be Lows.
†† Force all F outputs to be Highs.

SN54S381   SN74S381

Absolute Maximum Ratings

Supply Voltage, V_{CC} 7V
Input Voltage 5.5V
Storage Temperature Range .... −65°C to +150°C

Operating Conditions

SYMBOL	PARAMETER	MILITARY			COMMERCIAL			UNIT
		MIN	NOM	MAX	MIN	NOM	MAX	
V_{CC}	Supply voltage	4.5	5	5.5	4.75	5	5.25	V
T_A	Operating free-air temperature	−55		125	0		70	°C

Electrical Characteristics Over operating conditions

SYMBOL	PARAMETER	TEST CONDITIONS		MIN	TYP	MAX	UNIT
V_{IL}	Low-level input voltage					0.8	V
V_{IH}	High-level input voltage			2			V
V_{IC}	Input clamp voltage	V_{CC} = MIN I_I = −18mA				−1.2	V
I_{IL}	Low-level input current	V_{CC} = MAX V_I = 0.5V	Any S input			−2	mA
			Cn			−8	
			All others			−6	
I_{IH}	High-level input current	V_{CC} = MAX V_I = 2.7V	Any S input			50	μA
			Cn			250	
			All others			200	
I_I	Maximum input current	V_{CC} = MAX V_I = 5.5V				1	mA
V_{OL}	Low-level output voltage	V_{CC} = MIN V_{IH} = 2V V_{IL} = 0.8V I_{OL} = 20mA				0.5	V
V_{OH}	High-level output voltage	V_{CC} = MIN V_{IH} = 2V V_{IL} = 0.8V I_{OH} = −1mA	SN54S381	2.4	3.4		V
			SN74S381	2.7	3.4		
I_{OS}	Output short-circuit current*	V_{CC} = MAX		−40		−100	mA
I_{CC}	Supply current	V_{CC} = MAX			105	160	mA

* Not more than one output should be shorted at a time.

Switching Characteristics V_{CC} = 5 V, T_A = 25°C

SYMBOL	PARAMETER	FROM (INPUT)	TO (OUTPUT)	5/74S381		UNIT
				TYP	MAX	
t_P	Propagation delay time	C_n	Any F	10	17	ns
t_P	Propagation delay time	Any A or B	$\overline{G}$	12	20	ns
t_P	Propagation delay time	Any A or B	$\overline{P}$	11	18	ns
t_{PLH}	Propagation delay, low-to-high	Ai or Bi	Fi	18	27	ns
t_{PHL}	Propagation delay, high-to-low			16	25	ns
t_P	Propagation delay time	Any S	Fi, $\overline{G}$, $\overline{P}$	18	30	ns

SN54S381   SN74S381

Standard Test Load

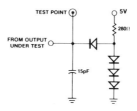

16-BIT ALU (USING 74S381)

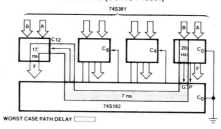

WORST CASE PATH DELAY

MAXIMUM DELAY OF ADDITION/SUBTRACTION.

	74S381
1-4 bits	27ns
5-16 bits	44ns
17-64 bits	64ns

Look-Ahead Carry Generators
SN54S182   SN74S182

Description

The SN54S182, and SN74S182 are high-speed, look-ahead carry generators capable of anticipating a carry across four binary adders or group of adders. They are cascadable to perform full look-ahead across n-bit adders. Carry, generate-carry, and propagate-carry functions are provided as enumerated in the pin designation table below.

When used in conjunction with 74S381, 67S581, 74S181, 2901, 6701 arithmetic logic units (ALU), these generators provide high-speed carry lookahead capability for any word length. Each 'S182 generates the look-ahead (anticipated carry) across a group of four ALU's and, in addition, other carry look-ahead circuits may be employed to anticipate carry across sections of four look-ahead packages up to n-bits.

The carry functions (inputs, outputs, generate, and propagate) of the look-ahead generators are implemented in the compatible forms for direct connection to the ALU. Logic equations for the 'S182 are:

$$C_{n+x} = G0 + P0\ C_n$$
$$C_{n+y} = G1 + P1\ G0 + P1\ P0\ C_n$$
$$C_{n+z} = G2 + P2\ G1 + P2\ P1\ G0 + P2\ P1\ P0\ C_n$$
$$\overline{G} = \overline{\overline{G3} + \overline{P3}\ \overline{G2} + \overline{P3}\ \overline{P2}\ \overline{G1} + \overline{P3}\ \overline{P2}\ \overline{P1}\ \overline{G0}}$$
$$\overline{P} = \overline{\overline{P3}\ \overline{P2}\ \overline{P1}\ \overline{P0}}$$

or

$$\overline{C}_{n+x} = \overline{Y0}\ (X0 + Cn)$$
$$\overline{C}_{n+y} = \overline{Y1}\ [X1 + Y0\ (X0 + Cn)]$$
$$\overline{C}_{n+z} = \overline{Y2}\ \{X2 + Y1\ [X1 + Y0\ (X0 + Cn)]\}$$
$$Y = Y3\ (X3 + Y2)\ (X3 + X2 + Y1)\ (X3 + X2 + X1 + Y0)$$
$$X = X3 + X2 + X1 + X0$$

Pin Configuration

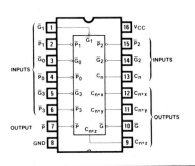

Ordering Information

PART NUMBER	PACKAGE	TEMPERATURE
SN54S182	J16,F16	Military
SN74S182	J16	Commercial

Summarizing Tables

FUNCTION TABLE FOR C_{n+y} OUTPUT

INPUTS				OUTPUT
$\overline{G}1$	$\overline{G}0$	$\overline{P}1$	$P0\ C_n$	C_{n+y}
L	X	X	X X	H
X	L	L	X X	H
X	X	L	L H	H
All other combinations				L

FUNCTION TABLE FOR $\overline{P}$ OUTPUT

INPUTS				OUTPUT
$\overline{P}3$	$\overline{P}2$	$\overline{P}1$	$\overline{P}0$	P
L	L	L	L	L
All other combinations				H

FUNCTION TABLE FOR C_{n+x} OUTPUT

INPUTS			OUTPUT
$\overline{G}0$	$\overline{P}0$	C_n	C_{n+x}
L	X	X	H
X	L	H	H
All other combinations			L

FUNCTION TABLE FOR $\overline{G}$ OUTPUT

INPUTS						OUTPUT
$\overline{G}3$	$\overline{G}2$	$\overline{G}1$	$\overline{G}0$	$\overline{P}3$	$\overline{P}2$ $\overline{P}1$	$\overline{G}$
L	X	X	X	X	X X	L
X	L	X	X	L	X X	L
X	X	L	X	L	L X	L
X	X	X	L	L	L L	L
All other combinations						H

FUNCTION TABLE FOR C_{n+z} OUTPUT

INPUTS						OUTPUT
$\overline{G}2$	$\overline{G}1$	$\overline{G}0$	$\overline{P}2$	$\overline{P}1$	$\overline{P}0$ $\overline{C}_n$	C_{n+z}
L	X	X	X	X	X X	H
X	L	X	L	X	X X	H
X	X	L	L	L	X X	H
X	X	X	L	L	L H	H
All other combinations						L

H = High Level, L = Low Level, X = Irrelevant. Any inputs not shown in a given table are irrelevant with respect to that output.

SN54S182   SN74S182

Absolute Maximum Ratings

Supply Voltage, V_{CC} 7V
Input Voltage 5.5V
Storage Temperature Range .... $-65°C$ to $+150°C$

Operating Conditions

SYMBOL	PARAMETER	MILITARY			COMMERCIAL			UNIT
		MIN	NOM	MAX	MIN	NOM	MAX	
V_{CC}	Supply voltage	4.5	5	5.5	4.75	5	5.25	V
T_A	Operating free-air temperature	-55		125	0		70	°C

Electrical Characteristics Over operating conditions

SYMBOL	PARAMETER	TEST CONDITIONS		MIN	TYP	MAX	UNIT
V_{IL}	Low-level input voltage					0.8	V
V_{IH}	High-level input voltage			2			V
V_{IC}	Input clamp voltage	V_{CC} = MIN I_I = -18mA				-1.2	V
I_{IL}	Low-level input current	V_{CC} = MAX V_I = 0.5V	C_n input			-2	mA
			$\overline{P}_3$ input			-4	
			$\overline{P}_2$ input			-6	
			$\overline{P}_0$, $\overline{P}_1$, or $\overline{G}_3$ input			-8	
			$\overline{G}_0$ or $\overline{G}_2$			-14	
			$\overline{G}_1$ input			-16	
I_{IH}	High-level input current	V_{CC} = MAX V_I = 2.7V	C_n input			50	μA
			$\overline{P}_3$ input			100	
			$\overline{P}_2$ input			150	
			$\overline{P}_0$, $\overline{P}_1$, or $\overline{G}_3$ input			200	
			$\overline{G}_0$ or $\overline{G}_2$			350	
			$\overline{G}_1$ input			400	
I_I	Maximum input current	V_{CC} = MAX V_I = 5.5V				1	mA
V_{OL}	Low-level output voltage	V_{CC} = MIN V_{IH} = 2V V_{IL} = 0.8V I_{OH} = -1mA				0.5	V
V_{OH}	High-level output voltage	V_{CC} = MIN V_{IH} = 2V V_{IL} = 0.8V I_{OL} = 20mA	SN74S182	2.7	3.4		V
			SN54S182	2.5	3.4		
I_{OS}	Output short-circuit current ∗	V_{CC} = MAX		-40		-100	mA
I_{CCL}	Supply current, all outputs low	V_{CC} = MAX See Note 1	SN74S182		69	109	mA
			SN54S182		69	99	
I_{CCH}	Supply current, all outputs high	V_{CC} = 5V See Note 2			35		mA

∗Not more than one output should be shorted at a time and duration of the short-circuit test should not exceed one second.

NOTES: 1. ICCL is measured with all outputs open; inputs $\overline{G}0$, $\overline{G}1$, and $\overline{G}2$ at 4.5 V, and all other inputs grounded.
       2. ICCH is measured with all outputs open, inputs $\overline{P}3$ and $\overline{G}3$ at 4.5 V, and all other inputs grounded.

SN54S182   SN74S182

Switching Characteristics V_{CC} = 5 V, T_A = 25 C

SYMBOL	PARAMETER	FROM (INPUT)	TO (OUTPUT)	TYP	MAX	UNIT
t_{PLH}	Propagation delay, low-to-high	$\overline{G}0, \overline{G}1, \overline{G}2, \overline{G}3,$	$C_{n+x}, C_{n+y}.$	4.5	7	ns
t_{PHL}	Propagation delay, high-to-low	$\overline{P}0, \overline{P}1, \overline{P}2,$ or $\overline{P}3$	or C_{n+z}	4.5	7	ns
t_{PLH}	Propagation delay, low-to-high	$\overline{G}0, \overline{G}1, \overline{G}2, \overline{G}3,$	$\overline{G}$	5	7.5	ns
t_{PHL}	Propagation delay, high-to-low	$\overline{P}1, \overline{P}2,$ or $\overline{P}3$		7	10.5	ns
t_{PLH}	Propagation delay, low-to-high	$\overline{P}0, \overline{P}1, \overline{P}2,$ or $\overline{P}3$	$\overline{P}$	4.5	6.5	ns
t_{PHL}	Propagation delay, high-to-low			6.5	10	ns
t_{PLH}	Propagation delay, low-to-high	C_n	$C_{n+x}, C_{n+y}.$	6.5	10	ns
t_{PHL}	Propagation delay, high-to-low		or C_{n+z}	7	10.5	ns

Standard Test Load

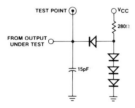

8x8 High Speed Schottky Multipliers
SN54/74S557   SN54/74S558

Features/Benefits

- Industry-standard 8x8 multiplier

- Multiplies two 8-bit numbers; gives 16-bit result

- Cascadable; 56x56 fully-parallel multiplication uses only 34 multipliers for the most-significant half of the product

- Full 8x8 multiply in 60ns worst case

- Three-state outputs for bus operation

- Transparent 16-bit latch in 'S557

- Plug-in compatible with original Monolithic Memories' 67558

Description

The 'S557/'S558 is a high-speed 8x8 combinatorial multiplier which can multiply two eight-bit unsigned or signed twos-complement numbers and generate the sixteen-bit unsigned or signed product. Each input operand X and Y has an associated Mode control line, X_M and Y_M respectively. When a Mode control line is at a Low logic level the operand is treated as an unsigned eight-bit number, while if the Mode control is at a High logic level the operand is treated as an eight-bit signed twos-complement number. Additional inputs, R_S and R_U, (R, S557) allow the addition of a bit into the multiplier array at the appropriate bit positions for rounding signed or unsigned fractional numbers.

The 'S557 internally develops proper rounding for either signed or unsigned numbers by combining the rounding input R with X_M, Y_M, $\overline{X_M}$, and $\overline{Y_M}$ as follows:

$R_U = \overline{X_M} \cdot \overline{Y_M} \cdot R$ = Unsigned rounding input to 2^7 adder.

$R_S = (X_M + Y_M) R$ = Signed rounding input to 2^6 adder.

Since the 'S558 does not require the use of pin 11 for the latch enable input G, R_S and R_U are brought out separately.

The most-significant product bit is available in both true and complemented form to assist in expansion to larger signed multipliers. The product outputs are three-state, controlled by an assertive-low Output Enable which allows several multipliers to be connected to a parallel bus or be used in a pipe-lined system. The device uses a single +5V power supply and is packaged in a standard 40-pin DIP.

Ordering Information

PART NUMBER	PACKAGE	TEMPERATURE
54S557, 54S558	J40, F42	Military
74S557, 74S558	J40	Commercial

Logic Symbol

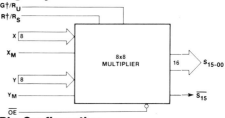

Pin Configuration

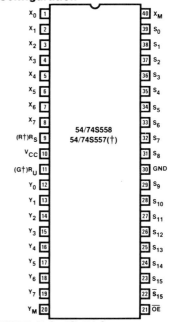

†For 54/74S557 Pin 9 is R and Pin 11 is G.

SN54/74S557   SN54/74S558

Logic Diagram

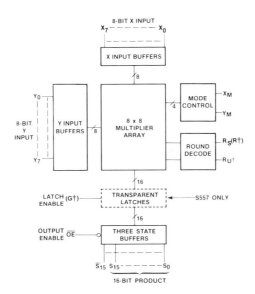

†For 54/74S557 Pin 9 is R and Pin 11 is G.

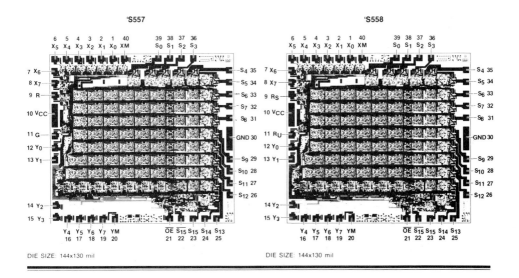

'S557

DIE SIZE: 144x130 mil

'S558

DIE SIZE: 144x130 mil

SN54/74S557 SN54/74S558

Absolute Maximum Ratings

Supply Voltage, V_{CC} 7V
Input Voltage 7V
Off-state output voltage 5.5V
Storage temperature .... −65° to +150°C

Operating Conditions

SYMBOL	PARAMETER	DEVICE	MILITARY			COMMERCIAL			UNITS
			MIN	TYP	MAX	MIN	TYP	MAX	
V_{CC}	Supply voltage	all	4.5	5	5.5	4.75	5	5.25	V
t_{su}	X_i, Y_i to G setup time	'S557	50			40			ns
t_h	X_i, Y_i to G hold time	'S557	0			0			ns
t_w	Latch enable pulse width	'S557	20			15			ns
T_A	Operating free-air temperature	all	−55		125*	0		75	°C

* Case temperature

Electrical Characteristics Over Operating Conditions

SYMBOL	PARAMETER	TEST CONDITIONS		MIN	TYP†	MAX	UNIT
V_{IL}	Low-level input voltage					0.8	V
V_{IH}	High-level input voltage			2			V
V_{IC}	Input clamp voltage	V_{CC} = MIN	I_I = −18mA			−1.5	V
I_{IL}	Low-level input current	V_{CC} = MAX	V_I = 0.5V			−1	mA
I_{IH}	High-level input current	V_{CC} = MAX	V_I = 2.4V			100	μA
I_I	Maximum input current	V_{CC} = MAX	V_I = 5.5V			1	mA
V_{OL}	Low-level output voltage	V_{CC} = MIN	I_{OL} = 8mA			0.5	V
V_{OH}	High-level output voltage	V_{CC} = MIN	I_{OH} = −2mA	2.4			V
I_{OZL}	Off-state output current	V_{CC} = MAX	V_O = 0.5V			−100	μA
I_{OZH}			V_O = 2.4V			100	μA
I_{OS}	Output short-circuit current*	V_{CC} = MAX	V_O = 0V	−20		−90	mA
I_{CC}	Supply current	V_{CC} = MAX			200	280	mA

* Not more than one output should be shorted at a time and duration of the short-circuit should not exceed one second.

† Typicals at 5.0V V_{CC} and 25°C T_A.

Switching Characteristics Over Operating Conditions

SYMBOL	PARAMETER	DEVICE	TEST CONDITIONS	MILITARY			COMMERCIAL			UNIT
				MIN	TYP†	MAX	MIN	TYP†	MAX	
t_{PD1}	X_i, Y_i to S_{7-0}	All			40	60		40	50	ns
t_{PD2}	X_i, Y_i to S_{15-8}	All			45	70		45	60	ns
t_{PD3}	X_i, Y_i to $\overline{S}_{15}$	All	C_L = 30pF		50	75		50	65	ns
t_{PD4}	G to S_i	'S557	R_L = 560Ω		20	40		20	35	ns
t_{PXZ}	$\overline{OE}$ to S_i	All	see test figures		20	40		20	30	ns
t_{PZX}	$\overline{OE}$ to S_i	All			15	40		15	30	ns

SN54/74S557   SN54/74S558

Timing Waveforms

Setup and Hold Times ('S557)

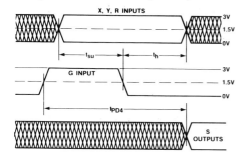

Test Waveforms

TEST	V_X		OUTPUT WAVEFORM — MEAS. LEVEL	
All t_{PD}	5.0V		V_{OH} —— 1.5V —— V_{OL}	
t_{PXZ}	for t_{PHZ}	for t_{PLZ}	V_{OH} —— 0.5V —— 2.8V	
	0.0V	5.0V	V_{OL} —— 0.5V —— 0.0V	
t_{PZX}	for t_{PZH}	for t_{PZL}	2.8V —— 1.5V —— V_{OH}	
	0.0V	5.0V	0.0V —— V_{OL}	

Propagation Delay

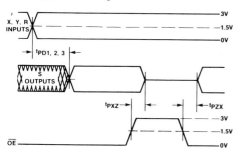

Load Test Circuit

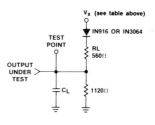

Latch Enable Pulse Width ('S557)

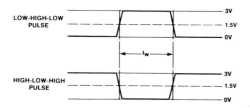

Definition of Timing Diagram

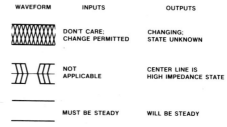

SN54/74S557 SN54/74S558

SUMMARY OF SIGNALS/PINS	
X_7-X_0	Multiplicand 8-bit data inputs
Y_7-Y_0	Multiplier 8-bit data inputs
X_M, Y_M	Mode control inputs for each data word; LOW for unsigned data and HIGH for twos-complement data
S_{15}-S_0	Product 16-bit output
$\overline{S}_{15}$	Inverted MSB for expansion
R_S, R_U	Rounding inputs for signed and unsigned data, respectively ('S558 only)
G	Transparent latch enable ('S557 only)
$\overline{OE}$	Three-state enable for S_{15}-S_0 and $\overline{S}_{15}$ outputs
R	Rounding input for signed or unsigned data; combined internally with X_M, Y_M ('S557 only)

ROUNDING INPUTS
'S557

INPUTS			ADDS	
X_M	Y_M	R	2^7	2^6
L	L	H	YES	NO
L	H	H	NO	YES
H	L	H	NO	YES
H	H	H	NO	YES
X	X	L	NO	NO

'S558

INPUTS		ADDS		USUALLY USED WITH	
R_U	R_S	2^7	2^6	X_M	Y_M
L	L	NO	NO	X	X
L	H	NO	YES	H†	H†
H	L	YES	NO	L	L
H	H	YES	YES	*	*

†In mixed mode, one of these could be Low but not both.
*Usually a nonsense operation. See applications section of data sheet.

74S557 FUNCTION TABLE

INPUTS		PRODUCT RESULT FROM ARRAY	LATCH CONTENTS (INTERNAL TO PART)	OUTPUTS	FUNCTION
$\overline{OE}$	G	T_i	Q_i	S_i	
L	L	X	L	L	Latched
L	L	X	H	H	
L	H	L	(L)*	L	Transparent
L	H	H	(H)*	H	
H	L	X	(L)	Z	Hi-Z; Latched Data not Changed
H	L	X	(H)	Z	
H	H	X	(X)*	Z	Hi-Z

* Identical with product result passing through latch.

MODE CONTROL INPUTS

OPERATING MODE	INPUT DATA		MODE CONTROL INPUTS	
	X_7-X_0	Y_7-Y_0	X_M	Y_M
Unsigned	Unsigned	Unsigned	L	L
Mixed	Unsigned	Twos-Comp.	L	H
	Twos-Comp.	Unsigned	H	L
Signed	Twos-Comp.	Twos-Comp.	H	H

SN54/74S557 SN54/74S558

Functional Description

The 'S557 and 'S558 multipliers are 8x8 combinatorial logic arrays capable of multiplying numbers in unsigned, signed twos-complement, or mixed notation. Each eight-bit input operand X and Y has associated with it a mode control which determines whether the array treats this number as signed or unsigned. If the mode control is at a High logic level, then the operand is treated as a twos-complement number with the most-significant bit having a negative weight; while, if the mode control is at a Low logic level, then the operand is treated as an unsigned number.

The multiplier provides all 16 product bits generated by the multiplication. For expansion during signed or mixed multiplication the most-significant product bit is available in both true and complemented form. This allows an adder to be used as a subtractor in many applications and eliminates the need for certain SSI circuits.

Two additional inputs to the array, R_S and R_U, allow the addition of a bit at the appropriate bit position so as to provide rounding to the best signed or unsigned fractional eight-bit result. These inputs can also be used for rounding in larger multipliers. In the 'S557, these two inputs are generated internally from the mode controls and a single R input.

The product outputs of the multiplier are controlled by an assertive-low Output Enable control. When this control is at a Low logic level the multiplier outputs are active, while if the control is at a High logic level then the outputs are placed in a high-impedance state. This three-state capability allows several multipliers to drive a common bus, and also allows pipelining of multiplication for higher-speed systems.

Rounding

Multiplication of two n-bit operands results in a 2n-bit product†. Therefore, in an n-bit system it is necessary to convert the double-length product into a single-length product. This can be accomplished by truncating or rounding. The following examples illustrate the difference between the two conversion techniques in decimal arithmetic:

$$\begin{matrix} 39.2 \rightarrow 39 \\ 39.6 \rightarrow 39 \end{matrix} \Bigg\} \text{ Truncating}$$

$$\begin{matrix} 39.2 + 0.5 = 39.7 \rightarrow 39 \\ 39.6 + 0.5 = 40.1 \rightarrow 40 \end{matrix} \Bigg\} \text{ Rounding}$$

Obviously, rounding maintains more precision than truncating, but it may take one more step to implement. The additional step involves adding one-half of the weight of the single-length LSB to the MSB of the discarded part; e.g., in decimal arithmetic rounding 39.28 to one decimal point is accomplished by adding 0.05 to the number and truncating the LSB:

$$39.28 + 0.05 = 39.33 \rightarrow 39.3$$

The situation in binary arithmetic is quite similar, but two cases need to be considered; signed and unsigned data representation. In signed multiplication, the two MSBs of the result are identical, except when both operands are –1; therefore, the best single-length product is shifted one position to the right with respect to the unsigned multiplications. Figure 1 illustrates these two cases for the 8x8 multiplier. In the signed case, adding one-half of the S_7 weight is accomplished by adding 1 in bit position 6, and in the unsigned case 1 is added to bit position 7. Therefore, the 'S558 multiplier has two rounding inputs, R_S and R_U. Thus, to get a rounded single-length result, the appropriate R input is tied to V_{CC} (logic High) and the other R input is grounded. If a double-length result is desired, both R inputs are grounded for the 'S558, and the single R input is grounded for the 'S557.

†In general: multiplication of an M-bit operand by an N-bit operand results in an (M + N)-bit product.

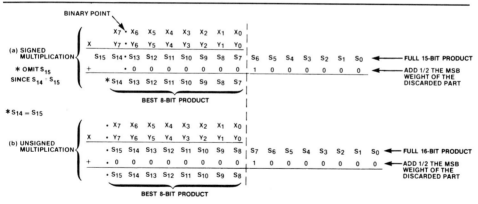

NOTES:

(a) In signed (twos-complement) notation, the MSB of each operand is the sign bit, and the binary point is to the right of the MSB. The resulting product has a redundant sign bit and the binary point is to the right of the second MSB of the product. The best eight-bit product is from S_{14} through S_7, and rounding is performed by adding "1" to bit position S_6.

(b) In unsigned notation the best 8-bit product is the most significant half of the product and is corrected by adding "1" to bit position S_7.

Figure 1. Rounding the Result of Binary Fractional Multiplication.

53/63XX-1

Pin Configurations

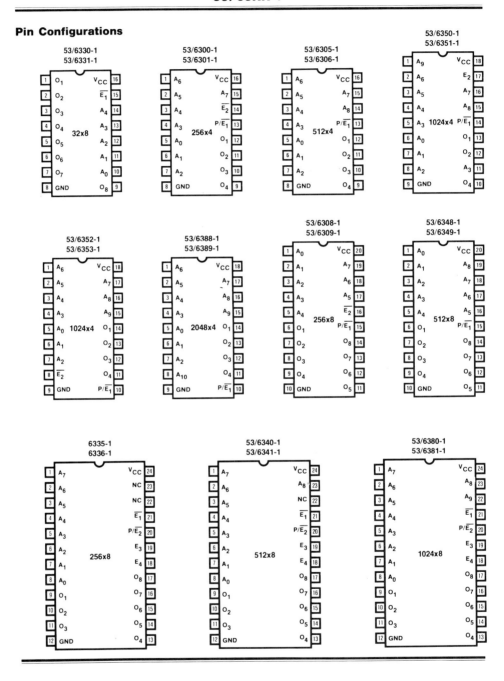

High Performance 1024x8 NiCr PROM
53/6380-2 53/6381-2

Features

- 8192 bit memory
- 55 ns max access time
- Reliability proven NiCr Fusible Links
- Available in 24-pin SKINNYDIP™
- Industry standard pin out

Applications

- Microprogram store
- Program store
- Look up table
- Programmable logic element
- Character generator

Description

The 6380/1-2 is a high speed 1Kx8 PROM which uses industry standard pin out. In addition, the device is available in the 24-pin (0.3 in.) SKINNYDIP™.

The family features low input current PNP inputs, full Schottky clamping, three-state and open collector outputs. The nichrome fuses store a logical high and are programmed to the low state. Special on-chip circuitry and extra fuses provide preprogramming tests which assure high programming yields and high reliability.

The 63 series is specified for operation over the commercial temperature and voltage range. The 53 series is specified for the military ranges.

Programming

This PROM is programmed with the same programming algorithm as all other NiCr PROMs.

Ordering Information

MEMORY		PACKAGE		COMMERCIAL		MILITARY	
SIZE	ORGANIZATION	PINS	TYPE	PART NUMBER	MAX TAA	PART NUMBER	MAX TAA
8K	1Kx8	OC / 24	J, JS	6380-2	70 ns	5380-2	90 ns
		TS		6381-2	55 ns	5381-2	70 ns

Pin Configurations

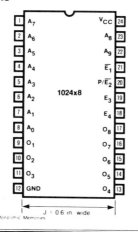

J = 0.6 in. wide

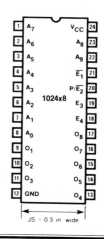

JS = 0.3 in. wide

SKINNYDIP is a registered trademark of Monolithic Memories

53/6380-2 53/6381-2

Absolute Maximum Ratings

Supply voltage, V_{CC} 7V
Input voltage 7V
Off-state output voltage 5.5V
Storage temperature .... –65° to +150°C

Operating Conditions

SYMBOL	PARAMETER	MILITARY			COMMERCIAL			UNIT
		MIN	TYP	MAX	MIN	TYP	MAX	
V_{CC}	Supply voltage	4.5	5	5.5	4.75	5	5.25	V
T_A	Operating free air temperature	–55		125	0		75	°C

Electrical Characteristics Over Operating Conditions

SYMBOL	PARAMETER	TEST CONDITIONS			MIN	TYP†	MAX	UNIT
V_{IL}	Low-level input voltage						0.8	V
V_{IH}	High-level input voltage				2			V
V_{IC}	Input clamp voltage	V_{CC} = MIN	I_I = –18mA				–1.5	V
I_{IL}	Low-level input current	V_{CC} = MAX	V_I = 0.45V				–0.25	mA
I_{IH}	High-level input current	V_{CC} = MAX	V_I = 4.5V (Program pin) V_I = V_{CC} MAX (Other pins)				40	μA
V_{OL}	Low-level output voltage	V_{CC} = MIN V_{IL} = 0.8V V_{IH} = 2V	MIL I_{OL} = 12mA				0.5	V
			COM I_{OL} = 16mA					
V_{OH}	High-level output voltage*	V_{CC} = MIN V_{IL} = 0.8V V_{IH} = 2V	MIL I_{OH} = –2mA		2.4			V
			COM I_{OH} = –3.2mA					
I_{OZL}	Off-state output current*	V_{CC} = MAX	V_O = 0.5V				–40	μA
I_{OZH}			V_O = 2.4V				40	μA
I_{CEX}	Open collector output current	V_{CC} = MAX	V_O = 2.4V				40	μA
			V_O = 5.5V				100	
I_{OS}	Output short-circuit current**	V_{CC} = 5V	V_O = 0V		–20		–90	mA
I_{CC}	Supply current	V_{CC} = MAX	All inputs grounded All outputs open	MIL		120	175	mA
				COM		120	170	

*Three-state only.
**Not more than one output should be shorted at a time and duration of the short-circuit should not exceed one second.
†Typicals at 5.0V V_{CC} and 25°C T_A.

53/6380-2 53/6381-2

Switching Characteristics
Over Operating Conditions

DEVICE TYPE	t_{AA} (ns) ADDRESS ACCESS TIME		t_{EA} AND t_{ER} (ns) ENABLE ACCESS AND RECOVERY TIME		CONDITIONS (See standard test load)	
	TYP†	MAX	TYP	MAX	R1(Ω)	R2(Ω)
6380-2	49	70	19	30		
6381-2	45	55	19	30	300	600
5380-2	49	90	19	40		
5381-2	45	70	19	40		

†Typicals at 5.0V V_{CC} and 25°C T_A

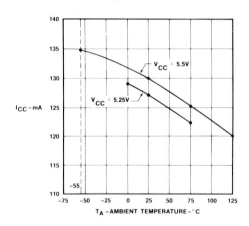

Typical I_{CC} vs Temperature

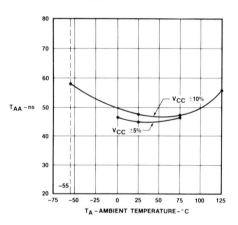

Typical T_{AA} vs Temperature

High Performance Registered 1024x4 PROM
53/63RA441

Features/Benefits

- Edge triggered "D" registers
- Advanced Schottky processing
- 4-bit-wide in 18 pin for high board density
- Lower system package counts
- Lower system power
- Faster cycle times
- 16mA I_{OL} output drive capability

Applications

- Pipelined microprogramming
- State sequencers
- Next address generation
- Mapping PROM

Description

A family of registered PROMs offers new savings for designers of pipelined microprogrammable systems. The wide instruction register which holds the microinstruction during execution, is now incorporated into the PROM chip.

Ordering Information

MEMORY		PACKAGE		DEVICE TYPE	
SIZE	ORGANIZATION	PINS	TYPE	MIL	COM
4K	1024x4	18	J, N	53RA441	63RA441

Edge Triggered Register

The PROM output is loaded into a 4-bit register on the rising edge of the clock. The use of the term "register" is to be distinguished from the term "latch," in that a register contains master slave flip-flops and the latch contains gated flip-flops. The advantages of using a register are that system timing is simplified, and faster micro cycle times can be obtained.

The output of the register is buffered by three-state drivers which are compatible with the new low-power Schottky three-state bus standard.

Pin Configuration

53/63RA441

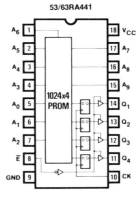

53/63RA441

Absolute Maximum Ratings

Supply voltage, V_{CC} 7V
Input voltage 7V
Off-state output voltage 5.5V
Storage temperature .... –65° to +150°C

Operating Conditions

SYMBOL	PARAMETER	MILITARY			COMMERCIAL			UNIT
		MIN	TYP	MAX	MIN	TYP	MAX	
V_{CC}	Supply voltage	4.5	5	5.5	4.75	5	5.25	V
t_{su}	Address set-up time	60	30		50	30		
t_h	Address hold time	0	–10		0	–10		
t_w	Clock pulse width	25	8		20	8		
T_A	Operating free-air temperature	–55		125	0		75	°C

Electrical Characteristics Over Operating Conditions

SYMBOL	PARAMETER	TEST CONDITIONS			MIN	TYP†	MAX	UNIT
V_{IL}	Low-level input voltage						0.8	V
V_{IH}	High-level input voltage				2			V
V_{IC}	Input clamp voltage	V_{CC} = MIN	I_I = –18mA				–1.5	V
I_{IL}	Low-level input current	V_{CC} = MAX	V_I = 0.4V				–0.25	mA
I_{IH}	High-level input current	V_{CC} = MAX	V_I = V_{CC}				40	µA
V_{OL}	Low-level output voltage	V_{CC} = MIN V_{IL} = 0.8V V_{IH} = 2V	I_{OL} = 16mA				0.5	V
V_{OH}	High-level output voltage	V_{CC} = MIN V_{IL} = 0.8V V_{IH} = 2V	MIL I_{OH} = –2mA		2.4			V
			COM I_{OH} = –3.2mA					
I_{OZL}	Off-state output current	V_{CC} = MAX	V_O = 0.5V				–40	µA
I_{OZH}			V_O = 2.4V				40	µA
I_{OS}	Output short-circuit current*	V_{CC} = 5V	V_O = 0V		–20		–90	mA
I_{CC}	Supply current	V_{CC} = MAX	All inputs grounded	MIL		120	175	mA
			All outputs open	COM		120	165	

* Not more than one output should be shorted at a time and duration of the short-circuit should not exceed one second.
† Typicals at 5.0V V_{CC} and 25°C T_A

Switching Characteristics
Over Operating Conditions

SYMBOL	PARAMETER	MILITARY			COMMERCIAL			UNIT
		MIN	TYP†	MAX	MIN	TYP†	MAX	
t_{pd}	Clock to output access time		20	35		20	30	
t_{ER}/t_{EA}	Enable to output access and recovery time		19	35		19	30	

Octal Buffers

SN54/74LS210 SN54/74S210
SN54/74LS240 SN54/74S240
SN54/74LS241 SN54/74S241
SN54/74LS244 SN54/74S244

Features/Benefits

- Three-state outputs drive bus lines

- Low current PNP inputs reduce loading

- 20-pin SKINNYDIP® saves space

- 8 bits matches byte boundaries

- Ideal for microprocessor interface

- Complementary-enable '210 and '241 types combine multiplexer and driver functions

Description

These octal buffers provide high speed and high current interface capability for bus organized digital systems. The three-state drivers will source a termination to ground (up to 133Ω) or sink a pull-up to V_{CC} as in the popular 220Ω/330Ω computer peripheral termination. The PNP inputs provide improved fan-in with 0.2 mA I_{IL} on the low-power Schottky buffers and 0.4 mA I_{IL} on the Schottky buffers.

The '240 and '244 provide inverting and non-inverting outputs respectively with assertive low enables. The '210 and '241 also provide inverting and non-inverting outputs respectively, but with complementary (both assertive-low and assertive-high) enables, to allow transceive or multiplexer operation.

All of the octal devices are packaged in the popular 20-pin SKINNYDIP®

Ordering Information

PART NUMBER	PKG	TEMP.	ENABLE	POLARITY	POWER
SN54LS210 SN74LS210	J,F N,J	mil com	HIGH- LOW	Invert	LS
SN54LS240 SN74LS240	J,F N,J	mil com	LOW		
SN54LS241 SN74LS241	J,F N,J	mil com	HIGH- LOW	Non- invert	
SN54LS244 SN74LS244	J,F N,J	mil com	LOW		
SN54S210 SN74S210	J,F N,J	mil com	HIGH- LOW	Invert	S
SN54S240 SN74S240	J,F N,J	mil com	LOW		
SN54S241 SN74S241	J,F N,J	mil com	HIGH- LOW	Non- Invert	
SN54S244 SN74S244	J,F N,J	mil com	LOW		

Logic Symbols

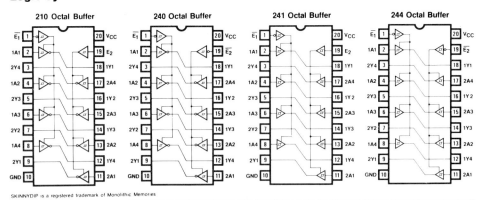

| 210 Octal Buffer | 240 Octal Buffer | 241 Octal Buffer | 244 Octal Buffer |

SKINNYDIP is a registered trademark of Monolithic Memories

SN54/74LS210 SN54/74LS240 SN54/74LS241 SN54/74LS244

Absolute Maximum Ratings

Supply Voltage V_{CC} 7V
Input Voltage 7V
Off-state output voltage 5.5V
Storage temperature .... $-65°$ to $+150°$C

Operating Conditions

SYMBOL	PARAMETER	MILITARY			COMMERCIAL			UNIT
		MIN	TYP	MAX	MIN	TYP	MAX	
V_{CC}	Supply voltage	4.5	5	5.5	4.75	5	5.25	V
T_A	Operating free-air temperature	-55		125	0		75	°C

Electrical Characteristics Over Operating Conditions

SYMBOL	PARAMETER	TEST CONDITIONS		MILITARY			COMMERCIAL			UNIT
				MIN	TYP	MAX	MIN	TYP	MAX	
V_{IL}	Low-level input voltage					0.7			0.8	V
V_{IH}	High-level input voltage			2			2			V
V_{IC}	Input clamp voltage	V_{CC} = MIN,	I_I = -18mA			-1.5			-1.5	V
ΔV_T	Hysteresis $(V_{T_+} - V_{T_-})$	V_{CC} = MIN		0.2	0.4		0.2	0.4		V
I_{IL}	Low-level input current	V_{CC} = MAX,	V_I = 0.4V			-0.2			-0.2	mA
I_{IH}	High-level input current	V_{CC} = MAX,	V_I = 2.7V			20			20	μA
I_I	Maximum input current	V_{CC} = MAX,	V_I = 7V			0.1			0.1	mA
V_{OL}	Low-level output voltage	V_{CC} = MIN, V_{IL} = MAX, V_{IH} = 2V	I_{OL} = 12mA			0.4			0.4	V
			I_{OL} = 24mA						0.5	
V_{OH}	High-level output voltage	V_{CC} = MIN, V_{IL} = 0.5V, V_{IH} = 2V	I_{OH} = -3mA	2.4	3.4		2.4	3.4		V
			I_{OH} = -12mA	2						
			I_{OH} = -15mA				2			
I_{OZL}	Off-state output current	V_{CC} = MAX, V_{IL} = MAX, V_{IH} = 2V	V_O = 0.4V			-20			-20	μA
I_{OZH}			V_O = 2.7V			20			20	μA
I_{OS}	Output short-circuit current *	V_{CC} = MAX		-40		-225	-40		-225	mA
I_{CC}	Supply Current	Outputs High	V_{CC} = MAX. Outputs open	LS210, LS240		17	27		17	27	mA
				LS241, LS244		17	27		17	27	
		Outputs Low		LS210, LS240		26	44		26	44	
				LS241, LS244		27	46		27	46	
		Outputs Disabled		LS210, LS240		29	50		29	50	
				LS241, LS244		32	54		32	54	

* Not more than one output should be shorted at a time and duration of the short-circuit should not exceed one second.

Switching Characteristics V_{CC} = 5 V, T_A = 25°C

SYMBOL	PARAMETER	TEST CONDITIONS (See Interface Test Load/Waveforms)	LS210, LS240			LS241, LS244			UNIT
			MIN	TYP	MAX	MIN	TYP	MAX	
t_{PLH}	Data to Output delay	C_L = 45pF R_L = 667Ω		9	14		12	18	ns
t_{PHL}				12	18		12	18	ns
t_{PZL}	Output Enable delay			20	30		20	30	ns
t_{PZH}				15	23		15	23	ns
t_{PLZ}	Output Disable delay	C_L = 5pF R_L = 667Ω		15	25		15	25	ns
t_{PHZ}				10	18		10	18	ns

SN54/74S210 SN54/74S240 SN54/74S241 SN54/74S244

Absolute Maximum Ratings

Supply Voltage V_{CC} 7V
Input Voltage 5.5V
Off-state output voltage 5.5V
Storage temperature .... -65° to +150°C

Operating Conditions

SYMBOL	PARAMETER	MILITARY			COMMERCIAL			UNIT
		MIN	TYP	MAX	MIN	TYP	MAX	
V_{CC}	Supply voltage	4.5	5	5.5	4.75	5	5.25	V
T_A	Operating free-air temperature	-55		125 *	0		75	°C

* The SN54S241/244J operating at free air temperature above 116°C requires a heat sink such that $R_{\theta CA}$ is not more than 40°C/W.

Electrical Characteristics Over Operating Conditions

SYMBOL	PARAMETER		TEST CONDITIONS		MILITARY			COMMERCIAL			UNIT
					MIN	TYP	MAX	MIN	TYP	MAX	
V_{IL}	Low-level input voltage						0.8			0.8	V
V_{IH}	High-level input voltage				2			2			V
V_{IC}	Input clamp voltage		V_{CC} = MIN	I_I = −18mA			−1.2			−1.2	V
ΔV_T	Hysteresis $(V_{T_+} - V_{T_-})$		V_{CC} = MIN		0.2	0.4		0.2	0.4		V
I_{IL}	Low-level input current	Any A	V_{CC} = MAX	V_I = 0.5V			−0.4			−0.4	mA
		Any E					−2			−2	
I_{IH}	High-level input current		V_{CC} = MAX	V_I = 2.7V			50			50	µA
I_I	Maximum input current		V_{CC} = MAX	V_I = 5.5V			1			1	mA
V_{OL}	Low-level output voltage		V_{CC} = MIN V_{IL} = 0.8V V_{IH} = 2V	I_{OL} = 48mA			0.55				V
				I_{OL} = 64mA						0.55	
V_{OH}	High-level output voltage		V_{CC} = MIN V_{IL} = 0.8V V_{IH} = 2V	I_{OH} = −1mA				2.7			V
				I_{OH} = −3mA	2.4	3.4		2.4	3.4		
				I_{OH} = −12mA	2						
				I_{OH} = −15mA				2			
I_{OZL}	Off-state output current		V_{CC} = MAX V_{IL} = 0.8V	V_O = 0.5V			−50			−50	µA
I_{OZH}			V_{IH} = 2V	V_O = 2.4V			50			50	µA
I_{OS}	Output short-circuit current †		V_{CC} = MAX		−50		−225	−50		−225	mA
I_{CC}	Supply Current	Outputs High	V_{CC} = MAX Outputs open	S210,S240		80	123		80	135	mA
				S241,S244		95	147		95	160	
		Outputs Low		S210,S240		100	145		100	150	
				S241,S244		120	170		120	180	
		Outputs Disabled		S210,S240		100	145		100	150	
				S241,S244		120	170		120	180	

† Not more than one output should be shorted at a time and duration of the short-circuit should not exceed one second.

Switching Characteristics V_{CC} = 5 V, T_A = 25°C

SYMBOL	PARAMETER	TEST CONDITIONS (See Interface Test Load/Waveforms)		S210, S240		S241, S244		UNIT
				MIN TYP	MAX	MIN TYP	MAX	
t_{PLH}	Data to Output delay	C_L = 50pF R_L = 90Ω		4.5	7	6	9	ns
t_{PHL}				4.5	7	6	9	ns
t_{PZL}	Output Enable delay			10	15	10	15	ns
t_{PZH}			S210	6.5	12	8	12	ns
			S240		10			ns
t_{PLZ}	Output Disable delay	C_L = 5pF R_L = 90Ω		10	15	10	15	ns
t_{PHZ}				6	9	6	9	ns

Octal Transceiver
SN54/74LS245

Features/Benefits

- 3-state outputs drive bus lines

- Low current PNP inputs reduce loading

- Symmetric -- equal driving capability in each direction

- 20-pin SKINNYDIP® saves space

- 8 bits matches byte boundaries

- Ideal for microprocessor interface

- Pin-compatible with SN54/74LS645 -- improved speed, I_{IL} and I_{OZL} specifications

Ordering Information

PART NUMBER	TYPE	TEMP	POLARITY	POWER
SN54LS245	J, F	mil	Non-invert	LS
SN74LS245	N,J	com		

Description

These octal bus transceivers are designed for asynchronous two-way communication between data buses. The control function implementation minimizes external timing requirements.

The device allows data transmission from the A bus to the B bus or from the B bus to the A bus depending upon the logic level at the direction control (DIR) input. The enable input (Ē) can be used to disable the device so that the buses are effectively isolated. All of the octal devices are packaged in the popular 20-pin SKINNYDIP®.

Function Table

ENABLE Ē	DIRECTION CONTROL DIR	OPERATION
L	L	B data to A bus
L	H	A data to B bus
H	X	Isolated

Logic Symbol

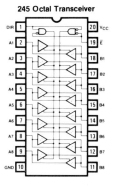

245 Octal Transceiver

SN54/74LS245

Absolute Maximum Ratings

Supply Voltage VCC 7V
Input Voltage 7V
Off-state output voltage 5.5V
Storage temperature .... -65° to +150°C

Operating Conditions

SYMBOL	PARAMETER	MILITARY			COMMERCIAL			UNIT
		MIN	TYP	MAX	MIN	TYP	MAX	
V_{CC}	Supply voltage	4.5	5	5.5	4.75	5	5.25	V
T_A	Operating free-air temperature	-55		125	0		75	°C

Electrical Characteristics Over Operating Conditions

SYMBOL	PARAMETER		TEST CONDITIONS		MILITARY			COMMERCIAL			UNIT
					MIN	TYP	MAX	MIN	TYP	MAX	
V_{IL}	Low-level input voltage						0.7			0.8	V
V_{IH}	High-level input voltage				2			2			V
V_{IC}	Input clamp voltage		V_{CC} = MIN.	I_I = -18mA			-1.5			-1.5	V
ΔV_T	Hysteresis $(V_{T_+} - V_{T_-})$ A or B		V_{CC} = MIN		0.2	0.4		0.2	0.4		V
I_{IL}	Low-level input current		V_{CC} = MAX.	V_I = 0.4V			-0.2			-0.2	mA
I_{IH}	High-level input current		V_{CC} = MAX.	V_I = 2.7V			20			20	μA
I_I	Maximum input current	A or B	V_{CC} = MAX,	V_I = 5.5V			0.1			0.1	mA
		DIR or $\bar{E}$		V_I = 7.0V			0.1			0.1	
V_{OL}	Low-level output voltage		V_{CC} = MIN, V_{IL} = MAX, V_{IH} = 2V	I_{OL} = 12mA		0.25	0.4		0.25	0.4	V
				I_{OL} = 24mA					0.35	0.5	
V_{OH}	High-level output voltage		V_{CC} = MIN, V_{IL} = MAX, V_{IH} = 2V	I_{OH} = -3mA	2.4	3.4		2.4	3.4		V
				I_{OH} = -12mA	2			2			
				I_{OH} = -15mA				2			
I_{OZL}	Off-state output current		V_{CC} = MAX, V_{IL} = MAX, V_{IH} = 2V	V_O = 0.4V			-200			-200	μA
I_{OZH}				V_O = 2.7V			10			10	μA
I_{OS}	Output short-circuit current *		V_{CC} = MAX		-40		-225	-40		-225	mA
I_{CC}	Supply Current	Outputs High	V_{CC} = MAX, Outputs open			48	70		48	70	mA
		Outputs Low				62	90		62	90	
		Outputs Disabled				64	95		64	95	

* Not more than one output should be shorted at a time and duration of the short-circuit should not exceed one second

Switching Characteristics VCC = 5 V, TA = 25°C

SYMBOL	PARAMETER	TEST CONDITIONS (See Interface Test Load/Waveforms)	A to B DIRECTION			B to A DIRECTION			UNIT
			MIN	TYP	MAX	MIN	TYP	MAX	
t_{PLH}	Data to Output delay	C_L = 45pF R_L = 667Ω		8	12		8	12	ns
t_{PHL}				8	12		8	12	ns
t_{PZL}	Output Enable delay			27	40		27	40	ns
t_{PZH}				25	40		25	40	ns
t_{PLZ}	Output Disable delay	C_L = 5pF R_L = 667Ω		15	25		15	25	ns
t_{PHZ}				15	25		15	25	ns

Octal Latches, Octal Registers
SN54/74LS373   SN54/74S373
SN54/74LS374   SN54/74S374

Features/Benefits

- 3-state outputs drive bus lines
- 20-pin SKINNYDIP® saves space
- 8 bits matches byte boundaries
- Hysteresis improves noise margin
- Low current PNP inputs reduce loading
- Ideal for microprocessor interface

Ordering Information

PART NUMBER	PKG	TEMP	POLARITY	TYPE	POWER
SN54LS373	J,F	mil		Latch	
SN74LS373	N,J	com			LS
SN54LS374	J,F	mil	Non-invert	Register	
SN74LS374	N,J	com			
SN54S373	J,F	mil		Latch	
SN74S373	N,J	com			S
SN54S374	J,F	mil		Register	
SN74S374	N,J	com			

Description

The latch passes eight (octal) bits of data from the inputs (D) to the outputs (Q) when the gate (G) is high. The data is "latched" when the gate (G) goes low. The register loads eight (octal) bits of input data and passes it to the output on the "rising edge" of the clock.[1]

The three-state outputs are active when $\overline{OE}$ is low, and high-impedance when $\overline{OE}$ is high. Schmitt-trigger buffers at the gate/clock inputs improve system noise margin by providing typically 400 mV of hysteresis.

All of the octal devices are packaged in the popular 20-pin SKINNYDIP®.

Function Tables

373 Octal Latch

$\overline{OE}$	G	D	Q
L	H	H	H
L	H	L	L
L	L	X	Q_0
H	X	X	Z

374 Octal Register

$\overline{OE}$	CK	D	Q
L	↑	H	H
L	↑	L	L
L	L	X	Q_0
H	X	X	Z

Logic Symbols

373 Octal Latch

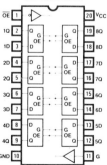

374 Octal Register

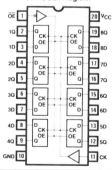

SN54/74LS373   SN54/74LS374

Absolute Maximum Ratings

Supply Voltage, VCC 7V
Input Voltage 7V
Off-state output voltage 5.5V
Storage temperature .... −65° to +150°C

Operating Conditions

SYMBOL	PARAMETER		MILITARY			COMMERCIAL			UNIT
			MIN	TYP	MAX	MIN	TYP	MAX	
V_{CC}	Supply voltage		4.5	5	5.5	4.75	5	5.25	V
T_A	Operating free air temperature		−55		125	0		75	°C
t_w	Width of Clock/Gate	High	15			15			ns
		Low	15			15			
t_{su}	Setup time		0↓			20↑			ns
t_h	Hold time		10↓			0↑			ns

Electrical Characteristics Over Operating Conditions

SYMBOL	PARAMETER	TEST CONDITIONS		MILITARY			COMMERCIAL			UNIT
				MIN	TYP	MAX	MIN	TYP	MAX	
V_{IL}	Low-level input voltage					0.7			0.8	V
V_{IH}	High-level input voltage			2			2			V
V_{IC}	Input clamp voltage	V_{CC} = MIN	I_I = −18mA			−1.5			−1.5	V
I_{IL}	Low-level input current	V_{CC} = MAX	V_I = 0.4V			−0.4			−0.4	mA
I_{IH}	High-level input current	V_{CC} = MAX	V_I = 2.7V			20			20	µA
I_I	Maximum input current	V_{CC} = MAX	V_I = 7V			0.1			0.1	mA
V_{OL}	Low-level output voltage	V_{CC} = MIN V_{IL} = MAX V_{IH} = 2V	I_{OL} = 12mA		0.25	0.4		0.25	0.4	V
			I_{OL} = 24mA					0.35	0.5	
V_{OH}	High-level output voltage	V_{CC} = MIN V_{IL} = MAX V_{IH} = 2V	I_{OH} = −1mA	2.4	3.4					V
			I_{OH} = −2.6mA				2.4	3.1		
I_{OZL}	Off-state output current	V_{CC} = MAX V_{IL} = MAX V_{IH} = 2V	V_O = 0.4V			−20			−20	µA
I_{OZH}			V_O = 2.7V			20			20	µA
I_{OS}	Output short-circuit current *	V_{CC} = MAX		−30		−130	−30		−130	mA
I_{CC}	Supply current	V_{CC} = MAX Outputs open	LS373		24	40		24	40	mA
			LS374		27	40		27	40	

* Not more than one output should be shorted at a time and duration of the short-circuit should not exceed one second

Switching Charcteristics V_{CC} = 5 V, T_A = 25°C

SYMBOL	PARAMETER	TEST CONDITIONS (See Interface Test Load/Waveforms)	LS373 MIN TYP MAX			LS374 MIN TYP MAX			UNIT
f_{MAX}	Maximum Clock frequency					35	50		MHz
t_{PLH}	Data to Output delay			12	18				ns
t_{PHL}				12	18				ns
t_{PLH}	Clock/Enable to output delay	C_L = 45pF R_L = 667Ω		20	30		15	28	ns
t_{PHL}				18	30		19	28	ns
t_{PZL}	Output Enable delay			25	36		21	28	ns
t_{PZH}				15	28		20	28	ns
t_{PLZ}	Output Disable delay	C_L = 5pF R_L = 667Ω		15	25		14	25	ns
t_{PHZ}				12	20		12	20	ns

SN54/74S373   SN54/74S374

Absolute Maximum Ratings

Supply Voltage, V_{CC} 7V
Input Voltage 5.5V
Off-state output voltage 5.5V
Storage temperature .... $-65°$ to $+150°C$

Operating Conditions

SYMBOL	PARAMETER	TEST CONDITIONS	MILITARY			COMMERCIAL			UNIT
			MIN	TYP	MAX	MIN	TYP	MAX	
V_{CC}	Supply voltage		4.5	5	5.5	4.75	5	5.25	V
T_A	Operating free air temperature		-55		125	0		75	$°C$
t_w	Width of Clock/Gate	High	6			6			ns
		Low	7.3			7.3			
t_{su}	Set up time	S373	0↓			0↓			ns
		S374	5↑			5↑			
t_h	Hold time	S373	10↓			10↓			ns
		S374	2↑			2↑			

Electrical Characteristics Over Operating Conditions

SYMBOL	PARAMETER	TEST CONDITIONS		MILITARY			COMMERCIAL			UNIT
				MIN	TYP	MAX	MIN	TYP	MAX	
V_{IL}	Low-level input voltage					0.8			0.8	V
V_{IH}	High-level input voltage			2			2			V
V_{IC}	Input clamp voltage	V_{CC} = MIN	I_I = -18mA			-1.2			-1.2	V
I_{IL}	Low-level input current	V_{CC} = MAX	V_I = 0.5V			-0.25			-0.25	mA
I_{IH}	High-level input current	V_{CC} = MAX	V_I = 2.7V			50			50	μA
I_I	Maximum input current	V_{CC} = MAX	V_I = 5.5V			1			1	mA
V_{OL}	Low-level output voltage	V_{CC} = MIN V_{IL} = 0.8V V_{IH} = 2V	I_{OL} = 20mA			0.5			0.5	V
V_{OH}	High-level output voltage	V_{CC} = MIN V_{IL} = 0.8V V_{IH} = 2V	I_{OH} = -2mA	2.4	3.4					V
			I_{OH} = -6.5mA				2.4	3.1		
I_{OZL}	Off-state output current	V_{CC} = MAX V_{IL} = 0.8V V_{IH} = 2V	V_O = 0.5V			-50			-50	μA
I_{OZH}			V_O = 2.4V			50			50	μA
I_{OS}	Output short-circuit current*	V_{CC} = MAX		-40		-100	-40		-100	mA
I_{CC}	Supply current	V_{CC} = MAX Outputs open	S373		105	160		105	160	mA
			S374		90	140		90	140	

* Not more than one output should be shorted at a time and duration of the short-circuit should not exceed one second.

Switching Characteristics V_{CC} = 5 V, T_A = 25°C

SYMBOL	PARAMETER	TEST CONDITIONS (See Interface Test Load/Waveforms)	S373			S374			UNIT
			MIN	TYP	MAX	MIN	TYP	MAX	
f_{MAX}	Maximum Clock frequency					75	100		MHz
t_{PLH}	Data to Output delay			7	12				ns
t_{PHL}		C_L = 15pF R_L = 280Ω		7	12				ns
t_{PLH}	Clock/Enable to output delay			7	14		8	15	ns
t_{PHL}				12	18		11	17	ns
t_{PZL}	Output Enable delay			11	18		11	18	ns
t_{PZH}				8	15		8	15	ns
t_{PLZ}	Output Disable delay	C_L = 5pF R_L = 280Ω		8	12		7	12	ns
t_{PHZ}				6	9		5	9	ns

INTRODUCTION TO PAL

The PAL family, [BIR 82], is similar to PLA except that in addition to AND-OR combinatorial functions, it can also implement sequential functions since it incorporates edge-triggered registers with internal feedback.

The best way to become familiar with PAL is to look through the combinatorial and sequential design examples in this section.

The following section is organized as follows:

- PAL Introduction

- PAL Legend

- Design Examples:

    Basic Gates

    Quad 4:1 MUX

    ALU Accumulator

    Octal Shift Register

    Binary to BCD Converter

- Data Sheet

- Logic Diagrams

PAL Introduction

PAL Input/Output/Function Chart

PART NUMBER	INPUT	OUTPUT	PROGRAMMABLE I/O'S	FEEDBACK REGISTER	OUTPUT POLARITY	FUNCTIONS	T_{PD} ns, TYP	I_{OL} mA	I_{CC} mA, TYP
PAL10H8	10	8			AND-OR	AND-OR Gate Array	25	8	55
PAL12H6	12	6			AND-OR	AND-OR Gate Array	25	8	55
PAL14H4	14	4			AND-OR	AND-OR Gate Array	25	8	55
PAL16H2	16	2			AND-OR	AND-OR Gate Array	25	8	55
PAL16C1	16	2			BOTH	AND-OR Gate Array	25	8	55
PAL20C1	20	2			BOTH	AND-OR Gate Array	25	8	60
PAL10L8	10	8			AND-NOR	AND-OR Invert Gate Array	25	8	55
PAL12L6	12	6			AND-NOR	AND-OR Invert Gate Array	25	8	55
PAL14L4	14	4			AND-NOR	AND-OR Invert Gate Array	25	8	55
PAL16L2	16	2			AND-NOR	AND-OR Invert Gate Array	25	8	55
PAL12L10	12	10			AND-NOR	AND-OR Invert Gate Array	25	8	60
PAL14L8	14	8			AND-NOR	AND-OR Invert Gate Array	25	8	60
PAL16L6	16	6			AND-NOR	AND-OR Invert Gate Array	25	8	60
PAL18L4	18	4			AND-NOR	AND-OR Invert Gate Array	25	8	60
PAL20L2	20	2			AND-NOR	AND-OR Invert Gate Array	25	8	60
PAL16L8	10	2	6		AND-NOR	AND-OR Invert Gate Array	25	24	120
PAL20L10	12	2	8		AND-NOR	AND-OR Invert Gate Array	35	24	90
PAL16R8	8	8		8	AND-NOR	AND-OR Invert Array w/Reg's	25	24	120
PAL16R6	8	6	2	6	AND-NOR	AND-OR Invert Array w/Reg's	25	24	120
PAL16R4	8	4	4	4	AND-NOR	AND-OR Invert Array w/Reg's	25	24	120
PAL20X10	10	10		10	AND-NOR	AND-OR-XOR Invert w/Reg's	35	24	120
PAL20X8	10	8	2	8	AND-NOR	AND-OR-XOR Invert w/Reg's	35	24	120
PAL20X4	10	4	6	4	AND-NOR	AND-OR-XOR Invert w/Reg's	35	24	120
PAL16X4	8	4	4	4	AND-NOR	AND-OR-XOR Invert w/Reg's	25	24	160
PAL16A4	8	4	4	4	AND-NOR	AND-CARRY-OR-XOR Invert w/Reg's	25	24	170

[1]Simultaneous AND-OR and AND-NOR outputs   Table 2

PALs For Every Task

The members of the PAL family and their characteristics are summarized in Table 2. They are designed to cover the spectrum of logic functions at reduced cost and lower package count. This allows the designer to select the PAL that best fits his application. PALs come in the following basic configurations:

Gate Arrays

PAL gate arrays are available in sizes from 12x10 (12 input terms, 10 output terms) to 20x2, with both active high and active low output configurations available. This wide variety of input/output formats allows the PAL to replace many different sized blocks of combinatorial logic with single packages.

Programmable I/O

A feature of the high-end members of the PAL family is programmable input/output. This allows the product terms to directly control the outputs of the PAL (Figure 9). One product term is used to enable the three-state buffer, which in turn gates the summation term to the output pin. The output is also fed back into the PAL array as an input. Thus the PAL drives the I/O pin when the three-state gate is enabled; the I/O pin is an input to the PAL array when the three-state gate is disabled. This feature can be used to allocate available pins for I/O functions or to provide bi-directional output pins for operations such as shifting and rotating serial data.

INPUTS, FEEDBACK AND I/O

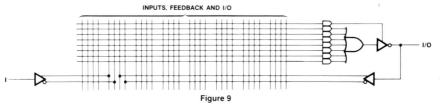

Figure 9

PAL Introduction

Registered Outputs with Feedback

Another feature of the high end members of the PAL family is registered data outputs with register feedback. Each product term is stored into a D-type output flip-flop on the rising edge of the system clock (Figure 10). The Q output of the flip-flop can then be gated to the output pin by enabling the active low three-state buffer.

In addition to being available for transmission, the Q output is fed back into the PAL array as an input term. This feedback allows the PAL to "remember" the previous state, and it can alter its function based upon that state. This allows the designer to configure the PAL as a state sequencer which can be programmed to execute such elementary functions as count up, count down, skip, shift, and branch. These functions can be executed by the registered PAL at rates of up to 20 MHz.

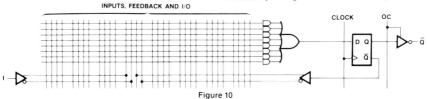

Figure 10

XOR PALs

These PALs feature an exclusive OR function. The sum of products is segmented into two sums which are then exclusive ORed (XOR) at the input of the D-type flip-flop. All of the

features of the Registered PALs are included in the XOR PALs. The XOR function provides an easy implementation of the HOLD operation used in counters.

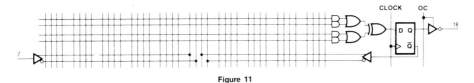

Figure 11

Arithmetic Gated Feedback

The arithmetic functions add, subtract, greater than, and less than are implemented by addition of gated feedback to the features of the XOR PALs. The XOR at the input of the D-type flip-flop allows carrys from previous operations to be XORed with two variable sums generated by the PAL array. The flip-flop

Q output is fed back to be gated with input terms I. This gated feedback provides any one of the 16 possible Boolean combinations which are mapped in the Karnaugh map (figure 14). Figure 13 shows how the PAL array can be programmed to perform these 16 operations. These features provide for versatile operations on two variables and facilitate the parallel generation of carrys necessary for fast arithmetic operations.

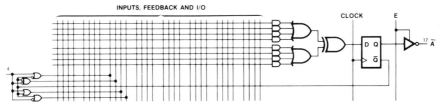

Figure 12

PAL Concepts

PAL Legend

Constants							
	LOW (L)	NEGATIVE (N)	ZERO (0)	GND	FALSE	×	FUSE NOT BLOWN
	HIGH (H)	POSITIVE (P)	ONE (1)	V_{CC}	TRUE	–	FUSE BLOWN

Operators	
(IN HIERARCHY OF EVALUATION)	; COMMENT FOLLOWS
	/ COMPLEMENT, PREFIX TO A PIN NAME
	* AND (PRODUCT)
	+ OR (SUM)
	:+: XOR (EXCLUSIVE OR)
	:*: XNOR (EXCLUSIVE NOR)
	( ) CONDITIONAL THREE-STATE (IF STATEMENT) OR FIXED SYMBOL
	= EQUALITY
	:= REPLACED BY AFTER THE LOW TO HIGH TRANSITION OF THE CLOCK

Equations		
	Standard $O_1 = I_1 \overline{I_2} + \overline{I_1} I_2$	PALASM O1 = I1*/I2 + /I1*I2

Function Table States		
H = HIGH LEVEL		C = TRANSITION FROM LOW TO HIGH
L = LOW LEVEL		Z = OFF (HIGH IMPEDANCE)
X = IRRELEVANT		

Test Conditions		
H = TEST HIGH	1 = DRIVE HIGH	C = DRIVE INPUT FROM LOW TO HIGH
L = TEST LOW	0 = DRIVE LOW	Z = TEST FOR HIGH IMPEDANCE
X = IRRELEVANT		

Conventional Symbology

PAL Symbology

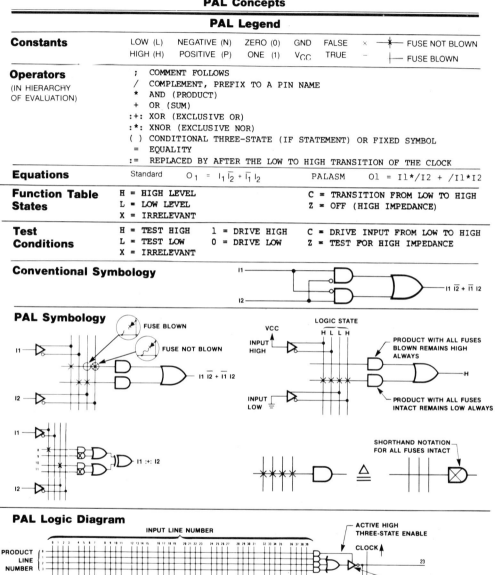

PAL Logic Diagram

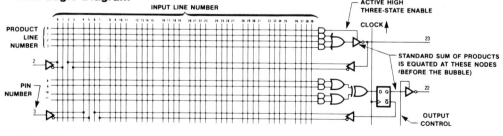

Basic Gates

PAL12H6   PAL DESIGN SPECIFICATION
BGATES   VINCENT COLI 06/12/81
BASIC GATES
MMI SUNNYVALE, CALIFORNIA
C D F G M N P Q I GND J K L R O H E B A VCC

B = /A   ; INVERTER   A ———|>o——— B

E = C*D   ; AND GATE   C —| \   C —| \o
                                                  D —| /— E   D —| /——— E

H = F + G   ; OR GATE   F —| \   F —| \o
                                                  G —| /— H   G —| /——— H

L = /I + /J + /K   ; NAND GATE   I   I
                                                  J —| \o— L   J —| \o——— L
                                                  K   K

O = /M*/N   ; NOR GATE   M —| \o   M —| \o
                                                  N —| /— O   N —| /——— O

R = P*/Q + /P*Q   ; EXCLUSIVE OR GATE   P —| \   P
                                                  Q —|))— R   Q   R

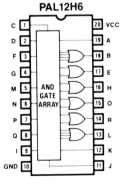

PAL12H6

Basic Gates

Basic Gates

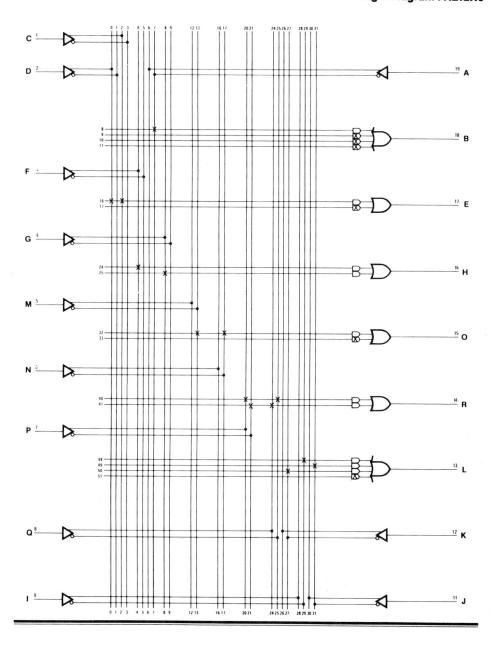

Quad 4:1 Mux

```
PAL18L4                                         PAL DESIGN SPECIFICATION
74LS453                                         BIRKNER/KAZMI/BLASCO 03/10/81
QUAD 4:1 MULTIPLEXER
MMI SUNNYVALE, CALIFORNIA
1C0 1C1 1C2 1C3 2C0 2C1 2C2 2C3 3C0 3C1 3C2 GND
3C3 4C0 4C1 4C2  4Y  3Y  2Y  1Y 4C3  B   A  VCC


/1Y  =  /B*/A * /1C0                      ;SELECT INPUT 1C0
     +  /B* A * /1C1                      ;SELECT INPUT 1C1
     +   B*/A * /1C2                      ;SELECT INPUT 1C2
     +   B* A * /1C3                      ;SELECT INPUT 1C3

/2Y  =  /B*/A * /2C0                      ;SELECT INPUT 2C0
     +  /B* A * /2C1                      ;SELECT INPUT 2C1
     +   B*/A * /2C2                      ;SELECT INPUT 2C2
     +   B* A * /2C3                      ;SELECT INPUT 2C3

/3Y  =  /B*/A * /3C0                      ;SELECT INPUT 3C0
     +  /B* A * /3C1                      ;SELECT INPUT 3C1
     +   B*/A * /3C2                      ;SELECT INPUT 3C2
     +   B* A * /3C3                      ;SELECT INPUT 3C3

/4Y  =  /B*/A * /4C0                      ;SELECT INPUT 4C0
     +  /B* A * /4C1                      ;SELECT INPUT 4C1
     +   B*/A * /4C2                      ;SELECT INPUT 4C2
     +   B* A * /4C3                      ;SELECT INPUT 4C3
```

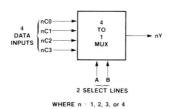

WHERE n = 1, 2, 3, or 4

Quad 4:1 Mux

Quad 4:1 Multiplexer   **Logic Diagram PAL18L4**

Quad 4:1

Application

4:1 Bus Select

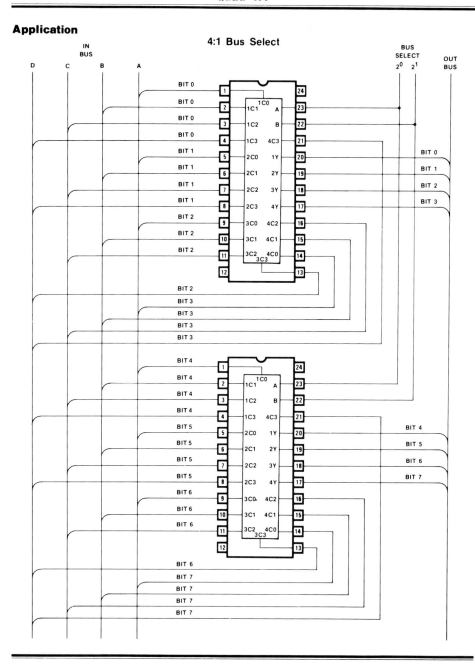

ALU/Accumulator

```
PAL16A4                                    PAL DESIGN SPECIFICATION
ALU                                        BIRKNER/COLI 07/15/81
ALU/ACCUMULATOR
MMI SUNNYVALE, CALIFORNIA
CLK I0   I1 B0 B1 B2 B3 I2 I3  GND
/OC LIO /P A3 A2 A1 A0 /G CIN VCC


CARRY0 .EQU   /I3*/I2*/I1*/I0 * CIN

CARRY1 .EQU   /I3*/I2*/I1*/I0 * (A0*B0)
          + /I3*/I2*/I1*/I0 * (A0+B0)*CIN

CARRY2 .EQU   /I3*/I2*/I1*/I0 * (A1*B1)
          + /I3*/I2*/I1*/I0 * (A1+B1)*(A0*B0)
          + /I3*/I2*/I1*/I0 * (A1+B1)*(A0+B0)*CIN

CARRY3 .EQU   /I3*/I2*/I1*/I0 * (A2*B2)
          + /I3*/I2*/I1*/I0 * (A2+B2)*(A1*B1)
          + /I3*/I2*/I1*/I0 * (A2+B2)*(A1+B1)*(A0*B0)
          + /I3*/I2*/I1*/I0 * (A2+B2)*(A1+B1)*(A0*B0)*CIN


/A0 :=  /I3*/I2*/I1*/I0*(A0:*:B0)    ;A0 PLUS B0
    +  /I3*/I2* I0*(/A0)             ;HOLD A0   (A0 AND)
    +  /I3*/I2* I1*(/B0)             ;LOAD B0   ( B0  )
    +  /I3* I2*/I1*/I0*(B0)          ;LOAD /B0
   :+: /I3* I2*/I1* I0*(/A0*/B0)     ;A0 OR B0
    +  /I3* I2* I1*/I0*/CIN          ;SHIFT LEFT A0
    +  /I3* I2* I1* I0*(/A1)         ;SHIFT RIGHT A0
    +   I3*(/A0)                     ;HOLD A0 (LSB)
    +   CARRY0                       ;A0 PLUS B0 PLUS 1

/A1 :=  /I3*/I2*/I1*/I0*(A1:*:B1)    ;A1 PLUS B1
    +  /I3*/I2* I0*(/A1)             ;HOLD A1   (A1 AND)
    +  /I3*/I2* I1*(/B1)             ;LOAD B1   ( B1  )
    +  /I3* I2*/I1*/I0*(B1)          ;LOAD /B1
   :+: /I3* I2*/I1* I0*(/A1*/B1)     ;A1 OR B1
    +  /I3* I2* I1*/I0*(/A0)         ;SHIFT LEFT A1
    +  /I3* I2* I1* I0*(/A2)         ;SHIFT RIGHT A1
    +   I3*(/A1)                     ;HOLD A1
    +   CARRY1                       ;A1 PLUS B1 PLUS 1

/A2 :=  /I3*/I2*/I1*/I0*(A2:*:B2)    ;A2 PLUS B2
    +  /I3*/I2* I0*(/A2)             ;HOLD A2   (A2 AND)
    +  /I3*/I2* I1*(/B2)             ;LOAD B2   ( B2  )
    +  /I3* I2*/I1*/I0*(B2)          ;LOAD /B2
   :+: /I3* I2*/I1* I0*(/A2*/B2)     ;A2 OR B2
    +  /I3* I2* I1*/I0*(/A1)         ;SHIFT LEFT A2
    +  /I3* I2* I1* I0*(/A3)         ;SHIFT RIGHT A2
    +   I3*(/A2)                     ;HOLD A2
    +   CARRY2                       ;A2 PLUS B2 PLUS 1
```

ALU/Accumulator

```
/A3 :=  /I3*/I2*/I1*/I0*(A3:*:B3)    ;A3 PLUS B3
    +   /I3*/I2* I0*(/A3)            ;HOLD A3    (A3 AND)
    +   /I3*/I2* I1*(/B3)            ;LOAD B3    ( B3  )
    +   /I3* I2*/I1*/I0*(B3)         ;LOAD /B3
  :+:   /I3* I2*/I1* I0*(/A3*/B3)    ;A3 OR B3
    +   /I3* I2* I1*/I0*(/A2)        ;SHIFT LEFT A3
    +   /I3* I2* I1* I0*/LIO         ;SHIFT RIGHT A3
    +    I3*(/A3)                    ;HOLD A3 (MSB)
    +   CARRY3                       ;A3 PLUS B3 PLUS 1

IF(VCC)  G  =  /I3*/I2*/I1*/I0 * (A3*B3)
            +  /I3*/I2*/I1*/I0 * (A3+B3)*(A2*B2)
            +  /I3*/I2*/I1*/I0 * (A3+B3)*(A2+B2)*(A1*B1)
            +  /I3*/I2*/I1*/I0 * (A3+B3)*(A2+B2)*(A1+B1)*(A0*B0)

IF(VCC)  P  =  /I3*/I2*/I1*/I0 * (A3+B3)*(A2+B2)*(A1+B1)*(A0+B0)
            +  /I3*/I2*/I1* I0 * (/A3)*(/A2)*(/A1)*(/A0)
            +  /I3*/I2* I1*/I0 * (/B3)*(/B2)*(/B1)*(/B0)
            +  /I3*/I2* I1* I0 * (/A3+/B3)*(/A2+/B2)*(/A1+/B1)*(/A0+/B0)
            +  /I3* I2*/I1* I0 * (/A3*/B3)*(/A2*/B2)*(/A1*/B1)*(/A0*/B0)
            +  /I3* I2* I1*/I0 * (/A2)*(/A1)*(/A0)*/CIN
            +  /I3* I2* I1* I0 * /LIO*(/A3)*(/A2)*(/A1)

IF (/I3* I2* I1*/I0) /LIO = (/A3)   ;SHIFT LEFT OUT

IF (/I3* I2* I1* I0) /CIN = (/A0)   ;SHIFT RIGHT OUT
```

DESCRIPTION

THE ALU ACCUMULATOR LOADS THE A-REGISTER WITH ONE OF EIGHT OPERANDS ON
THE RISING EDGE OF THE CLOCK.   G AND P OUTPUT GENERATE AND PROPAGATE
ON THE ADD INSTRUCTION.   P OUTPUTS OP = ZERO ON INSTRUCTIONS 1,2,3,5,6,7.

OPERATIONS TABLE:

/OC	CLK	I3	I2	I1	I0	LIO	CIN	A3-A0	OPERATION	
H	X	X	X	X	X	X	X	Z	HI-Z	A =Z
L	C	L	L	L	L	X	L	A PLUS B	ADD	A:=A PLUS B
L	C	L	L	L	L	X	H	A PL B PL 1	ADD	A:=A PLUS B PLUS 1
L	C	L	L	L	H	X	X	A	HOLD	A:=A
L	C	L	L	H	L	X	X	B	LOAD	A:=B
L	C	L	L	H	H	X	X	A AND B	AND	A:=A*B
L	C	L	H	L	L	X	X	/B	LOAD COMP	A:=/B
L	C	L	H	L	H	X	X	A OR B	OR	A:=A+B
L	C	L	H	H	L	X	LI	SL(A)	SHIFT LEFT	
L	C	L	H	H	H	RI	X	SR(A)	SHIFT RIGHT	
L	C	H	X	X	X	X	X	A	HOLD	A:=A

ALU/Accumulator

```
ALU/ACCUMULATOR

             11 1111 1111 2222 2222 2233
     0123 4567 8901 2345 6789 0123 4567 8901

 0  X--- X--- ---- ---- ---- ---- X--- -X--  /I3*I2*I1*I0
 1  ---- ---- XX-- ---- ---- ---- ---- ----  /A0

 8  ---- ---- ---- ---- ---- ---- ---- ----
 9  -X-- -X-- ---- ---- ---- X-XX -X-- -X--  /I3*/I2*/I1*/I0*A3*B3
10  -X-- -X-- ---- ---- X-XX --X- -X-- -X--  /I3*/I2*/I1*/I0*A3+B3*A2*B2
11  -X-- -X-- ---- X-XX --X- --X- -X-- -X--  /I3*/I2*/I1*/I0*A3+B3*A2+B2*A1-
12  -X-- -X-- X-XX --X- --X- --X- -X-- -X--  /I3*/I2*/I1*/I0*A3+B3*A2+B2*A1-

16  -X-- -X-- X--X ---- ---- ---- -X-- -X--  /I3*/I2*/I1*/I0*A0:*:B0
17  X--- ---- XX-- ---- ---- ---- -X-- -X--  /I3*/I2*I0*/A0
18  ---- X--- -X-X ---- ---- ---- -X-- -X--  /I3*/I2*I1*/B0
19  -X-- -X-- X-X- ---- ---- ---- X--- -X--  /I3*I2*/I1*/I0*B0
20  X--- -X-- XX-X ---- ---- ---- X--- -X--  /I3*I2*/I1*I0*/A0*/B0
21  -X-X X--- ---- ---- ---- ---- X--- -X--  /I3*I2*I1*/I0*/CIN
22  X--- X--- ---- XX-- ---- ---- X--- -X--  /I3*I2*I1*I0*/A1
23  ---- ---- XX-- ---- ---- ---- X--- ----  I3*/A0

24  -X-- -X-- ---- X--X ---- ---- -X-- -X--  /I3*/I2*/I1*/I0*A1:*:B1
25  X--- ---- XX-- ---- ---- ---- -X-- -X--  /I3*/I2*I0*/A1
26  ---- X--- ---- -X-X ---- ---- -X-- -X--  /I3*/I2*I1*/B1
27  -X-- -X-- ---- X-X- ---- ---- X--- -X--  /I3*I2*/I1*/I0*B1
28  X--- -X-- ---- XX-X ---- ---- X--- -X--  /I3*I2*/I1*I0*/A1*/B1
29  -X-- X--- XX-- ---- ---- ---- X--- -X--  /I3*I2*I1*/I0*/A0
30  X--- X--- ---- ---- XX-- ---- X--- -X--  /I3*I2*I1*I0*/A2
31  ---- ---- ---- XX-- ---- ---- X--- ----  I3*/A1

32  -X-- -X-- ---- ---- X--X ---- -X-- -X--  /I3*/I2*/I1*/I0*A2:*:B2
33  X--- ---- ---- ---- XX-- ---- -X-- -X--  /I3*/I2*I0*/A2
34  ---- X--- ---- ---- -X-X ---- -X-- -X--  /I3*/I2*I1*/B2
35  -X-- -X-- ---- ---- X-X- ---- X--- -X--  /I3*I2*/I1*/I0*B2
36  X--- -X-- ---- ---- XX-X ---- X--- -X--  /I3*I2*/I1*I0*/A2*/B2
37  -X-- X--- ---- XX-- ---- ---- X--- -X--  /I3*I2*I1*/I0*/A1
38  X--- X--- ---- ---- ---- XX-- X--- -X--  /I3*I2*I1*I0*/A3
39  ---- ---- ---- ---- XX-- ---- X--- ----  I3*/A2

40  -X-- -X-- ---- ---- ---- X--X -X-- -X--  /I3*/I2*/I1*/I0*A3:*:B3
41  X--- ---- ---- ---- ---- XX-- -X-- -X--  /I3*/I2*I0*/A3
42  ---- X--- ---- ---- ---- -X-X -X-- -X--  /I3*/I2*I1*/B3
43  -X-- -X-- ---- ---- ---- X-X- X--- -X--  /I3*I2*/I1*/I0*B3
44  X--- -X-- ---- ---- ---- XX-X X--- -X--  /I3*I2*/I1*I0*/A3*/B3
45  -X-- X--- ---- ---- XX-- ---- X--- -X--  /I3*I2*I1*/I0*/A2
46  X--- X--- ---- ---- ---- ---- X--- -X-X  /I3*I2*I1*I0*/LIO
47  ---- ---- ---- ---- ---- XX-- ---- X---  I3*/A3

48  ---- ---- ---- ---- ---- ---- ---- ----
49  -X-- -X-- --X- --X- --X- --X- -X-- -X--  /I3*/I2*/I1*/I0*A3+B3*A2+B2*A1-
50  X--- -X-- XX-- XX-- XX-- XX-- -X-- -X--  /I3*/I2*/I1*I0*/A3*/A2*/A1*/A0
51  X--- X--- -X-X -X-X -X-X -X-X X--- -X--  /I3*/I2*I1*/I0*/B3*/B2*/B1*/B0
52  X--- X--- -X-- -X-- -X-- -X-- -X-- -X--  /I3*/I2*I1*I0*/A3+/B3*/A2+/B2*-
53  X--- -X-- XX-X XX-X XX-X XX-X X--- -X--  /I3*/I2*I1*/I0*/A3*/B3*/A2*/B2*-
54  -X-X X--- XX-- XX-- XX-- ---- X--- -X--  /I3*I2*I1*/I0*/A2*/A1*/A0*/CIN
55  X--- X--- ---- XX-- XX-- XX-- X--- -X-X  /I3*I2*I1*I0*/LIO*/A3*/A2*/A1
56  -X-- X--- ---- ---- ---- ---- X--- -X--  /I3*I2*I1*/I0
57  ---- ---- ---- ---- ---- XX-- ---- ----  /A3

LEGEND:  X : FUSE NOT BLOWN (L,N,0)   - : FUSE BLOWN   (H,P,1)
NUMBER OF FUSES BLOWN = 1270
```

ALU/Accumulator

ALU/Accumulator   **Logic Diagram PAL16A4**

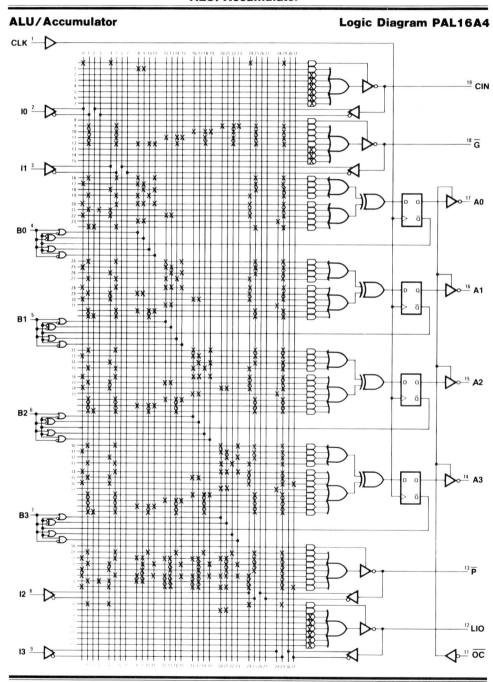

Octal Shift Register

```
PAL20X8                                    PAL DESIGN SPECIFICATION
74LS498                                    UDI GORDON 02/20/81
OCTAL SHIFT REGISTER
MMI SUNNYVALE, CALIFORNIA
CLK  I0  D0 D1 D2 D3 D4 D5 D6 D7  I1  GND
/OC RILO Q7 Q6 Q5 Q4 Q3 Q2 Q1 Q0 LIRO VCC


/Q0 :=  /I1*/I0*/Q0                    ;HOLD Q0
    +   /I1* I0*/Q1                    ;SHIFT RIGHT
    :+:  I1*/I0*/LIRO                  ;SHIFT LEFT
    +    I1* I0*/D0                    ;LOAD D0

/Q1 :=  /I1*/I0*/Q1                    ;HOLD Q1
    +   /I1* I0*/Q2                    ;SHIFT RIGHT
    :+:  I1*/I0*/Q0                    ;SHIFT LEFT
    +    I1* I0*/D1                    ;LOAD D1

/Q2 :=  /I1*/I0*/Q2                    ;HOLD Q2
    +   /I1* I0*/Q3                    ;SHIFT RIGHT
    :+:  I1*/I0*/Q1                    ;SHIFT LEFT
    +    I1* I0*/D2                    ;LOAD D2

/Q3 :=  /I1*/I0*/Q3                    ;HOLD Q3
    +   /I1* I0*/Q4                    ;SHIFT RIGHT
    :+:  I1*/I0*/Q2                    ;SHIFT LEFT
    +    I1* I0*/D3                    ;LOAD D3

/Q4 :=  /I1*/I0*/Q4                    ;HOLD Q4
    +   /I1* I0*/Q5                    ;SHIFT RIGHT
    :+:  I1*/I0*/Q3                    ;SHIFT LEFT
    +    I1* I0*/D4                    ;LOAD D4

/Q5 :=  /I1*/I0*/Q5                    ;HOLD Q5
    +   /I1* I0*/Q6                    ;SHIFT RIGHT
    :+:  I1*/I0*/Q4                    ;SHIFT LEFT
    +    I1* I0*/D5                    ;LOAD D5

/Q6 :=  /I1*/I0*/Q6                    ;HOLD Q6
    +   /I1* I0*/Q7                    ;SHIFT RIGHT
    :+:  I1*/I0*/Q5                    ;SHIFT LEFT
    +    I1* I0*/D6                    ;LOAD D6

/Q7 :=  /I1*/I0*/Q7                    ;HOLD Q7
    +   /I1* I0*/RILO                  ;SHIFT RIGHT
    :+:  I1*/I0*/Q6                    ;SHIFT LEFT
    +    I1* I0*/D7                    ;LOAD D7

IF(/I1*I0) /LIRO = /Q0                 ;LEFT IN RIGHT OUT

IF(I1*/I0) /RILO = /Q7                 ;RIGHT IN LEFT OUT
```

Octal Shift Register

DESCRIPTION

THIS PAL IS AN 8-BIT SHIFT REGISTER WITH PARALLEL LOAD AND HOLD CAPABILITY.
TWO FUNCTION SELECT INPUTS (I0,I1) PROVIDE ONE OF FOUR OPERATIONS WHICH OCCUR
SYNCHRONOUSLY ON THE RISING EDGE OF THE CLOCK (CLK). THESE OPERATIONS ARE:

/OC	CLK	I1	I0	D7-D0	Q7-Q0	OPERATION
H	X	X	X	X	Z	HI-Z
L	C	L	L	X	L	HOLD
L	C	L	H	X	SR(Q)	SHIFT RIGHT
L	C	H	L	X	SL(Q)	SHIFT LEFT
L	C	H	H	D	D	LOAD

TWO OR MORE OCTAL SHIFT REGISTERS MAY BE CASCADED TO PROVIDE LARGER SHIFT
REGISTERS. RILO AND LIRO ARE LOCATED ON PINS 14 AND 23 RESPECTIVELY, WHICH
PROVIDES FOR CONVENIENT INTERCONNECTIONS WHEN TWO OR MORE OCTAL SHIFT REGISTERS
ARE CASCADED TO IMPLEMENT LARGER SHIFT REGISTERS.

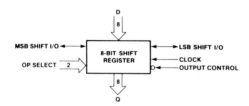

Octal Shift Register

Octal Shift Register

Logic Diagram PAL20X8

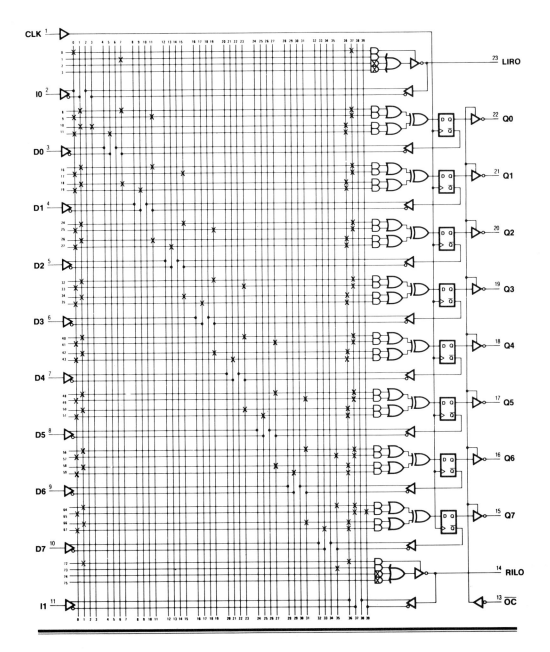

Binary to BCD Converter

Serial Binary to Parallel BCD Conversion

The purpose of this circuit is to convert a serial stream of binary data into a parallel BCD representation as depicted by Figure 1.

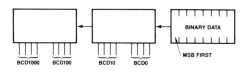

BINARY DATA

MSB FIRST

BCD1000   BCD100   BCD10   BCD0

Figure 1. Conceptual Diagram of Binary to BCD Converter

Couleur's Technique (BIDEC)

In this conversion technique (Ref. 1), the input binary data is shifted left (starting with the MSB) into the BCD register. The beauty of this method is that after each clock pulse, the BCD output contains correct BCD representation for the "relative" binary data shifted so far. We illustrate the last statement in Figure 2.

Logic Design

The overall conversion problem can be segmented into four-bit binary blocks. Each block represents one BCD digit and is expandable by C_{IN} and C_{OUT}. The BCD building block, is shown in Figure 3 as a state machine.

The combinational network can be designed from a "next-state" truth table. The truth table can be constructed by observing that a left shift is a multiplication by 2, and a carryin adds 1 to the LSB.

In equation form:

BCD (next state): $= 2*$ BCD (present state) $+ C_{IN}$

Of course, if it were binary it will be simply,

$$Q_n := Q_{n-1}$$

However, BCD requires some corrections as will be shown shortly. For simplicity we analyze the three relevent cases:

a) BCD (present state): $= 0 - 4$
   then BCD (next state): $= 0 - 8$ which are representable in BCD format

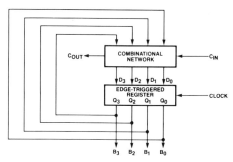

B_3 B_2 B_1 B_0

Figure 3, BCD Converter Building Block.

b) BCD (present state): $= 5 - 9$
   then BCD (next state): $= 10 - 18$ which are not representable in one BCD digit, and a carry out is generated.
   e.g. If BCD (present state): $= 6$
   then BCD (next state): $= 2$ and $C_{OUT} = 1$

c) If $C_{IN} = 1$ then it is simply shifted into the LSB of the BCD digit (the old LSB was shifted left leaving a zero in its original position).
   Thus, regardless of the BCD (present state) value, the following is true:

$$B0 \text{ (next state): } = C_{IN}$$

Truth Table

The preceding discussion is summarized by Tables 1 and 2.

PRESENT STATE B_3-B_0	NEXT STATE B_3-B_0	C_{OUT}
0-4	0-8	0
5-9	0-8	1
10-15	DON'T CARE	DON'T CARE

Table 1, General Truth Table.

n	PRESENT STATE B_3 B_2 B_1 B_0	NEXT STATE B_3 B_2 B_1 B_0	C_{OUT}
0	0 0 0 0	0 0 0 C_{IN}	0
1	0 0 0 1	0 0 1 C_{IN}	0
2	0 0 1 0	0 1 0 C_{IN}	0
3	0 0 1 1	0 1 1 C_{IN}	0
4	0 1 0 0	1 0 0 C_{IN}	0
5	0 1 0 1	0 0 0 C_{IN}	1
6	0 1 1 0	0 0 1 C_{IN}	1
7	0 1 1 1	0 1 0 C_{IN}	1
8	1 0 0 0	0 1 1 C_{IN}	1
9	1 0 0 1	1 0 0 C_{IN}	1
10-15		X X X X	X

Table 2: Detailed Truth Table.

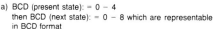

CONVERSION REGISTER

10^2	10^1	10^0	(conversion register)

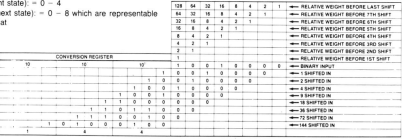

128	64	32	16	8	4	2	1	
128	64	32	16	8	4	2	1	← RELATIVE WEIGHT BEFORE LAST SHIFT
	64	32	16	8	4	2	1	← RELATIVE WEIGHT BEFORE 7TH SHIFT
		32	16	8	4	2	1	← RELATIVE WEIGHT BEFORE 6TH SHIFT
			16	8	4	2	1	← RELATIVE WEIGHT BEFORE 5TH SHIFT
				8	4	2	1	← RELATIVE WEIGHT BEFORE 4TH SHIFT
					4	2	1	← RELATIVE WEIGHT BEFORE 3RD SHIFT
						2	1	← RELATIVE WEIGHT BEFORE 2ND SHIFT
							1	← RELATIVE WEIGHT BEFORE 1ST SHIFT
1	0	0	1	0	0	0	0	← BINARY INPUT
1	0	0	1	0	0	0		← 1 SHIFTED IN
1	0	0	1	0	0			← 2 SHIFTED IN
1	0	0	1	0				← 4 SHIFTED IN
1	0	0	1					← 9 SHIFTED IN
1	0	0						← 18 SHIFTED IN
1	0							← 36 SHIFTED IN
1								← 72 SHIFTED IN
								← 144 SHIFTED IN

Figure 2: Tabular Representation of the Conversion Cycle.

Binary to BCD Converter

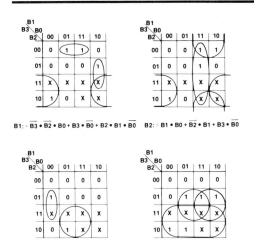

B1: $= \overline{B3} \cdot \overline{B2} \cdot B0 + B3 \cdot \overline{B0} + B2 \cdot B1 \cdot \overline{B0}$ B2: $= \overline{B1} \cdot B0 + \overline{B2} \cdot B1 + B3 \cdot \overline{B0}$

B3: $= B2 \cdot \overline{B1} \cdot \overline{B0} + B3 \cdot B0$ COUT: $= B3 + B2 \cdot B0 + B2 \cdot B1$

Figure 4. Karnaugh Maps

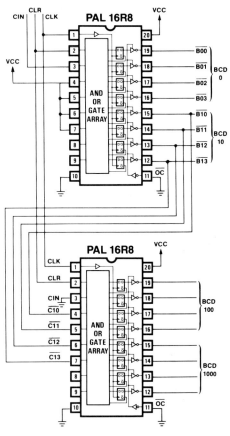

Figure 5. Logic Schematic

PAL Implementation

The PAL16R8 implements two BCD digits. One of the pins is assigned to the clear (CLR) function. The BCD conversion register must be initialized to zero before shifting of the binary input data is started. The eight output registers are assigned to the two BCD digits.

At this point, it seems that we are short of one output pin for the C_{OUT} in expanding to more BCD digits. However, the basic equations indicate that C_{OUT} is a function of the four preceding BCD bits. Therefore, by inputting these four bits to the next stage, the C_{OUT} is derived internally by the latter stage. A similar trick is used in each chip to cascade internally.

This expansion solution implies that in the least significant BCD stage the equation is:

(1) BO: $= C_{IN}$

whereas in later stages the equation is:

(2) BO: $= C_{13} + C_{12} \cdot C_{10} + C_{12} \cdot C_{11}$

where the C terms are driven by the corresponding B terms of a preceding stage. However, in order to have a universal solution, we OR the two equations. If the PAL is used as the least significant stage C_{10}, C_{11}, C_{12} and C_{13} are grounded and equation (1) holds. If the PAL is used as an intermediate stage, C_{IN} is grounded and equation (2) holds.

Summary

A similar algorithm was described in Ref. 2, where the two BCD digits were implemented with four ICs and could be clocked at 80 ns. Here we described one chip implementation that can be clocked at 60 ns.

References

1 "Binary to BCD Conversion Techniques" by B. MacDonald, EDN Dec. 1, 1969.
2 "Special PROM Mode Effects Binary to BCD Converter", by D.M. Brockman, Electronics.

Binary to BCD Converter

```
PAL16R8                                    PAL DESIGN SPECIFICATION
BBCD                                       S. WASER/V. COLI 09/14/81
BINARY TO BCD CONVERTER
MMI SUNNYVALE, CALIFORNIA
CLK /CLR CIN /C10 /C11 /C12 /C13 NC NC GND
/OC /B13 /B12 /B11 /B10 /B03 /B02 /B01 /B00 VCC


B00 := /CLR* CIN                           ;CONVERT B00 (LSB)
    + /CLR* C13
    + /CLR* C12* C10
    + /CLR* C12* C11

B01 := /CLR*/B03*/B02* B00                 ;CONVERT B01
    + /CLR* B03*/B00
    + /CLR* B02* B01*/B00

B02 := /CLR* B01* B00                       ;CONVERT B02
    + /CLR*/B02* B01
    + /CLR* B03*/B00

B03 := /CLR* B02*/B01*/B00                  ;CONVERT B03
    + /CLR* B03* B00

B10 := /CLR* B03                            ;CONVERT B10
   ,+ /CLR* B02* B00
    + /CLR* B02* B01

B11 := /CLR*/B13*/B12* B10                  ;CONVERT B11
    + /CLR* B13*/B10
    + /CLR* B12* B11*/B10

B12 := /CLR* B11* B10                        ;CONVERT B12
    + /CLR*/B12* B11
    + /CLR* B13*/B10

B13 := /CLR* B12*/B11*/B10                   ;CONVERT B13 (MSB)
    + /CLR* B13* B10
```

Binary to BCD Converter

BINARY TO BCD CONVERTER

```
               11 1111 1111 2222 2222 2233
      0123 4567 8901 2345 6789 0123 4567 8901

 0 X--- X--- ---- ---- ---- ---- ---- ---- /CLR*CIN
 1 X--- ---- ---- ---- ---- -X-- ---- ---- /CLR*C13
 2 X--- ---- -X-- ---- -X-- ---- ---- ---- /CLR*C12*C10
 3 X--- ---- ---- -X-- -X-- ---- ---- ---- /CLR*C12*C11

 8 X--X ---- --X- --X- ---- ---- ---- ---- /CLR*/B03*/B02*B00
 9 X-X- ---- ---- ---X ---- ---- ---- ---- /CLR*B03*/B00
10 X-X- ---X ---X ---- ---- ---- ---- ---- /CLR*B02*B01*/B00

16 X--X ---X ---- ---- ---- ---- ---- ---- /CLR*B01*B00
17 X--- ---X --X- ---- ---- ---- ---- ---- /CLR*/B02*B01
18 X-X- ---- ---- ---X ---- ---- ---- ---- /CLR*B03*/B00

24 X-X- --X- ---X ---- ---- ---- ---- ---- /CLR*B02*/B01*/B00
25 X--X ---- ---- ---X ---- ---- ---- ---- /CLR*B03*B00

32 X--- ---- ---- ---X ---- ---- ---- ---- /CLR*B03
33 X--X ---- ---X ---- ---- ---- ---- ---- /CLR*B02*B00
34 X--- ---X ---X ---- ---- ---- ---- ---- /CLR*B02*B01

40 X--- ---- ---- ---- ---X ---- --X- --X- /CLR*/B13*/B12*B10
41 X--- ---- ---- ---- --X- ---- ---- ---X /CLR*B13*/B10
42 X--- ---- ---- ---- --X- ---X ---X ---- /CLR*B12*B11*/B10

48 X--- ---- ---- ---- ---X ---X ---- ---- /CLR*B11*B10
49 X--- ---- ---- ---- ---X --X- ---- /CLR*/B12*B11
50 X--- ---- ---- ---- --X- ---- ---- ---X /CLR*B13*/B10

56 X--- ---- ---- ---- --X- --X- ---X ---- /CLR*B12*/B11*/B10
57 X--- ---- ---- ---- ---X ---- ---- ---X /CLR*B13*B10
```

LEGEND: X : FUSE NOT BLOWN (L,N,0)   - : FUSE BLOWN   (H,P,1)

NUMBER OF FUSES BLOWN =   664

Binary to BCD Converter

Binary to BCD Converter   **Logic Diagram PAL16R8**

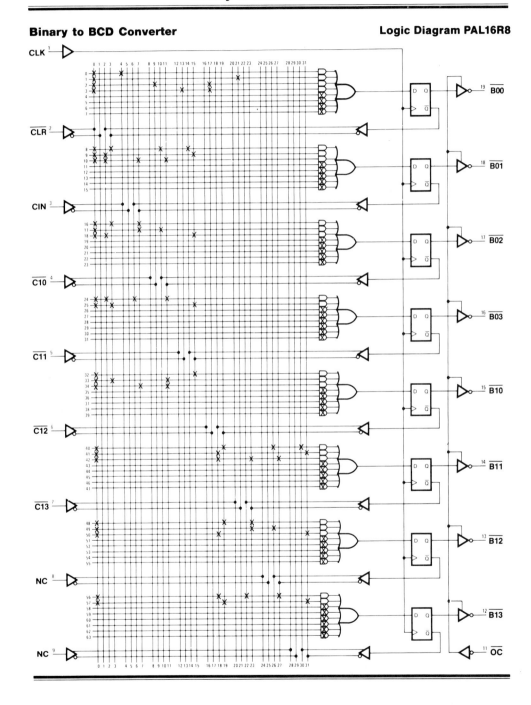

High Speed Programmable Array Logic Family

PAL® Series 20A

U.S. Patent 4124899

March 1982

Features/Benefits

- 15ns typical propagation delay
- Programmable replacement for TTL logic
- Reduces IC inventories
- Reduces chip count by greater than 4 to 1
- Expedites prototyping and board layout
- Saves space with 20-pin SKINNYDIP™ packages
- Programmed on standard PROM programmers
- Programmable three-state outputs
- Last fuse prevents duplication on a PROM/PAL programmer

PART NUMBER	PKG	GATE ARRAY DESCRIPTION
PAL16L8A	N,J,F,L	Octal 16 Input And-Or-Invert
PAL16R8A	N,J,F,L	Octal 16 Input Registered And-Or
PAL16R6A	N,J,F,L	Hex 16 Input Registered And-Or
PAL16R4A	N,J,F,L	Quad 16 Input Registered And-Or

Unused inputs are tied directly to V_{CC} or GND. Product terms with all fuses blown assume the logical high state, and product terms connected to both true and complement of any single input assume the logical low state. Registers consist of D type flip-flops which are loaded on the low to high transition of the clock. PAL Logic Diagrams are shown with all fuses blown, enabling the designer use of the diagrams as coding sheets.

Description

The PAL Series 20A family utilizes Monolithic Memories advanced self-aligned washed emitter high speed bipolar process and the bipolar PROM fusible link technology to provide user programmable logic for replacing conventional SSI/MSI gates and flip-flops at reduced chip count.

The family lets the systems engineer "design his own chip" by blowing fusible links to configure AND and OR gates to perform his desired logic function. Complex interconnections which previously required time-consuming layout are thus "lifted" from the PC board and are placed on silicon where they can be easily modified during prototype check-out or production.

The PAL transfer function is the familiar sum of products. Like the PROM, the PAL has a single array of fusible links. Unlike the PROM, the PAL is a programmable AND array driving a fixed OR array (the PROM is a fixed AND array driving a programmable OR array). In addition the PAL provides these options:

- Variable input/output pin ratio
- Programmable three-state outputs
- Registers with feedback

PAL* is a registered trademark of Monolithic Memories

The entire PAL family is programmed on inexpensive conventional PROM programmers with appropriate personality and socket adapter cards. Once the PAL is programmed and verified, two additional fuses may be blown to defeat verification. This feature gives the user a proprietary circuit which is very difficult to copy.

Ordering Information

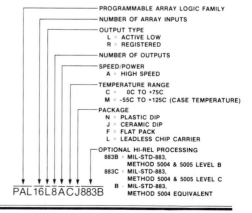

```
PROGRAMMABLE ARRAY LOGIC FAMILY
NUMBER OF ARRAY INPUTS
OUTPUT TYPE
    L = ACTIVE LOW
    R = REGISTERED
NUMBER OF OUTPUTS
SPEED/POWER
    A = HIGH SPEED
TEMPERATURE RANGE
    C =   0C TO +75C
    M = -55C TO +125C (CASE TEMPERATURE)
PACKAGE
    N = PLASTIC DIP
    J = CERAMIC DIP
    F = FLAT PACK
    L = LEADLESS CHIP CARRIER
OPTIONAL HI-REL PROCESSING
    883B = MIL-STD-883,
              METHOD 5004 & 5005 LEVEL B
    883C = MIL-STD-883,
              METHOD 5004 & 5005 LEVEL C
       B = MIL-STD-883,
              METHOD 5004 EQUIVALENT

PAL 16 L 8 A C J 883B
```

PAL Series 20A

Absolute Maximum Ratings

	Operating	Programming
Supply Voltage, V_{CC}	–0.5 to 7.0V	–0.5 to 12.0V
Input Voltage	–1.5 to 5.5V	–1.0 to 12.0V⊕
Off-state output Voltage	5.5V	12.0V
Storage temperature		–65° to +150°C

Operating Conditions

SYMBOL	PARAMETER		MILITARY			COMMERCIAL			UNIT
			MIN	TYP	MAX	MIN	TYP	MAX	
V_{CC}	Supply voltage		4.5	5	5.5	4.75	5	5.25	V
t_w	Width of clock	Low	20	10		15	10		ns
		High	20	10		15	10		
t_{su}	Set up time from input or feedback to clock	16R8A 16R6A 16R4A	30	16		25	16		ns
t_h	Hold time		0	–10		0	–10		ns
T_A	Operating free-air temperature		–55			0	25	75	°C
T_C	Operating case temperature				125				°C

Electrical Characteristics Over Operating Conditions

SYMBOL	PARAMETER	TEST CONDITIONS			MIN	TYP	MAX	UNIT
V_{IL}*	Low-level input voltage						0.8	V
V_{IH}*	High-level input voltage				2			V
V_{IC}	Input clamp voltage	V_{CC} = MIN	I_I = –18mA			–0.8	–1.5	V
I_{IL}	Low-level input current †	V_{CC} = MAX	V_I = 0.4V			–0.02	–0.25	mA
I_{IH}	High-level input current †	V_{CC} = MAX	V_I = 2.4V				25	µA
I_I	Maximum input current	V_{CC} = MAX	V_I = 5.5V				1	mA
V_{OL}	Low-level output voltage	V_{CC} = MIN V_{IL} = 0.8V V_{IH} = 2V	MIL	I_{OL} = 12mA		0.3	0.5	V
			COM	I_{OL} = 24mA				
V_{OH}	High-level output voltage	V_{CC} = MIN V_{IL} = 0.8V V_{IH} = 2V	MIL	I_{OH} = –2mA	2.4	2.8		V
			COM	I_{OH} = –3.2mA				
I_{OZL}	Off-state output current †	V_{CC} = MAX V_{IL} = 0.8V V_{IH} = 2V		V_O = 0.4V			–100	µA
I_{OZH}				V_O = 2.4V			100	µA
I_{OS}	Output short-circuit current **	V_{CC} = 5V		V_O = 0V	–30	–70	–130	mA
I_{CC}	Supply current	V_{CC} = MAX				120	180	mA

† I/O pin leakage is the worst case of I_{OZX} or I_{IX} e.g., I_{IL} and I_{OZH}.

†† All typical values are at V_{CC} = 5V, T_A = 25°C.

* These are absolute voltages with respect to pin 10 on the device and includes all overshoots due to system and/or tester noise. Do not attempt to test these values without suitable equipment.

** Only one output shorted at a time.

⊕ Pins 1 and 11 may be raised to 22V max.

PAL Series 20A

Switching Characteristics

Over Operating Conditions

SYMBOL	PARAMETER				TEST CONDITIONS	MILITARY			COMMERCIAL			UNIT
						MIN	TYP	MAX	MIN	TYP	MAX	
t_{PD}	Input or feed-back to output	16R6A	16R4A	16L8A			15	30		15	25	ns
t_{CLK}	Clock to output or feedback						10	20		10	15	ns
t_{PZX}	Pin 11 to output enable						10	25		10	20	ns
t_{PXZ}	Pin 11 to output disable				$R_1 = 200\Omega$ $R_2 = 390\Omega$		11	25		11	20	ns
t_{PZX}	Input to output enable	16R6A	16R4A	16L8A			10	30		10	25	ns
t_{PXZ}	Input to output disable	16R6A	16R4A	16L8A			13	30		13	25	ns
f_{MAX}	Maximum frequency	16R8A	16R6A	16R4A		20	30		25	30		MHz

Test Load

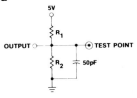

Available Programmers

MANUFACTURER	PERSONALITY CARD SET	SOCKET ADAPTER CONFIGURATION
Data I/O Corporation	909-1427	715 1428-1 715 1428-2 715 1428-3
Pro-Log Corporation	PM9068	
Stag Systems	PM202	AM10H8 AM10L8 AM12H6 AM12L6 AM14H4 AM14L4 AM16H2 AM16L2 AM16C1
Structured Design	SD20/24	
Kontron	MPP-80S	

Schematic of Inputs and Outputs

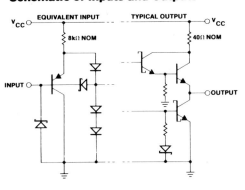

PAL Series 20A

Programming

PAL fuses are programmed using a low-voltage linear-select procedure which is common to all 4 PAL types. The array is divided into two groups, products 0 thru 31 and products 32 thru 63, for which pin identifications are shown in Pin Configurations below. To program a particular fuse, both an input line and a product line are selected according to the following procedure:

Step 1 Raise Output Disable, OD, to V_{IHH}

Step 2 Select an input line by specifying $I_0, I_1, I_2, I_3, I_4, I_5, I_6, I_7$ and L/R as shown in Table 1.

Step 3 Select a product line by specifying A_0, A_1 and A_2 one-of-eight select as shown in Table 2.

Step 4 Raise V_{CC} (pin 20) to V_{IHH}

Step 5 Program the fuse by pulsing the output pins, O, of the selected product group to V_{IHH} as shown in Programming Waveform.

Step 6 Lower V_{CC} (pin 20) to 6.0 V

Step 7 Pulse the CLOCK pin and verify the output pin, O, to be Low for active Low PAL types or High for active High PAL types.

Step 8 Lower V_{CC} (pin 20) to 4.5 V and repeat step 7.

Step 9 Should the output not verify, repeat steps 1 thru 8 up to five (5) times.

This procedure is repeated for all fuses to be blown (see Programming Waveforms).

To prevent further verification, two last fuses may be blown by raising pin 1 and pin 11 to V_P. V_{CC} is not required during this operation.

Voltage Legend

L = Low-level input voltage, V_{IL}
H = High-level input voltage, V_{IH}
HH = High-level program voltage, V_{IHH}
Z = High impedance (e.g., 10kΩ to 5.0V)

INPUT LINE NUMBER	PIN IDENTIFICATION								
	I_7	I_6	I_5	I_4	I_3	I_2	I_1	I_0	L/R
0	HH	HH	HH	HH	HH	HH	HH	L	Z
1	HH	HH	HH	HH	HH	HH	HH	H	Z
2	HH	HH	HH	HH	HH	HH	HH	L	HH
3	HH	HH	HH	HH	HH	HH	HH	H	HH
4	HH	HH	HH	HH	HH	HH	L	HH	Z
5	HH	HH	HH	HH	HH	HH	H	HH	Z
6	HH	HH	HH	HH	HH	HH	L	HH	HH
7	HH	HH	HH	HH	HH	HH	H	HH	HH
8	HH	HH	HH	HH	HH	L	HH	HH	Z
9	HH	HH	HH	HH	HH	H	HH	HH	Z
10	HH	HH	HH	HH	HH	L	HH	HH	HH
11	HH	HH	HH	HH	HH	H	HH	HH	HH
12	HH	HH	HH	HH	L	HH	HH	HH	Z
13	HH	HH	HH	HH	H	HH	HH	HH	Z
14	HH	HH	HH	HH	L	HH	HH	HH	HH
15	HH	HH	HH	HH	H	HH	HH	HH	HH
16	HH	HH	HH	L	HH	HH	HH	HH	Z
17	HH	HH	HH	H	HH	HH	HH	HH	Z
18	HH	HH	HH	L	HH	HH	HH	HH	HH
19	HH	HH	HH	H	HH	HH	HH	HH	HH
20	HH	HH	L	HH	HH	HH	HH	HH	Z
21	HH	HH	H	HH	HH	HH	HH	HH	Z
22	HH	HH	L	HH	HH	HH	HH	HH	HH
23	HH	HH	H	HH	HH	HH	HH	HH	HH
24	HH	L	HH	HH	HH	HH	HH	HH	Z
25	HH	H	HH	HH	HH	HH	HH	HH	Z
26	HH	L	HH	HH	HH	HH	HH	HH	HH
27	HH	H	HH	HH	HH	HH	HH	HH	HH
28	L	HH	HH	HH	HH	HH	HH	HH	Z
29	H	HH	HH	HH	HH	HH	HH	HH	Z
30	L	HH	HH	HH	HH	HH	HH	HH	HH
31	H	HH	HH	HH	HH	HH	HH	HH	HH

Table 1 Input Line Select

PRODUCT LINE NUMBER	PIN IDENTIFICATION						
	O_3	O_2	O_1	O_0	A_2	A_1	A_0
0, 32	Z	Z	Z	HH	Z	Z	Z
1, 33	Z	Z	Z	HH	Z	Z	HH
2, 34	Z	Z	Z	HH	Z	HH	Z
3, 35	Z	Z	Z	HH	Z	HH	HH
4, 36	Z	Z	Z	HH	HH	Z	Z
5, 37	Z	Z	Z	HH	HH	Z	HH
6, 38	Z	Z	Z	HH	HH	HH	Z
7, 39	Z	Z	Z	HH	HH	HH	HH
8, 40	Z	Z	HH	Z	Z	Z	Z
9, 41	Z	Z	HH	Z	Z	Z	HH
10, 42	Z	Z	HH	Z	Z	HH	Z
11, 43	Z	Z	HH	Z	Z	HH	HH
12, 44	Z	Z	HH	Z	HH	Z	Z
13, 45	Z	Z	HH	Z	HH	Z	HH
14, 46	Z	Z	HH	Z	HH	HH	Z
15, 47	Z	Z	HH	Z	HH	HH	HH
16, 48	Z	HH	Z	Z	Z	Z	Z
17, 49	Z	HH	Z	Z	Z	Z	HH
18, 50	Z	HH	Z	Z	Z	HH	Z
19, 51	Z	HH	Z	Z	Z	HH	HH
20, 52	Z	HH	Z	Z	HH	Z	Z
21, 53	Z	HH	Z	Z	HH	Z	HH
22, 54	Z	HH	Z	Z	HH	HH	Z
23, 55	Z	HH	Z	Z	HH	HH	HH
24, 56	HH	Z	Z	Z	Z	Z	Z
25, 57	HH	Z	Z	Z	Z	Z	HH
26, 58	HH	Z	Z	Z	Z	HH	Z
27, 59	HH	Z	Z	Z	Z	HH	HH
28, 60	HH	Z	Z	Z	HH	Z	Z
29, 61	HH	Z	Z	Z	HH	Z	HH
30, 62	HH	Z	Z	Z	HH	HH	Z
31, 63	HH	Z	Z	Z	HH	HH	HH

Table 2 Product Line Select

PAL Series 20A

Pin Configurations

PRODUCTS 0 THRU 31

```
 1  OD          VCC  20
 2  I0            O0  19
 3  I1            O1  18
 4  I2            O2  17
 5  I3            O3  16
 6  I4            A0  15
 7  I5            A1  14
 8  I6            A2  13
 9  I7            LR  12
10  GND        CLOCK  11
```

PRODUCTS 32 THRU 63

```
 1  CLOCK        VCC  20
 2  I0            LR  19
 3  I1            A0  18
 4  I2            A1  17
 5  I3            A2  16
 6  I4            O0  15
 7  I5            O1  14
 8  I6            O2  13
 9  I7            O3  12
10  GND           OD  11
```

Programmer Requirement $T_A = 25°C$

SYMBOL	DEFINITION		LIMITS			UNIT
			MIN	TYP	MAX	
V_{IHH}	Program-level input voltage		11	11.5	12	V
I_{IHH}	Program-level input current	Output Program Pulse			50	mA
		OD, L/R			25	
		All Other Inputs			5	
I_{CCH}	Program Supply Current				400	mA
T_P	Program Pulse Width		10		50	μS
t_D	Delay time		100			ns
t_{DV}	Delay Time to Verify		100			μS
	Program Pulse duty cycle				25	%
V_P	Verify-Protect-input voltage		20	21	22	V
I_P	Verify-Protect-input current				400	mA
T_{PP}	Verify-Protect Pulse Width		20		50	msec

Programming Waveforms

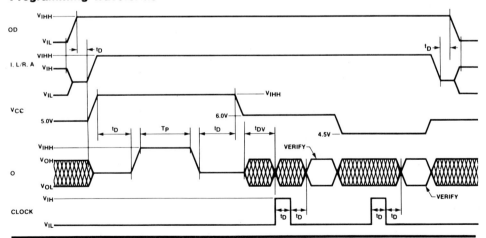

PAL Series 20

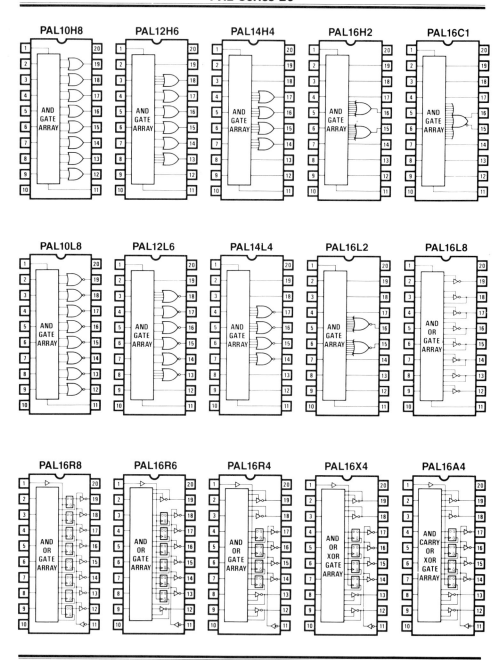

PAL Series 20

Logic Diagram PAL16L8

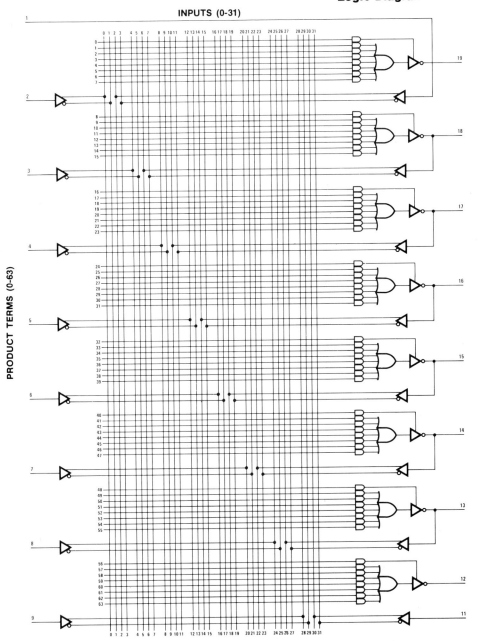

PAL Series 20

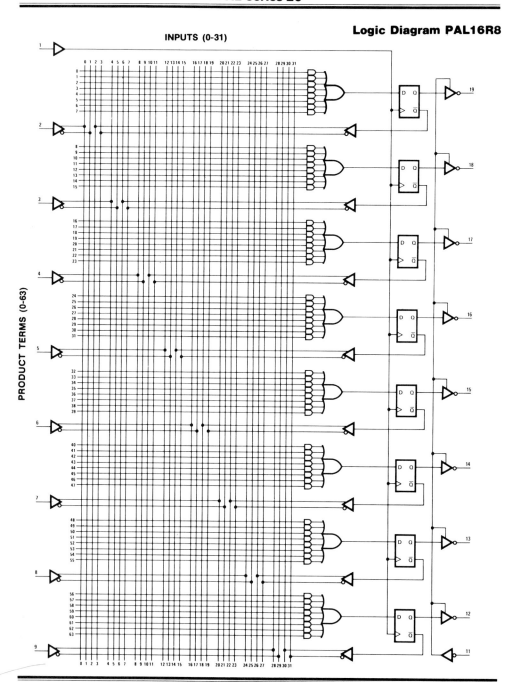

INPUTS (0-31)

Logic Diagram PAL16R8

PRODUCT TERMS (0-63)

PAL Series 20

Logic Diagram PAL16R6

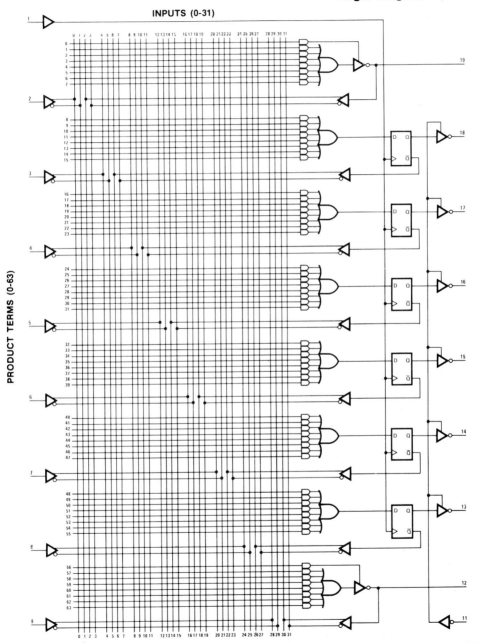

PAL Series 24

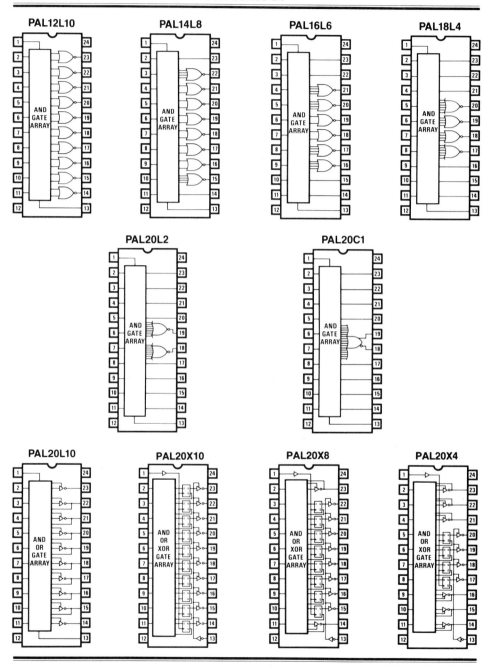

PAL Series 24

Logic Diagram PAL20X 8

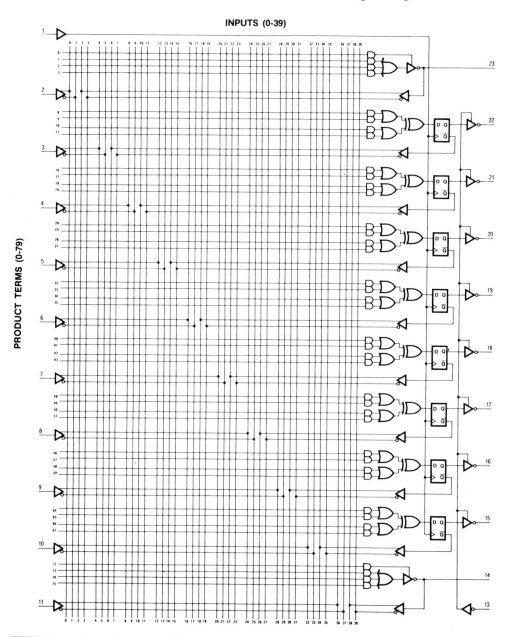

REFERENCES

[AMD 82]   "Am29516 16 $\times$ 16 bit parallel multiplier," Advanced Micro Devices, 901 Thompson Place, Sunnyvale, CA. 94086, February 1982.

[AND 67]   **Anderson, F. S., et al.**, "The IBM System 360/91 Floating Point Execution Unit," *IBM J. Res. Devel.*, Vol. 11, No. 1, January 1967, pp. 34–53.

[ATK 68]   **Atkins, D. E.**, "Higher-Radix Division Using Estimates of the Divisor and Partial Remainders," *IEEE Trans. Computers*, Vol. C-17, No. 10, October 1968, pp. 925–934.

[BAN 74]   **Banerji, D. K.**, "A Novel Implementation Method for Addition and Subtraction in Residue Number Systems," *IEEE Trans. Computers*, Vol. C-23, No. 1, pp106–108. January 1974.

[BIR 79]   **Birkner, D. A.**, "High Speed Array Processor Using Serial Techniques," Conf. Record, WESCON, 1979, paper no. 7/3.

[BIR 80]   **Birkner, D. A.**, "High Speed Matrix Processor Using Floating Point Representation," Conf. Record, WESCON, 1980, paper no. 14/3.

[BIR 82]   **Birkner, J. and Coli, V.**, "PAL, Programmable Array Logic Handbook," Monolithic Memories, Inc., 1165 E. Arques Avenue, Sunnyvale, CA. 94086., February, 1982.

[BOO 51]   **Booth, A. D.**, "A Signed Binary Multiplication Technique," *Qt. J. Mech. Appl. Math.*, Vol. 4, Part 2, 1951.

[BRE 68]   **Brennan, J. F.**, "The Fastest Time of Addition and Multiplication," *IBM Research Reports*, Vol. 4, No. 1, 1968.

[BRE 73]   **Brent, R. P.**, "On the Precision Attainable with Various Floating Point Number Systems," *IEEE Trans. Computers*, Vol. C-22, No. 6, June 1973, pp. 601–607.

[BUR 46]   **Burks, A. W., et al.**, "Preliminary Discussion of the Logical Design of an Electronic Computing Instrument," reprinted in [SWA 76].

[CHE 61]   **Cheney, P. W.**, "A Digital Correlator Based on the Residue Number System," *IRE Trans. Electronic Computer*, Vol. EC-10, No. 3, March 1961, pp. 63–70.

[CHE 80]   **Cheng, S. and Rallapalli K.**, "Am 9512: Single Chip Floating Point Processor," Conf. Record, WESCON, 1980, paper no. 14/4.

[COD 73]   **Cody, W. J., Jr.**, "Static and Dynamic Numerical Characteristics of Floating Point Arithmetic," *IEEE Trans. Computers*, Vol. C-22, No. 6, June 1973, pp. 598–601.

[COD 81]   **Cody, W. J., Jr.**, "Analysis of Proposals for the Floating Point Standard," *Computer*, March 1981.

[COH 81]   **Cohler, E. U. and Storer, J. E.**, "Functionally Parallel Architecture for Array Processors," *Computer*, September 1981.

[COO 79]   **Coonen, J. T.**, "Specifications for a Proposed Standard for Floating Point Arithmetic," University of California Memorandum No. UCB/ERL M78/72, January 25, 1979.

[COO 80]   **Coonen, J. T.**, "An Implementation Guide to a Proposed Standard for Floating Point Arithmetic," *Computer*, January 1980.

[COO 81]   **Coonen, J. T.**, "Underflow and the Denormalized Numbers," *Computer*, March 1981.

[DAD 65]   **Dadda, L.**, "Some Schemes for Parallel Multipliers," *Alta Frequenza*, Vol. 34, March 1965, pp. 349–356.

[DAV 74]   **Davis, R.L.**, "Uniform Shift Networks," *Computer*, September 1974, pp. 60–71.

[DEV 75]   **Deverell, J.**, "Pipeline Iterative Arithmetic Arrays," *IEEE Trans. Computers*, Vol. C-24, No. 3, March 1975, pp. 317–322.

[EAR 65]   **Earle, J. G.**, "Latched Carry-Save Adder," *IBM Technical Disclosure Bull.*, Vol. 7, March 1965, pp. 909–910.

[FAW 75]   **Fawcett, B. K.**, "Maximal Clocking Rates for Pipelined Digital Systems," M.S. Thesis, Dept. Elec. Eng., University of Illinois at Urbana–Champaign, 1975.

[FLY 70]   **Flynn, M. J.**, "On Division by Functional Iteration," *IEEE Trans. Computers*, Vol. C-19, No. 8, August 1970, pp. 702–706.

[FPS 78]   "AP-120B, Array-Processor Handbook," Floating Point Systems, Inc., 10520 S.W. Cascade Blvd., Portland, OR, 1978.

[FRA 78]   **Fraley, B.**, "Zeros and Infinities Revisited and Gradual Underflow," HP Laboratories, 3500 Deer Creek Road, Palo Alto, CA 94304, December 28, 1978.

[GAJ 78]   **Gajski, D. D., and Rubinfield, L. P.**, "Design of Arithmetic Elements for Burroughs Scientific Processor," *Proc. Fourth Symposium on Computer Arithmetic*, October 1978, pp. 245–256.

[GAJ 80]   **Gajski, D. D.** "Parallel Compressors," *IEEE Trans. Computers*, Vol. C-29, No. 5, May 1980. pp 393–398.

[GAR 59]   **Garner, H. L.**, "The Residue Number System," *IRE Trans. Electronic Computers*, Vol. EC-8, June 1959.

[GAR 65]   **Garner, H. L.**, "Number Systems and Arithmetic," *Advances in Computers*, Vol. 6, 1965, pp. 131–194.

[GAR 76]   **Garner, H. L.**, "A Survey of Some Recent Contributions to Computer Arithmetic," *IEEE Trans. Computers*, Vol. C-25, No. 12, December 1976, pp. 1277–1282.

[GAR 78]   **Garner, H. L.**, "Theory of Computer Addition and Overflows," *IEEE Trans. Computers*, Vol. C-27, No. 4, April 1978, pp. 297–301.

[GHE 71] **Ghest, R. C.**, "A Two's Complement Digital Multiplier, the Am25S05," Advanced Micro Devices, 901 Thompson Place, Sunnyvale, CA, 1971.

[GIN 77] **Ginsberg, M.**, "Numerical Influences on the Design of Floating Point Arithmetic for Microcomputers," *Proc. 1st Annual Rocky Mountain Symp. Microcomputers*, August 1977, pp. 24–72.

[GOR 82] **Gordon, E. and Hastings, C.**, "Big, Fast and Simple Algorithms, Architecture and Components for High-end Super Minis," Conf. Record, SOUTHCON, 1982, paper no. 21/3.

[GSC 67] **Gschwind, H. W.**, *Design of Digital Computers*, New York, Springer-Verlag, 1967.

[HAL 72] **Hallin, T. G. and Flynn, M. J.**, "Pipelining of Arithmetic Functions," *IEEE Trans. Computers*, Vol. C-21, No. 8, August 1972, pp. 880–886.

[HAS 77] **Hasitume, B.**, "Floating Point Arithmetic," *Byte*, November 1977.

[HAS 79] **Hastings, C.**, "Shift Matrices: The Missing Teeth in the Number Cruncher," Conf. Record, WESCON, 1979, paper no. 18/3.

[HOU 81] **Hough, D.**, "Applications of the Proposed IEEE-754 Standard for Floating Point Arithmetic," *Computer*, March 1981.

[HWA 78] **Hwang, K.**, *Computer Arithmetic: Principles, Architecture, and Design* New York, John Wiley and Sons, Inc., 1978.

[JUL 78] **Jullien, G. A.**, "Residue Number Scaling and Other Operations Using ROM Arrays," *IEEE Trans. Computers*, Vol. C-27, No. 4, April 1978, pp. 325–336.

[KAR 81] **Karplus, W. J., and Cohen, D.**, "Architectural and Software Issues in the Design and Application of Peripheral Array Processors," *Computer*, September 1981.

[LIN 81] **Ling, H.**, "High-Speed Binary Adder," *IBM J. Res. Devel.*, Vol. 25, Nos. 2 and 3, May 1981, pp. 156–166.

[LOU 81] **Louie, T.**, "Array Processors: A Selected Bibliography," *Computer*, September 1981.

[MAC 61] **MacSorley, O. L.**, "High-Speed Arithmetic in Binary Computers," *Proc. IRE*, Vol. 49, January 1961. Note: this article has been reprinted in a book edited by Swartzlander, [SWA 76].

[MAJ 76] **Majithia, J. C.**, "Some Comments Concerning Design of Pipeline Arithmetic Arrays," *IEEE Trans. Computers*, Vol. C-25, No. 11, November 1976, pp. 1132–1134.

[MAR 73] **Marasa, J. D., and Matula, D. W.**, "A Simulative Study of Correlated Error Propagation in Various Finite Precision Arithmetic," *IEEE Trans. Computers*, Vol. C-22, No. 6, June 1973, pp. 587–597.

[MAR 81] **Maron, N., and Brengle, T. A.**, "Integrating an Array Processor into a Scientific Computing System," *Computer*, September 1981.

[MER 64] **Merrill, R. D., Jr.,** "Improving Digital Computer Performance Using Residue Number Theory," *IEEE Trans. on Electronic Computers*, Vol. EC-13, No. 2, April 1964, pp. 93–101.

[MCM 80] **McMinn, C.**, "The Intel 8087: A Numeric Data Processor," Conf. Record, WESCON, 1980, paper no. 14/5.

[MMI 82a]   "Bipolar LSI Data Book", Monolithic Memories, Inc., 1165 E. Arques Ave., Sunnyvale, CA; 1982.

[MMI 82]   "74S516 Data Sheet", Monolithic Memories, Inc., 1165 E Arques Ave., Sunnyvale, CA; 1982.

[MOT 78]   "Motorola, MC10808-MECL LSI Programmable 16-Bit Shifter Function," Motorola Semiconductor, P.O. Box 20912, Phoenix, AZ, May 1978.

[NEW 56]   **Newman, J. R.**, *The World of Mathematics*, New York, Simon and Schuster, 1956.

[PAL 77]   **Palmer, J.**, "The Intel Standard for Floating Point Arithmetic," *Proc. COMSAC*, November 1977, pp. 107–112.

[PAR 66]   **Parker, F. D.**, *The Structure of Number Systems*, Englewood Cliffs, NJ., Prentice-Hall, 1966.

[PAY 78]   **Payne, M., and Strecker W.**, "Draft Proposal for Floating Point Standard," Digital Equipment Corporation, 146 Main St., Naynard, MA. 01754, December 11, 1978.

[PEZ 70]   **Pezaris, S. D.**, "A 40 ns 17-Bit by 17-Bit Array Multiplier," *IEEE Trans. Computers*, Vol. C-20, No. 4, April 1971, pp 442–227.

[REI 79]   **Reinsch, C.**, Private Correspondence, Leibniz-Rechenzentrum, D-8000 Munich 2, Germany, January 11, 1979.

[ROB 58]   **Robertson, J. E.**, "A New Class of Digital Division Methods," *IRE Trans. Electronic Computers*, Vol. EC-5, June 1956, pp. 65–73.

[SHA 79]   **Shapiro, G.**, "Exploit LSI Memory Components Today, Instead of Waiting for Arithmetic Devices," Conf. Record, WESCON, 1979, paper no. 18/5.

[SKL 60]   **Sklansky, J.**, "Conditional Sum Addition Logic," *Trans. IRE*, Vol. EC-9, No. 2, June 1960, pp. 226–230.

[SPA 81]   **Spaniol, O.**, *Computer Arithmetic: Logic and Design*, New York, John Wiley and Sons, Inc., 1981.

[SPI 73]   **Spira, P. M.**, "Computation Times of Arithmetic and Boolean Functions in (d, r) Circuits," *IEEE Trans. Computers*, Vol. C-22, No. 6, June 1973, pp. 552–555.

[STE 71]   **Steinard, M. L., and Munro, W. D.**, *Introduction to Machine Arith metic*, Reading, MA. Addison-Wesley, 1971.

[STE 74]   **Sterbenz, P. H.**, *Floating Point Computation*, Englewood Cliffs, NJ. Prentice-Hall, 1974.

[STE 77]   **Stenzel, W. J.**, et al., "A Compact High-Speed Multiplication Scheme," *IEEE Trans. Computers*, Vol. C-26, No. 10, October 1977, pp. 948–957.

[STE 81]   **Stevenson, D.**, "A Proposed Standard for Binary Floating Point Arithmetic," *Computer*, March 1981.

[STO 73]   **Stone, H. S.**, *Discreet Mathematical Structures*, Chicago, Science Research Associates, 1973.

[STO 75]   **Stone, H. S.**, *Introduction to Computer Architecture*, Chicago, Science Research Associates, 1975.

[SWA 76]   **Swartzlander, E. E.**, *Computer Design Development, Principal Papers*, Hayden Book Company, Rochelle Park, NJ. 1976.

[SZA 67]   **Szabo, N. S., and Tanaka, R. I.,** *Residue Arithmetic and its Applications to Computer Technology,* New York, McGraw-Hill, 1967.

[TAY 82]   **Taylor, F. J. and Huang, C. H.,** "An Autoscale Residue Multiplier," *IEEE Trans. Computers,* Vol. C-31, No. 4, April 1982, pp. 321–325.

[THE 81]   **Theis, D. J.,** "Array Processor Architecture: Guest Editor Introduction," *Computer,* September 1981.

[THO 62]   **Thomas, G. B.,** *Calculus and Analytic Geometry,* Reading, MA. Addison-Wesley, 1962, pp. 451–452.

[TI 81]   "TTL Data Book," Texas Instruments, Inc., P.O. Box 5012, Dallas, TX, 1976.

[TRW 81]   TRW LSI Products, "MPY-Series Multipliers," P.O. Box 2472, La Jolla, CA; 1981.

[UND 80]   **Undheim, T.,** "Combinatorial Floating Point Processors as an Integral Part of the Computer" Conf. Record, WESCON, 1980, paper no. 14/1.

[WAL 64]   **Wallace, C. S.,** "A Suggestion for a Fast Multiplier," *IEEE Trans. Electronic Computers,* Vol. EC-13, February 1964, pp. 14–17.

[WAR 79]   **Warren, H. S., Jr., and Fox, A. S., and Markstein, P. W.,** "Modulus Division on a Two's Complement Machine," IBM Research Report No. RC7712, Yorktown Heights, New York, June 1979.

[WAS 78a]   **Waser, S.,** "State of the Art in High-Speed Arithmetic ICs," *Computer Des.,* July 1978.

[WAS 78b]   **Waser, S.,** "High Speed Monolithic Multipliers for Real-Time Digital Signal Processing," *Computer,* October 1978.

[WAT 66]   **Watson, R. W. and Hastings, C. W.,** "Self-Checked Computation using Residue Arithmetic," Proceedings of the IEEE, Vol. 54, no. 12, pp.1920–1931, December, 1966.

[WIE 56]   **Weinberger, A. and Smith, J. L.,** "A One-Microsecond Adder Using One-Megacycle Circuitry," *IRE Trans. Electronic Computers,* Vol. EC-5, June 1956, pp. 65–73.

[WIE 66]   **Wiegel, R. E.,** "Methods of Binary Additions," Report No. 195, Department of Computer Science, University of Illinois, Urbana, February 1966.

[WIN 79]   **Winnigstad, C. N.,** "Using LSI to Crunch Numbers at High Speed: An Overview," Conf. Record, WESCON, 1979, paper no. 18/1.

[WIN 65]   **Winograd, S.,** "On the Time Required to Perform Addition," *J. ACM,* vol. 12, no. 2, 1965, pp. 277–285.

[WIN 67]   **Winograd, S.,** "On the Time Required to Perform Multiplication," *J. ACM,* vol. 14, no. 4, 1967, pp. 793–802.

[WIT 78]   **Wittmayer, W. R.,** "Array Processor Provides High Throughput Rate," *Computer Des.,* March 1978, pp. 93–100.

[YOH 73]   **Yohe, J. M.,** "Roundings in Floating Point Arithmetic," *IEEE Trans. Compters,* Vol. C-22, No. 6, June 1973, pp. 577–586.

Index

Initial book design was done by Barbara Laddaga.
Final book design was the effort of Kathleen Flynn.
Hand-drawn illustrations were the responsibility
of Stanford University's Word Graphics.
This book was set in Computer Modern Roman times ten
with 368 points to a line and 8.00 true inches per vertical page.
The TEX formatting system, with macros designed by
Max Diaz, was used to produce the final manuscript.
Photocomposition was done at Stanford University using Alphatype.